DANISH YEARBOOK
OF
PHILOSOPHY

VOLUME 48–49

DANISH YEARBOOK
OF
PHILOSOPHY

VOLUME 48–49

2013–2014

MUSEUM TUSCULANUM PRESS
UNIVERSITY OF COPENHAGEN 2016

The present double issue of the *Danish Yearbook of Philosophy* has its origins in an international symposium, held at the University of Copenhagen (18–19 April 2013) and organized by Søren Gosvig Olesen, University of Copenhagen, Hans Ruin, Södertörn University (Stockholm) and Thomas Schwarz Wentzer, Aarhus University.

We would like to express our gratitude to the Riksbankens jubileumsfond & Time, Memory and Representation and the Department of Media, Cognition and Communication at the University of Copenhagen for supporting the symposium. We would also like to thank the Danish Research Council for the Humanities for its financial commitment to the symposium as well as to the journal.

Published for
Dansk Filosofisk Selskab
in cooperation with
the Philosophical Societies of Aarhus and Odense
and with financial support from
the Danish Research Council for the Humanities

*

*

Articles for consideration and all editorial communications should be sent in three copies to:
Danish Yearbook of Philosophy
University of Copenhagen, Department of Philosophy
Karen Blixens Vej 4, DK-2300 Copenhagen S, Denmark

Business communications, including subscriptions and orders for reprints, should be addressed to the publishers:
MUSEUM TUSCULANUM PRESS
Birketinget 6
DK-2300 Copenhagen S
Denmark

*

ISBN 978 87 635 4399 6
ISSN 0070 2749

CONTENTS

PREFACE

The Phenomenon History – Das Phänomen Geschichte
– Le phénomène de l'histoire
International Symposium at the University of Copenhagen

SØREN GOSVIG OLESEN, HANS RUIN, AND THOMAS SCHWARZ WENTZER

Description

Philosophy was traditionally defined through its relation to eternal truths and values in contrast to temporal and transitory phenomena. But as philosophy in the modern era, through Descartes and Kant, is founded in human awareness and consciousness, in the "I think", its relation to time is also transformed. Rather than constituting the beginning, the timeless is now seen as an endpoint that can be achieved only through different forms and strategies of doubt and criticism.

As a consequence of this, modern philosophy has preoccupied itself with the changeable, rather than with the eternal. Also it has exposed itself to various forms of self-criticism. Most philosophical schools during the 20th century have oriented themselves historically. In many cases "the historical" itself has become the main theme of exploration. "History" no longer designates a specific domain of reality in contrast to "nature". Instead, history and historicity now appear as fundamental conditions for human life. But what is the philosophical meaning of this new and encompassing sense of the "historical". What is the phenomenon "history"? That was the question for this meeting.

The theme of the conference was primarily philosophical, not historical. It concerns the philosophy of history, rather the history of philosophy, even though the distinction itself needs continually to be questioned. Individual contributions naturally concerned themselves with the work of Hegel, Heidegger, Merleau-Ponty, Derrida, and others. But it is the concept and phenomenon of history that is in focus.

Beschreibung

Die Philosophie zeichnet sich traditionellerweise durch ihren Bezug auf zeitlose oder ewige Werte aus, die sich historischer Veränderlichkeit entziehen. Doch insofern die Philosophie der Moderne, beginnend mit Descartes und Kant, menschlich wird und ihr Fundament im Bewusstsein des ‚ich denke' zu legen sucht, ist dieses Fundament nicht so sehr der Ausgangspunkt philosophischer Bemühungen, als ihr Schlusspunkt, nachdem sie durch Formen des methodischen Zweifels oder der Kritik hindurchgegangen ist.

Als eine Folge beschäftigt sich die moderne Philosophie eher mit dem Veränderlichen als mit dem Ewigen. Entsprechend unterzieht sich das philosophische Denken zunehmend verschiedenen Formen der Selbstkritik. Alle philosophischen Richtungen des 20. Jahrhunderts orientieren sich historisch; für viele Philosophen wird ‚Geschichte' ein Hauptthema. ‚Geschichte' markiert jetzt kein bestimmtes Gegenstandsgebiet etwa im Gegensatz zu ‚Natur'. Vielmehr bezeichnet Geschichte und Geschichtlichkeit eine bzw. die Bedingung menschlicher Existenz. Doch was genau meint ‚Geschichte' in dieser neuen und umfassenden Bedeutung? Dies war die Frage dieser Tagung.

Das Thema der Tagung war geschichtsphilosophisch und nicht philosophiegeschichtlich zu verstehen; der vermeintliche Unterschied von systematischer Philosophie und Philosophiegeschichte spielt keine Rolle. Natürlich bezogen sich die einzelnen Beiträge auf Hegel, Heidegger, Merleau-Ponty, Derrida und andere. Doch ist es der Begriff der Geschichte selbst, der im Fokus des Interesses steht.

Contexte

De par sa tradition, la philosophie a eu tendance à éviter le temporaire, elle a cherché plutôt la vérité "éternelle". Or, devenant résolument humaine à partir de Descartes et de Kant, c'est-à-dire lorsqu'elle cherche à se fonder sur le cogito, la philosophie fait l'expérience que ce point de départ ne se trouve qu'à l'issue de la méthode du doute ou de la critique.

C'est ainsi que la philosophie se rapportera plus au temporel qu'à l'éternel. Et c'est ainsi qu'elle devra réviser son statut. Tous les grands courants du XX° siècle sont d'orientation historique, et chez un grand nombre des philosophes de ce siècle l'histoire constitue un thème majeur. On ne considère plus alors l'histoire comme une région particulière (opposée à celle de la nature); on va jusqu'à l'identifier avec l'existence humaine. Or, comment concevoir l'histoire, si elle doit avoir un sens aussi englobant? Tel était la question réunissant les thèmes de ce congrès.

Le congrès s'est organisé autour de la philosophie de l'histoire et non autour de l'histoire de la philosophie; la distinction entre philosophie systématique et historique n'aura pas cours ici. Il va de soi que les contributions se sont référées à Hegel, à Heidegger, à Merleau-Ponty, à Derrida, etc., mais c'est la notion même de l'histoire qui forme le centre des discussions.

*Danish Yearbook of Philosophy, Vol. **48–49** (2013–2014), 9–20*

EXPERIENCE AND HISTORY

DAVID CARR

1. Introduction

The project in this paper, to explore the intersection between experience and history, can be seen in part as a response to recent trends in the philosophy of history. For several decades, theoretical reflections on history have been dominated by two themes: *representation* and *memory*. Each is conceived as a relation to the past: representation can be of the past, and memory is by its nature of the past. Sometimes these themes are treated together and sometimes separately. In either case, philosophical reflection on these two themes has revealed some important things about history, but it has also raised certain problems that, if it restricts itself to these themes, it is incapable of solving. As a way of overcoming the weaknesses and solving the problems of this dual focus on representation and memory, I propose a phenomenological approach which puts *experience* in their place as the central focus of a philosophy of history.

While I have been interested in theories of representation, especially narrative representation, as a phenomenologist I am more interested in the experience that lies behind it. What is the presentation behind the representation? How is history given, how does it enter our lives, how do we encounter it directly? This inquiry is of course in keeping with the theme of this conference: the phenomenon of history, or history as it appears or is given, rather than history as an object of knowledge or as an element in a metaphysical theory.

At first glance, this connection between experience and history might seem to involve a simple four-step progression. Experience is essentially temporal; experience is essentially intersubjective; history is intersubjective temporality; thus experience is essentially historical. But each of these steps, especially the third, needs elaboration, and this is what I propose in the following. Much of my account of these four steps depends on notions of spatial, temporal and social continuities, but historical experience in crucial cases turns on discontinuity and rupture as well. Accordingly, after an account of experiential continuities, I will consider several types of discontinuity. I conclude by looking at the concept of historicity, with its background in the German historicist tradition, and relate it to my account of historical experience.

2. Temporality, intentionality, world

First, temporality: The temporal flow of consciousness is essential to the concept of subjectivity, and phenomenology, beginning with Husserl,[1] has developed an account of consciousness that is unified while spanning past, present
and future. Husserl's great accomplishment is his introduction of the notion of
retention and the sharp distinction he makes between it and memory in the
usual sense, which he calls "recollection" or sometimes "reproduction." What
Husserl is trying to describe here is the experience of both the presentness of
the present and the *continuity* of the present. Retention is definitely a consciousness of something past: e.g., the previous note of a melody, for example,
is gone forever. Yet I am conscious of it *together with* the present and it makes
the present possible.

The use by Husserl of small-scale, compact examples like hearing a melody
is valuable because it permits us to focus on the main features that are new in
Husserl's account, namely retention and the temporal *Gestalt*. But Husserl
chose it partly because it allows him to abstract, for purposes of analysis, from
elements that belong to the larger sphere of our experience. Our experience is
not in our heads but relates us to a world. Consciousness, as Husserl famously
recognized, is not wrapped up in itself, but is always *of something.* As Sartre
would later insist,[2] interpreting Husserl, consciousness is entirely outside of
itself, *in the world.* So we must bring in what these phenomenologists call *intentionality.*

Thus the concept of subjectivity comprises both its temporality and its intentionality. Consciousness flows, and has its retentional-protentional structure. It
is *in* the here-and-now, the present, but only because the present stands out
from a kind of temporal field that encompasses past and future. And it is *of* the
here-and-now in the sense that it relates intentionally to objects that are other
than and outside itself.

The introduction of intentionality into the discussion of experience means
that we cannot properly speak of experience without discussing *what* is intended, *as* it is intended. It is not just that we want to consider those "objects
that are other than and outside" the intention; we *must* consider them if we
want to understand experience. Husserl spoke of "temporal objects" (*Zeitob-
jekte*) as a special class of objects – things that take time or unfold in time, and
must do so in order to be what they are, and to be experienced *as* what they are.
The melody is one example, but so is the dancer's twirl, the tree's sway in the
breeze, a conversation. But we have a perfectly good word to describe such

"objects:" they are *events*. Things that don't take time, or just persist through time, like my pen, can be distinguished from events. Of course, my experience, even of my pen, is itself an event; that is, it unfolds in time, even if my pen just sits there. So, when we talk of experiencing an event, like hearing a melody, we must distinguish between the event of hearing and the event that is heard, the melody itself.

As we further develop our treatment of subjectivity in relation to history, the concept of event assumes major importance, and needs to be further broken down and elaborated with some subtlety. For the moment suffice it to say that the experience, of the here and now, is intentionally related to things and events as its "objects," in the broadest sense. But as *intentional* objects, things and events have *meaning* –and this leads us to the concept of *world*.

This is one of those terms that have developed a special sense in the context of phenomenology, largely thanks to the work of Husserl and Heidegger. "World" can mean just the totality of what is, the universe, all the things that exist, and so on. The phenomenological understanding of world retains the sense of totality, but includes the idea of things and events *as intended*, that is, as having meaning – for consciousness, for someone, for human existence – meanings they have in relation to one another and in relation to the totality itself. Things and events added together may make up a universe, but things and events that have meaning for someone make up a world, at least in the phenomenological sense. This does not mean that these things and events, or their meanings, or the world itself, are "merely subjective." Indeed one of the meanings they have is, as we have seen, that they are other than or outside consciousness. In virtue of intentionality, experience relates itself to what is beyond itself. In this sense, the subject is in the world, and the world, as a complex of meaningful things and events, is as essential to it as intentionality itself.

3. Intersubjectivity

The phenomenological account of time and subjectivity is initially tied to the first-person singular point of view. And yet this focus seems highly inappropriate for talking about history. History, it is fair to say, is not itself focused on individuals, but concerns the social world. If we are to find a connection between subjectivity and history, then consciousness is in some sense going to have to concern more than just the individual. This is where intersubjectivity comes in. We are going to have to talk about the experience of the social world, and, at the limit, about experience itself as something that occurs *socially*.

A significant part of *what* we experience, among the things and events that make up our world, are 1) other people and groups of other people; 2) events involving other people; 3) the actions, sufferings, and experiences of other people; 4) human artifacts and other productions, not only physical but also institutional, procedural and developmental. The concept of subjectivity in modern philosophy came to prominence in response to epistemological concerns, and these were conceived in relation to the newly developing sciences of nature. The only *objects* of experience that were considered important, accordingly, were physical and natural objects. This focus on *things* meant that our encounter with other people was conceived in terms of our perception of their bodies as physical objects and led to the notorious problem of "other minds."

This supposed problem, certainly insoluble as it is formulated, has long been recognized as bogus. We experience persons as persons, their bodies as human bodies, not as physical objects. Thus our world is primarily, indeed overwhelmingly, a human and social world. Once this human world moves to the center of our concern, and becomes more fully elaborated, we can return to the *temporality* of experience in relation to the social world and to social existence. We can now shift our attention from the simple act of hearing a melody to the music itself as a product belonging to the inventory of our cultural environment. We and our contemporaries live in a world that includes, besides music, also literature and art, pop-culture, the financial system, businesses, trends, movements, etc. But the material inventory of our cultural world is much nearer to us and more pervasive. Most of us live in a world of houses and buildings, of streets, traffic and means of transportation. Houses and streets (except when they are being torn down and built up) are more or less immobile objects, but they provide the surroundings for the movements and actions of those who live in and use them. As artifacts, they also refer implicitly to the activity of their builders. The human world is thus a world not just of things but of events and processes, of actions and developments, which we experience as continuities thanks to the retentional-protentional structure. Like the natural world the human world is temporal, and we experience it as temporal continuity, but the temporality of the human world is different from that of the natural world.

Houses and streets, cities and their configurations, have a past which is given with them as horizon and background when we experience them in the present. Indeed, we can say the same thing of other people. This horizon of pastness is given in retention, and thanks to retention we have something like an experience of the past – but only as background for the present. Further, we can say that many of these objects, and many of these people, are older than we are – i.e. older than I, the particular subject of any given experience. In these cases the horizon of pastness reaches back into the time before our birth. Thus the depth and breadth of this past, receding into the indefinite, as horizon and background for the present, is always given in every experience of the human world. In this sense what is experienced is not limited to the lifetime of the experiencing subject.

Merging the phenomenological account of temporality with that of the social world we can say that the direct experience of persons, groups and other social entities, such as artifacts, buildings, streets, etc. bears its past along with it in the manner of retentional consciousness. To have an experience in this first sense is to be in the presence of an object that stands out from its temporal background. To experience an action or event is likewise to see it emerge from its antecedents. In each of these cases the retained past is part of what gives meaning to the present and makes it what it is. Each object and event, in other words, comes to us with its past attached. Without this past it would not only be meaningless, it could not even be an item in our experience. If it is true that our experience is in the present and connects us with the present, it is equally true that it gives an unmediated connection with the past.

This past extends indefinitely into the temporal "distance" and has its contours and features, some more distinct than others. The retained past has patterns that accumulate and bear upon the present. One way of stating this is that what is given in immediate and direct experience can make sense or have meaning for us in virtue of falling into a pattern or structure. It is recognized as an exemplar or instance of a type provided by our past experience. As Hume saw, we build up expectations. Yet because consciousness is also open to the future, those expectations can be rudely disappointed, or happily surprised, by the new and the unexpected.

4. Community

To correctly describe and fully understand this relation to others, we need to introduce an indispensable new term, namely that of the group to which I and the others belong. It is precisely as fellow members of a group that others are encountered in this way, and so we need to explore what "group" means in this context, to understand how it exists, how far it extends, etc. What we have in mind here is not merely an objective collection of individuals, united by some common objective characteristic like size, shape, hair color or complexion, or geographical location. The relevant sense of group for our purposes is united from the inside, not from the outside. The word most often used to convey this sense of group is *community*, *Gemeinschaft*. These terms derive from the common or the shared, but this must be understood in a special way.

If the community makes possible a certain kind of encounter with others, how do I encounter the community itself? It too is not primarily an object standing over against me as something to be perceived or known, as if I were an anthropologist or sociologist. I relate to it rather in terms of membership, adherence or belonging. The sign of this relation is my use of the "we" to characterize the subject of certain experiences and actions. The possibility that the community can emerge as a "we"-subject affords a way of understanding not only the nature of the community but also the peculiar character of being with others that makes it up.

One thing to be noted is how such a community relates to the possibility of phenomenological understanding. Phenomenology is often characterized by the first-person character of its descriptions. By shifting our attention from the "I" to the "we," it is not necessary to leave the first-person point of view behind; we merely take up the plural rather than the singular first person. Describing this plural subject phenomenologically involves reflecting on those occasions and experiences in which I identify myself with a group or community by enlisting, so to speak, in the "we." It happens when the experience or action in which I am engaged is attributed not just to me but to "us," when I take myself to be a participant in a collective action or experience. But the action or experience must be enduring or ongoing, and with it the existence of the collective subject, the "we." To say that we build a house is not equivalent to saying that I build a house, you build a house, she builds a house, etc. The common project is articulated into subtasks distributed among the participants such that the agent cannot be any of the members singly but only the group as such.

To say that I enlist in or participate in such collective endeavors or experiences is to say that I identify myself with the group in question, and this sense of "identifying oneself" deserves our attention. The identity of the subject of experience is not a given but constitutes itself over time as a sort of project, and I identify myself in relation to others. This brings us into the territory of "identity" as it is used in such phrases as "identity crisis" and "identity politics." As

an individual I identify myself with certain groups and thus construe my identity in terms of my belonging. Among these are family, profession, religion,
nationality, culture, etc.

Thus individuals identify themselves with groups that range from small and
intimate to larger and more encompassing. But it must not be thought that these
groups nest easily inside each other like a series of concentric circles. Groups
criss-cross one another, and I identify myself sometimes more with one than
another, depending on circumstances. Furthermore, participation in one may
not always be compatible with participation in another. Family may conflict
with profession, class with country, religion with civic duty, etc., to name only
a few of the classic conflicts. These conflicts can be personal and psychologi-
cal, "identity crises" in which the individual is torn between conflicting com-
mitments and allegiances; and through the individuals involved the conflicts
can be social as well, pitting groups against each other in collective action and
enmity.

Much of our focus here has been on temporality, but spatiality has also
cropped up at certain important junctures, and we need to take note of this. Just
as phenomenologists are not speaking of clock-time, or objective time, but of
lived time, so the space of our experience is not objective or geometrical space
but lived space. The phenomenology of perception, in the hands of Husserl and
Merleau-Ponty, has taught us the bodily and oriented space of our immediate
surroundings, its correlation to movement and practical projects of our spatial
being in the world. Once we move to the level of the community, the spatial
field, like the temporal field, opens up and takes on new dimensions. Here
space has the characteristics of terrain and territory, the place of habitation and
dwelling, the qualities of home and away-from-home, the familiar and the
strange.

Much more could be said about various aspects and implications of the We-
relation, but I want to turn now to its relevance to our topic. We have been
looking for a connection between subjectivity and history that could be described as the experience of historical existence. I want to contend that it is in
the experience of membership in communities that time is genuinely historical
for us. As a member of a community I become part of a We-subject with an
experience of time that extends back before my birth and can continue even
after my death. Since the We is experienced as genuinely subjective, it has the
same sort of temporality as the I-subject. That is, it is not just an entity persist-
ing in time, or a series of nows, but a occupies a prospective-retrospective

temporal field encompassing past and future. Just as we attribute agency and experience to the we-subject, so we can speak of its expectations and its memories. History is sometimes spoken of as "society's memory," the manner in which a community retains its past such that the past plays an enduring role in the life of the present. To put it another way: just as the present is for the I-subject the vantage point which gives access to a temporal field encompassing past and future; likewise, for the we-subject, the present similarly functions as a vantage-point. But the field which is opened up in this case is much broader. It is to this field that I gain access in virtue of my membership and participation in a community.

But there is more to it than this. Engaged in a community by using the term "we," I enjoy a special relationship with my fellow members, as we have seen. But these fellow members are temporally differentiated in significant ways. Alfred Schutz spoke of the difference between contemporaries, predecessors and successors, but this distinction is much too simple.[3] My contemporaries are further differentiated into elder and younger, distinctions which are more than just chronological. In both family, ethnic and professional contexts, elders are traditionally considered more knowledgeable and more experienced, and act as parents, guides and mentors to the younger. In any case, these intergenerational relations show that being a member of a community means belonging to a temporally continuous entity whose temporality exceeds that of my own subjectivity. With regard to the past, its reach gradually expands in a kind of relay-form from elders to ancestors and predecessors who came "before my time," that is, before my experience and before my birth.

One thing to be emphasized about our account of subjectivity and history is that it remains anchored, like the concept of experience itself, firmly in the present, the here-and-now. But one great advantage of the phenomenological approach to temporality, on which we have drawn extensively, is that it shows there can be no experience of the present, and no presence as experienced, without its horizon or background of past – and future. The "here-and-now" is possible only as emerging from the past and anticipating the future. This is true of the flow of our experience itself, and it is true of the meaningful events, objects, persons and other entities that occur around us and make up our world.

5. Four types of discontinuity

There has been much emphasis on continuity in what I have said so far: the continuity of time-consciousness, which brings past and future into our purview; the continuities of intersubjectivity, especially in the solidarity of membership in the community. But I think the relation between subjectivity and history is marked as much, if not more, by discontinuity and rupture, and I want to turn now to four sorts of discontinuity peculiar to historical experience.

1) We have already spoken, with reference to the identity of the individual, of conflicts that arise from divided loyalties and allegiances. But similar problems arise with the establishment of communities. First, the establishment of the we-subject is not possible without otherness. The community demarcates itself from other communities, just as the individual subject must distinguish itself from others. The intersubjective character of the individual is also affected: I relate to my fellows as members of the same community, with whom I say "we." And I relate to others not just as other individuals but as members of an opposing group: "them" versus "us."

2) The intergenerational continuity of predecessors and successors is also marked, perhaps necessarily, by discontinuity as well: Just as important as the benign relationships of filiation and tradition is the agonistic, indeed, Oedipal, struggle in which the young rebel against the domination of the old, break away and establish their independence.

3) The "historical" is often experienced more by the discontinuity than the continuity of events. Think of the fall of the Berlin Wall in 1989, and the attacks on New York and Washington in 2001, events within the living memories of most of us here. Both were shocking and unexpected, catching everyone by surprise. They were immediately recognized as marking historical turning points, playing out, thanks to television, before our very eyes.

4) This suggests a fourth discontinuity, this time in temporality itself. Claude Lévi-Strauss wrote that history,[4] like any other science, uses a code to gain access to its objects, and that history's code is that of dates and chronology. But dates, he said, are not arrayed along a single axis but belong to different levels or strata. 1610, 1648, 1715 belong to one sequence, that of the French monarchy; the first and second millennia belong to another; ancient, medieval and modern make up a third, and so on. The point is that human temporality occurs on different planes, perhaps starting with the bodily cycles of sleep, waking and digestion. Superimposed on this is the personal history of the individual life-story. Events are experienced within these frameworks, and get their mean-

ing from them. The idea of different levels or strata of temporality introduces a significant new feature to our whole account of temporality and historical time. It suggests that the experience of these large-scale historical events, in which we participate as members of the community of spectators, catapults us onto a different plane of temporality, that of historical time.

What can these events, and our experience of them, tell us about the connection between experience and history? They are, of course, abnormal, exceptional; that's why they were chosen. But the abnormal can often enlighten us about the normal, and I think that's the case here. Paying attention to the peculiar *intentionality* of these examples, let's talk first about the events *as* experienced, then about the experience *of* these events, and finally about the *subject* of that experience.

1) My claim is that these events are directly experienced *as* historical events, which means among other things that we experience them as belonging on the same plane stratum as other historical events, past and future. That is, they are not just events that occur in sequence with other events; their significance derives from their relation to a particular class of events. Both events are experienced as "turning points," even though we may not know what they are turning toward or where they lead. But they are turning points of a peculiar sort: not turning points in *my* life or that of my family or of some particular group, but historical turning points that belong to the class of historical events. The fact that this whole class or stratum comes to our awareness with these extraordinary events suggests that it exists as a permanent possibility in all our experience, even if most of the time we don't notice it. After all, other strata or levels of events – we spoke of the stratum of bodily rhythms and that of the personal life-story – can recede into the background, especially when nothing unusual is going on. So we could venture the claim that we are always open to the historical plane, that it always figures as a permanent possibility in our world, in what we might call the ontology of our lives.

2) This ontology is reflected in the character of our *experience* itself, in particular, in the temporality of our experience. All our experience is temporal, but we are conscious of time by being conscious of events in time. What this investigation reveals is that the temporality of our experience is linked to that of the events which are its objects; the horizon of retention and protention, to use Husserl's language, that is, what lies within the scope of our anticipations and in the background of the past, is situated on the same historical plane as the event we experience in the past. The unexpected and shocking events we have

considered shatter our expectations and reorder our sense of the past, but it is not just the past and future *tout court,* but the *historical* future and the *historical* past, that are reordered by the experience of these events. So the temporality of our experience has a place reserved, we may say, for historical time, situated on a plane that can be activated as the need and the occasion arise.

3) And what of the *subject* of these experiences? Here we recall our analysis of the *we*-subject, the first-person plural. It seems to me that in these cases we become members of a special kind of collective subject that correlates to the historical plane of the events experienced. As we saw, the first-person plural turns up in many contexts: we say "we," in all sorts of different situations, thereby expressing our membership in or identification with some community or other: it can be family, political or social solidarity, professional of vocational allegiance, and so on. In the extreme cases of the Berlin Wall and of 9/11, observing these astonishing and obviously momentous events, we have, as noted before, the sense that "everyone" is watching. These events, I would argue, take us beyond particular identities of any kind. Perhaps there is a hint of the universal subject, humanity as such, with which we identify so rarely, but which can reveal itself as a possibility on these special occasions.

6. Conclusion

What we have been trying to describe here is what the German philosophers called the *Geschichtlichkeit,* or historicity, of human existence. Dilthey wrote that "we are historical beings first, before we are observers of history, and only because we are the former do we become the latter . . . The historical world is always there, and the individual not only observes it from the outside but is intertwined with it."[5] Dilthey, Husserl, Heidegger and others who used this term, in keeping with the historicist tradition, thought of historicity as something like an essential human trait, something bound to subjectivity itself. What my analysis shows, I think, is that it is primarily as members of communities of various sorts that we experience the reality of the past in our present lives. It is here that such terms as "tradition," "inheritance," "legacy" come into play. In the agency of the "we" the past is not just passively given; we take it over or, as Heidegger put it, we "hand down" to ourselves the legacy of the past.[6] Communal existence is active in many ways, but a constant feature of its activity is the manner in which it appropriates its past. That this is an activity is evident from the varying forms this takes. We select from the past what we wish to take over and neglect what we wish to forget. Indeed, remembering and forgetting are central activities by which communities constitute themselves. Remembering leads to commemoration and memorialization, in which we celebrate our heroes and achievements in monuments and popular songs on national holidays. The silence of forgetting can seek to evade responsibility for evils such as slavery or genocide; but it can in some cases have the beneficial effect of overcoming past resentments and grievances. Some communities remember too little; others remember too much.

Let us summarize the results of our account of historicity. We exist historically by virtue of our participation in communities that predate and outlive our individual lives. Through the we-relation historical reality enters directly into our lived experience and becomes part of our identity. Our membership gives us access to a past, a tradition, and a temporal span that it not so much something we know about as something that is part of us. This is the primary sense in which we are, in Dilthey's sense, historical beings before we are observers of history; this is the sense in which we are "intertwined" with history.

Notes

1 Edmund Husserl, *Zur Phänomenologie des inneren Zeitbewusstseins (1893–1917),* ed. R. Boehm (Husserliana X), Haag: Martinus Nijhoff.
2 Jean-Paul Sartre, *La Transcendence de l'ego,* Paris: Vrin.
3 Alfred Schutz, *The Phenomenology of the Social World,* trans. George Walsh and Frederick Lehnert, Evanston: Northwestern University Press, 1967, p. 208.
4 Claude Lévi-Strauss, *La Pensée sauvage,* Paris: Plon, 1962, pp. 342ff.
5 Wilhelm Dilthey, *Der Aufbau der geschichtlichen Welt in den Geisteswissenschaften.* Einleitung von Manfred Riedel, Frankfurt: Suhrkamp Verlag, 1970, p. 346.
6 Martin Heidegger, *Sein und Zeit,* Tübingen: Max Niemeyer Verlag, p. 383.

Danish Yearbook of Philosophy, Vol. 48–49 (2013–2014), 21–36

THE PLACE OF FRIENDSHIP:
MAURICE BLANCHOT AND ROBERT ANTELME

CHRISTOPHER FYNSK

My ambition in this essay is to draw forth the significance of a most remarkable commemorative piece that Maurice Blanchot wrote for his departed friend, Robert Antelme (1917–1990).[1] This brief text is arresting and deeply haunting in itself, eminently worthy of attention. But when read in the light of Blanchot's earlier work, it is nothing less than astonishing – so unexpected that one is moved to enquire as to how such a statement could have been possible. To approach this essay, therefore, I would like to begin by taking up an earlier text that has an almost canonical status as regards Blanchot's approach to commemoration and friendship itself. This earlier essay, written after the passing of Georges Bataille,[2] would actually appear to exclude the gesture made in "*Dans la nuit surveillée*," even as it indicates the threshold of for the step Blanchot makes in this later text.

"*L'amitié*," we might note immediately, did not seek to commemorate or somehow preserve in memory the man or the friendship that had bound Maurice Blanchot to him. Indeed, we might say that it was written to preserve the man and the friendship *from* the appropriation of memory or any historicizing approach. There could be no witness to the excessive "truth" of this now disappearing existence, no matter how veridical the testimony; the void that marked it, that gave it, would always escape. Only in friendship could the immensity of this passing be known, and this friendship was itself destined to effacement. I will permit myself to quote in its entirety the opening section of this astounding statement:

> How could one agree to speak of this friend? Neither in praise nor in the interest of some truth. The traits of his character, the forms of his existence, the episodes of his life, even in keeping with the search for which he felt himself responsible to the point of irresponsibility, belong to no one. There are no witnesses. Those who were closest say only what was close to them, not the distance that affirmed itself in this proximity, and distance ceases as soon as presence ceases. Vainly do we try to maintain, with our words, with our writings, what is absent; vainly do we offer it the appeal of our memories and a sort of figure, the joy of remaining with the day, life prolonged by a truthful appearance. We are only looking to fill a void, we cannot bear the pain: the affirmation of this void. Who could agree to receive its insignificance, an insignificance so enormous that we do not have a memory capable of

containing it and such that we ourselves must already slip into oblivion in order to sustain it, for the time of this slippage, into the very enigma this insignificance represents? Everything we say tends to veil the one affirmation: that all must fade and that we can remain loyal only so long as we watch over this movement that fades, to which something in us that rejects all memory already belongs. (A 326/289)

Blanchot begins, as we have heard, with a refusal that *defends*. The existence of the individual that has now passed belongs to no one. And whether or not the implicit admonition to those closest is directed in some specific way, it clearly extends to any gesture that would seek to appropriate or say the inappropriable, which was surely a temptation for Blanchot himself. What was there, Blanchot insists, even as absence, is no longer there. The distance in Georges Bataille's inestimable presence, of which Maurice Blanchot would speak elsewhere so eloquently in describing the way it was harboured in his language (his speech, first of all, but also his books),[3] is declared here to have ceased; the passing is irrevocable. The event itself exceeds our hold and renders vain any effort to contain or supplement the void with memory or some figure, however life-like or *apparently* veridical this prolonging fiction might be. Any effort to hold back something from this absenting only serves to avoid its fact, its insistence: *l'affirmation de ce vide*. But who, Blanchot continues, could face this presence of an absence, this insistent cessation, given the immeasurability of its insignificance? No remembrance or anamnesis can hold this void that only forgetting, if we could accept such a thing (for it contains the forgetting of ourselves), could bear in the time of a furtive slippage, carrying us into the heart of its enigma. The meaning of this passing is exorbitant, and anything we could say would obscure what Blanchot terms the one affirmation – an affirmation that necessarily exceeds Blanchot's own phrasing of it: "...that all must fade [*que tout doit s'effacer*] and that we can remain loyal only so long as we watch over this movement that fades [*ce movement qui s'efface*], to which something in us that rejects all memory already belongs."

Blanchot's statement will go on to suggest what it meant to watch over the movement of effacement already in Bataille's lifetime. Friendship, he says, dictated a discretion founded on a fundamental distance that measured everything between them. This discretion (extending quite beyond the mere reserve that would already render any divulgence regarding the person unthinkable) did not inhibit communication, Blanchot insists; rather, it brought the two into the difference of speech and the silence it borders: a speech that was already an "infinite conversation." To watch over meant to preserve an "*entente*" and to maintain (here, *entretenir*) the movement of the conversation. But this discretion was always shaped by awareness of what awaited it and what it would become, which Blanchot names abruptly in the course of his meditation "the fissure of death" (A 329/291). At this term, the furtive, imminent presence to which discretion always answered gave way to a radical effacement of the separation that held in relation, a dissipation of the distance-between from which there could be no return.[4] Even his own presence, Blanchot notes, would suffer this last, inexorable effacement. Thus his concluding paragraph will underscore again that however tempting recollection and some figuration of what has passed might be, this restorative gesture will remain vain. To "watch over" during the life of the friendship meant to preserve a speech and a silence; after the closing of this relation, there was nothing more than accompanying this friendship into forgetting.

In sum, there was no recalling to life, by any figuration, what had spoken in Georges Bataille's existence. What its passing left to thought (to the extent that something of reflective thought could itself survive, however briefly, in thought's own struggle with the invisible and thus "accompany" friendship into forgetting [A 330/292]) was no more than the enigma to which this passing in its measureless insignificance pointed: that all must give way to effacement (*que tout doit s'effacer*). It is true that this phrase, so simple in appearance that it could be passed along (and over) as common wisdom, actually points to something more than a necessity or a destiny, as we learn in the succeeding clause. For this necessity becomes in human existence an exigency that shapes the meaning of friendship and fidelity for the fact that "something in us" belongs to this movement. But does the exigency of watching over the finitude of Being from the ground of human finitude and what the latter dictates in the way of accompaniment somehow direct us toward the possibility of the gesture Blanchot will make in his text on Antelme? Has the interdiction of any figuration or semblance of a dialogue not prohibited such a statement?

My rapid and somewhat brutal translation of "effacement" with "finitude" (a translation that cannot fail to afflict in return the notion of finitude itself) will signal the level and extent of questioning required here, which is both existential and ontological. And clearly, we are left with a forbidding question as to what Blanchot might mean by the phrase, "watching over," which offers the link between the two commemorative texts under consideration. What survival (in/of thought) was implied by this term? It goes without saying that there can be no adequate treatment, in the space of this essay, of the questions that have opened here. But in following a few textual links, it may be possible to evoke the steps Blanchot has taken in that space that separates the two statements.

We may note, first of all, that the phrase "*tout doit s'effacer, tout s'effacera*" will recur more than once in Blanchot's work (while the motif of effacement will itself be developed extensively).[5] Its appearance in *Le pas au-delà* (1973) is of particular interest for us on this occasion. The passage in question does not define "watching over," but it does describe one response to the exigency of effacement:

> Everything must give way to effacement, everything will efface itself [*Tout doit s'effacer, tout s'effacera*]. It is in accord with the infinite exigency of effacement that writing takes place and has its place. (PA 76/53)

These words are then followed immediately by a form of (unmarked) exchange:

> Even if writing leaves traces, and, in leaving them, makes it so that traces are engendered or produced out of the life of traces? One can answer: to write is to go by way of the world of traces towards the effacement of traces and of all traces, since traces are opposed to totality and always already disperse themselves.

Writing meets the "infinite exigency" of effacement and thereby finds its place. The ground for this accord, however, remains elusive inasmuch as writing is normally understood as *perduring* in its traces and calls, in the obscurity of these traces that outlive or simply exceed any order of meaning, for further writing. This multiplication would hardly seem to serve the exigency of effacement. But a possible answer is offered with an account of writing that is in keeping with Blanchot's unfolding reflections on fragmentation in the period to which *Le pas au-delà* belongs. Writing, the possible interlocutor offers, engages the "dispersive" character of the trace (Derrida would call this "dissemination"), its resistance to any gathering in meaning, in such a way as to approach the suspension of presentation that belongs to what Blanchot terms "*le neutre*."[6] To write would be to approach the "neutral" of effacement, or, perhaps better, it would be to approach *le neutre* in its guise of effacement. We see again, in any case, that "*tout s'efface, tout doit s'effacer*" does not refer to the inexorable character of time to which all must answer – or not simply; it names a disruption in time that compromises any "horizonal" offering (as Heidegger understood it in the existential analytic, for example, in arguing that time was the horizon for the understanding of Being) by which we would have a relation to history or to passing (mortality) in general. It disrupts, from the start, the formation of the *"tout"* (*"le tout"*) that we may now hear in *"tout doit s'effacer"* – the order gathered by a logos or a memory. Where writing engages effacement, the horizon of all legibility and all evidence is left behind or breached. The order of meaning and appearance is scattered, leaving an excessive "insignificance" in a neutral, interrupted space where the very meaning of "exigency" is altered, no less than the freedom of the one who undertakes to answer. It is in this space that thought "must struggle with the invisible where everything falls back into indifference" as Blanchot put it in his essay on Bataille (A 330/292). But it will also be apparent now that "indifference" is not the mere absence of those differential relations ordered by the negative (and thus ultimately the dialectic). The "affirmation of the void" holds something else for thought; it calls to another form of relation – something undoubtedly comparable to what Blanchot had evoked already a decade before his commemorative essay on Bataille in his brief narrative, *La folie du jour*. There, effacement is given an epochal or quasi-messianic meaning, and a narrating voice that has evidently suffered this catastrophe not only brings a form of effacement to the fore in and by the very strangeness of its speech and mode of enunciation (*"je,"* we would say in employing a Blanchotian shorthand, is already in the grips of an *"il"*), but ecstatically affirms the eclipse that will come with its eventual return, enigmatically pointing to some form of act: *"ce jour s'effaçant, je m'effacerai avec lui."* It is an astonishing declaration that requires long consideration, but it will at least alert us here to the fact that while Blanchot's notion of writing invites an extreme of passivity, it also points to an affirmative turn that we will again encounter in Blanchot's text on Antelme.

Following the reference to writing opened by the passage we have considered in *Le pas au-delà*, we may perhaps now approach a still later passage in *L'écriture du désastre* (1980) wherein Blanchot contrasts a construction of a relation to death (through the work of psychoanalysis, for example) that seeks escape from its undefined menace when it presents itself in its "immemorial" character with a writing that *allows* what "in us" belongs to effacement. Again, we see a reference to an act of exception comparable to the *"je m'effacerai"* of *La folie du jour*:

> Dying means: you are dead already, in an immemorial past, of a death which was not yours, which you have thus neither known nor lived, but under the threat of which you believe you are called upon to live; you await it henceforth in the future, constructing a future to make

> it possible at last – possible as something that will take place and will belong to the realm of experience.
>
> To write is no longer to situate death in the future – the death which is always already past; to write is to accept that one has to die without making death present and without making oneself present to it. To write is to know that death has taken place even though it has not been experienced, and to recognize it in the forgetfulness that it leaves – in the traces which, effacing themselves, call upon one to *except oneself from the cosmic order* and to abide where the disaster makes the real impossible and desire undesirable. (ED 108–109/66)

The discussion in *L'écriture du désastre* that follows this paragraph identifies the dimension of experience to which we are exposed by our finitude as "the impossible necessary death" – a dying that thought bears in it and that bears it, but which cannot be received except in a form of forgetting. Blanchot's pages will focus on conceptual tools offered by psychoanalysis (the motif of a dying *infans*, offered by Winnicott and Leclaire) and by the Hegelian dialectic, emphasizing that this death cannot be assumed by the concept, which can only ever re-mark the exigency it represents.[7] But some figuration, a "fictive relation of singularity" is nonetheless essential to speech and life. Some fiction is required by a movement of effacement that Blanchot links to an effacement in time itself:

> A child already dead is dying, by a murderous death, a child of whom we know nothing (even if we characterize him as marvellous, terrifying, tyrannical, or indestructible) except this: that the possibility of speaking and of life depend on the fictive establishment, through death and murder, of a relation of singularity with a mute past, with a prehistory, with a past, then, which is outside the past and of which the eternal infans is the figure at the same time that he is concealed therein. "A child is being killed." Let us make no mistake about this present: it signifies that the operation could never take place once and for all, that it is not accomplished at any privileged moment of time, that it operates inoperably and thus tends to be none but the very time that destroys (effaces) time, an effacement, or a destruction, or a gift that has always already avowed itself in the precession of a Saying outside any said, a work of writing whereby this effacement, far from effacing itself in its turn, is perpetuated without term even in the *interruption* that constitutes its mark. (ED 116/71)

"*On tue un enfant*" is presumably a fictive saying that meets the necessity Blanchot identifies for speech and life and would bring to language a forever prior saying ("*Dire*") that will have already avowed the event of effacement itself. This fictive saying ("*on tue un enfant*") is in turn destined to a form of effacement if ever it is brought to sound ("a phrase immediately torn from every language, for it draws us outside consciousness and unconsciousness each time it is given to us, other than ourselves and in a relation of impossibility with the other, to pronounce this unpronounceable" [ED 117/72]), but in its extreme insufficiency and obscurity, it nonetheless relays what is at once destruction and a gift (what Blanchot names "survival" will be inseparable from this gift) that Blanchot will attempt to capture with the motif of a watch and an awakening:

> What does "to survive" mean then, if not to live in and by acquiescence to refusal, in the exhaustion of emotion, withdrawn from any interest in oneself, dis-interested, extenuated to a state of utter calmness, expecting nothing?
> – Consequently, waiting and watching, for suddenly wakened and, knowing this full well henceforth, never wakeful enough." (ED 179/116)

Effacement/Writing and the Exigency of Fiction/Affirmation and Watching. These hardly constitute a bridge to the brief text on Antelme, but they hint, I believe, at its possibility. The possibility inheres in a term that was noticeably absent from the meditation on Bataille's passing and its meaning for the relation of friendship: writing. "To watch over the movement of effacement" in the essay for Bataille entailed refusing the temptation of any re-vivifying figuration, any appeal to semblance (by a dialogue, for example) in the name of the strictest possible understanding of loss. But Blanchot's meditation on the *exigency* that lies in effacement (the exigency that gives writing its place) directs him not just to another sense of responsibility pertaining to friendship, but to the assertion of a right that bears on fiction. Let me thus turn to this text now and attempt to approach its singular movement.

*

In *L'écriture du désastre*, the phrase, "a child is being killed" was offered as an impossible saying of effacement. In *"Dans la nuit surveillée,"* something comparable is offered, though the words emerge from a friendship sinking into forgetting and call to something like its accompaniment. These words that come in the night of a sleep deprived of sleep do not mark the presence of Antelme; they indicate, rather, his absenting. There is a nearness of the phrase itself, we are told, but it is given in a removed proximity, and the phrase itself, in its very repetition, effectively says effacement. We could say that an uncertain identification ("I persuaded myself") is brought to focus ("I understood immediately") with a firm link to Robert Antelme, but this identification is given only to cede immediately to another naming; the *"je"* effaces itself in its repetition to allow – or even to insist upon – the hearing of the names of the camps enumerated. Listen to these names again, the voice says: they are slipping away. Perhaps they have never been recalled more powerfully, and this is precisely what seems to shock the narrating voice who pursues a dialogue without speech. Are we forgetting? (The *"je"* marked in the first paragraph is now replaced by a more anonymous *"nous."*) Yes, you forget, comes the answer. You forget all the more for remembering and by a memory that allows you to survive and preserve your love for me. And then the incredible words: "But one does not love a dead person…"

Is this not, in fact, the lesson given in the essay on Bataille? Have the self-effacing words, *"je m'éloigne,"* in their very becoming anonymous, not recalled the narrator to "an insignificance so unmeasured that we do not have a memory capable of containing it"? One can love, certainly, but then one has lost the meaning of death or non-being, which is the very impossibility of meaning, or the "impossibility" of non-being. One has failed the more severe imperative of watching over effacement. Here, however, and this is crucial to our larger discussion, the effacement belongs to history itself, to what Robert Antelme's experience gave of a relation to the immemorial of those names. Robert's *"je m'éloigne"* effectively echoes *"je m'efface"* as a statement about history while reiterating the impossible of the imperative to which Blanchot gave insistent attention in the 1980's and thereafter: "Don't forget." *"Je m'éloigne"* says the fact of history thought from effacement, and this enjoins the impossible task of watching over "that for which there is no memory…but which is always, in one way or another, and always in anguish, the immemorial."[8]

From here, or rather from an indeterminate temporal passage that is marked by a subsequent reading of the dialogue that has preceded, the narrator, or the one we may now recognize as a writer, knows his blinding (I will refer to this narrating figure henceforth as "Blanchot," recognizing that this identification cannot be taken simply for granted). Robert Antelme will have already been lost to sight. The words that follow thus come in a tone of lament that is conveyed by the past tense ("the incomparable friend that I knew") and then the delicacy of the following phrase: "He was so simple." But the sober awareness of losing from sight this friend, this sobriety of the day, so to speak, appears to allow another form of statement, which is itself sobering in the directness of its prose. Here, Blanchot refers to the teaching of *L'espèce humaine* as Blanchot had elucidated it in paired essays published in *L'entretien infini*, the first devoted to Jewish thought and what Levinas allows us to understand of the teaching that occurs in the relation to the infinite alterity of the other, the second devoted to *L'espèce humaine* itself (EI, 180–200/123–136). What is conveyed in *L'espèce humaine* is not easily summarized, but I will restate Blanchot's own rapid evocation of it with the following: that even the oppressor cannot escape the indestructible element of the human relation which they seek to destroy and that this very violence brings to the fore. Antelme's wisdom was such that he was able to draw forth the human truth of this unfathomable ground of human relation, affirming it against the efforts of the oppressor and refusing to deny it even to that oppressor.[9]

But Blanchot adds another step to what his essay on Antelme had brought forth regarding the burden of the ethical relation. Or, to put this more precisely, he draws out something that his meditation on "the indestructible" revealed about the human truth to which he refers, namely that what is proper to the human is exposure to an abyss – an "inhuman," that can never be appropriated. The point is illustrated with reference to an incident recounted in *L'espèce humaine* in which Antelme finds himself unable to recognize a dying friend. Here is the exposure to effacement in its most terrible form, because the other, K., presents, in his unrecognizability, an unfathomable void, a nothing that attends life itself. Blanchot's brief evocation of this encounter in the text we are reading is powerful in itself, but it is noteworthy that for the republication of the text in a collective volume published by Gallimard, he requested that the relevant pages from *L'espèce humaine* be reprinted next to his statement.[10] It is as though Blanchot's simple account of the lesson of that passage could not be enough – that the written testimony was required for the saying of this exposure Blanchot sought to recall. Such a saying was required, we might presume, for the passage Blanchot makes to the statement of the imperative and the affirmation with which this paragraph concludes.

What did the passage regarding Robert's visit to the infirmary underscore or reinforce in Blanchot's meditation? To begin to answer this question, I believe it is crucial to recognize that Blanchot understands *L'espèce humaine* not merely as a form of historical testimony (twice he refuses this word for the book), but rather as a rendering of the experience of the camps in what he terms a "just" or "true" speech.[11] *L'espèce humaine* thus brings to its writing a hospitable word that receives the unknown or the foreign that is humankind when it is exposed as that ever-receding limit Blanchot names the indestructible. I follow Blanchot's reading of Levinas in asserting that only such a hospitable word can transmit what I have called a teaching. Citing *L'espèce humaine* in the republication of *"Dans la nuit surveillée,"* Blanchot has implicitly deferred to this hospitable word, opening again to the questioning it bears and the exigency it transmits. I say "opening again" because it is difficult not to hear in the scene from the infirmary multiple, if muffled, echoes of what had been written in *"Dans la nuit surveillée."* Whether or not Blanchot intended such an echoing (and it is hard to imagine he did not recognize it), it is evident that Antelme's account somehow implicated Blanchot. He too, as we have read, had been visited at his bedside by Robert Antelme, and he too (but the roles are reversed now), was forced to acknowledge that he had lost his friend from sight. Neither the visit by night (where Antelme gives voice to his effacement in visiting Blanchot's sleep without sleep), nor the awareness of the day conveyed in the two paragraphs of reflection, can be strictly correlated with the scene in the infirmary, even if Antelme's last words to K. bring their own terrible echo (*"Bonsoir, mon vieux,"* he had said, acknowledging his departure into the night).[12] But it seems evident that Blanchot has somehow received the words of Antelme's account or has been received by them in such a way that a teaching and an exigency have formed for him. This encounter, transmitted in these words (like an encounter we read in *Le pas au-delà*[13]), calls for its translation. What Antelme learned or understood in that encounter becomes a lesson for Blanchot and an imperative: "We must learn to live with this void. We will maintain plenitude even in nothingness."

We have heard something of this imperative in the pages from *L'écriture du désastre* cited earlier. There, it will be recalled, Blanchot contrasts a refusal or avoidance of "the impossible necessary death" with an acceptance of it, via writing and the reception of the exigency it brings: to except oneself from the sidereal order and to open onto the vacant night of what he terms *le dés-astre.* Here, Blanchot actually performs that acceptance with the astonishing words "We will maintain plenitude even onto nothing." "Plenitude" is not a very Blanchotian word, and I will not try to do more here than underscore its enigma.[14] But here I want to stress how the acceptance or acquiescence affords a kind of passage. The moral or ethical decision, which gathers the *"we"* enunciated in an ethical imperative ("we must") into a community that holds at its heart exposure to a nothing ("we will maintain"), gives way to another form of affirmation: "This is why, Robert, I still have my place next to you." The latter conclusion, also giving a "we" of sorts, is still coloured by the ethical decision that precedes, but the right or the place that it asserts is existentially grounded, if I may draw here from an early Heideggerian vocabulary. What Blanchot is describing, or claiming, is a being-with, or, more precisely, a dying-with that he now feels empowered to claim and to draw forth in a form of writing.

I am proceeding now to a rather firm interpretation of a few extremely difficult lines, so I would like to back up slightly to sketch my understanding of the passage I have briefly evoked – the passage from an account of a teaching and the lesson drawn from it, to an affirmation and then a striking re-assertion and even grounding of the relation that was evoked in the opening of the text. To put this briefly, I want to emphasize that such a passage was only possible because Blanchot received Antelme's teaching in what I have termed a hospitable writing. I have tried to suggest that Blanchot found himself implicated in Antelme's account of the encounter (with nothing) in the infirmary. I would add, or emphasize, that this implication was not a matter of simple identification (if such a thing could ever be simple); it was rather that Antelme had communicated his exposure to an unfathomable void in the living presence of the other and had confided – in French, this would be *confié* – his understanding of the exigency that formed in this exposure. He had in effect related a trace of the exposure to alterity in a responsive word (a "just" or "true" word as Blanchot put it in his essay in *L'espèce humaine*) and had given it over to the fidelity, the keeping of the other. The declaration of the concluding paragraph, I want to suggest, was made in such a fidelity. It is then from this answerable response that Blanchot could claim his place next to his departing friend. Because this place forms *by the writing of the other*, or, more precisely, in a kind of relay of that writing (whereby another – Blanchot – writes in the place opened by Antelme[15]), I believe we are perhaps justified in understanding it as comparable to the one that was evoked at the opening of the brief narrative that Blanchot offered in the pages following his meditation on "the impossible necessary death" in *L'écriture du désastre* – a narrative that appears to give a kind of figuration to an experience of the event of effacement, or at least to the "impossible" words that transcribe it: "*on tue un enfant.*" That narrative, offered as what is perhaps a primal scene, opens as follows: "You who live later, close to a heart that beats no more, suppose, suppose this…" (ED 117/72).[16] The text addresses one who has lived *near* an event of effacement, a passing of some kind, and invites to *suppose* such a passing, or, more precisely, a figuration of this passing. Later in *L'écriture du désastre*, Blanchot returns to the status of this supposition and states that such an act of fictioning is required because otherwise, "speaking of the child who has never spoken (the *infans*) would be to draw back into history, into experience or into the real….what has ruined them (history, experience, or the real)" (ED 178/114). Thus, only something like sup-position can entertain the effacement in question and then what it might mean to survive this effacement: "waiting and watching, for suddenly awakened, and, knowing this full well henceforth, never wakeful enough" (ED 179/116, as cited above).

"*Dans la nuit surveillée*," I would argue, remains in the order of supposition, even if it affirms the right to such supposition:

> And this "night watched over" in which you come to see me is not an illusion where eve-rything would disappear but my right to make you live, even in the void I feel approaching.

But is "the night watched over" itself an expression of this right to make the other live (the syntax of the sentence and the quotation marks themselves hint that this night is something claimed and thus brought to some form of saying or figuration), or does its event, its "fact," confer the right? The latter interpre-tation seems most immediately compelling and almost evident: the trace of Antelme's departure/effacement has brought Blanchot this right. But it is also clear at this point in the meditation that Blanchot himself has come to assume, or is assuming, the watch in the night, that he is now writing from the place of the other. The exposure to the approaching void that Blanchot evoked in the preceding paragraph has come to found a knowledge of the night in which Blanchot sensed the approaching withdrawal of his friend. It has given him that night in the space/time of a kind of survival, thus rendering possible the as-sumption and the very writing of "the night watched over," a literary act. The night, attended by the trace of Robert Antelme's passing (as transcribed in the words "*je m'éloigne, je m'éloigne*"), may thus be understood as both the origin and the issue of this piece of meditative writing; it *becomes* the condition of the right to fiction affirmed in the text, which folds upon itself as this right is af-firmed. We have here, though I offer this suggestion with great reserve, a most astonishing recollection of the haunting title of Blanchot's great essay on liter-ary language: "Literature and the Right to Death."[17] If we follow this echo, we are perhaps prompted to read the phrase "right to death" as something like "the right to figure an accompaniment onto death—the right to a saying of a dying-with." But I have to acknowledge that I use the word "figure" here with even greater reserve, because the necessary paucity of such a figuration has already been indicated to us; in this very piece of writing, it consists of nothing more than the exchanged words we have read. "To make you live": this is *entretenir*, to be sure, but in the manner of sustaining that opening onto the effacing names and the impossible relation that they carry or into which they are carried in this exchange – sustaining a relation to the anonymous and ultimately unthinkable suffering to which those names point, the effacement of that suffering. *Faire vivre*: this is nothing more, even if it involves what he called a "plenitude," than retaining relation to the effacement to which this other has afforded relation.

I stress again the way *"je m'éloigne"* opens onto a form of historical testimony on the ground of Blanchot's insistence that these words spoke not of Robert Antelme, but of what he came to bear through his experience of the camps. But Blanchot's way of introducing his understanding of *"la nuit surveillée"* also drives us in a comparable direction (toward a real). That night is not an illusion, he insists. Were it a mere dream or some comparable fantasy (we might even say "fiction," in the traditional sense of this term), then all would in fact be lost; the relation to Robert Antelme would be lost in a night of a different kind. We might be tempted to interpellate the assertion at this point: No, it is not an illusion, it is real, even if it is brought to us in writing. And perhaps that interpellation is not mistaken (keeping in mind all of Blanchot's wariness with regard to the term"real"). But we can say, at least, following Blanchot, that this night is real in the manner of a legitimating condition of an act of writing (*"faire vivre"*) in which the *entretien* I have described would find justification. In this night, Blanchot declares, I have a right to this commemoration and to keeping a vigil in relation to the names upon which Robert Antelme's own opens – a right to accompany the friendship even onto nothing, as Blanchot declared in the essay on Bataille. I have been given the right and the obligation to bring to language an instance of the effacement that is the abyssal ground of history itself.

Notes

1   *"Dans la nuit surveillée,"* in *Maurice Blanchot: Écrits politiques, 1953–1993* (Paris: Gallimard, 2008), 251–53; translated by Zakir Paul in *Maurice Blanchot: Political Writings* (New York: Fordham University Press, 2010), 251–52. The text is brief enough to cite here in its entirety:
In The Night That Is Watched Over
It is slowly, in those nights when I sleep without sleeping, that I became conscious (this word is inappropriate) of your proximity, which is distant nonetheless. I persuaded myself that you were here: not you, but this repeated phrase: "I am going far away, I am going far away."
I immediately understood that Robert, so generous, so little concerned about himself, was not speaking to me about or for himself, but of all the places of extermination, of which (if it was him speaking) he listed a few: "Listen to them, listen to the names: Treblinka, Chelmno, Belzec, Majdanek, Auschwitz, Sobibor, Birkenau, Ravensbrück, Dachau."

"But," I say, speaking, not speaking, "do we forget?" – "Yes, you forget; you forget all the more for remembering. Your memory does not impede you from living, from surviving, nor even from loving me. But one does not love a dead person, because then the meaning escapes you, the impossibility of meaning, the nonbeing and impossibility of nonbeing."

When I reread these lines, I know that I have already lost sight of Robert Antelme, the incomparable friend I knew. He was so simple, and at the same time so rich, with a knowledge that the greatest minds lacked. In the experience of servitude that was his, even if he shared it with others, he kept the human truth from which he knew not to exclude even those who oppressed him.

But he went even further: not recognizing a companion (K.) he had come to see in the infirmary, who was still alive, he understood that there is a nothingness in life itself, an unfathomable void against which one has to defend oneself, even while acknowledging its approach. We must learn to live with this void. We will maintain plenitude even in nothingness.

This is why, Robert, I still have my place next to you. And this "night watched over" in which you come to see me is not an illusion where everything would disappear but my right to make you live, even in the void I feel approaching.

November 1993

2   This essay, originally published in 1962, appears in the collection of essays to which it gives its name: *L'amitié* (Paris: Gallimard, 1971), 326–30. This volume is translated by Elizabeth Rottenberg: *Friendship* (Stanford: Stanford University Press, 1997), 289–92. I follow Rottenberg's excellent translation closely, but as with the other translations offered in this essay, I have made slight alterations that derive from the perspective afforded me by my guiding questions. Subsequent citations in the body of this essay will be followed with the abbreviation "A," followed by the French and English page numbers.

3   I refer to the essay on Bataille (also published originally in 1962) collected in *L'entretien infini* (Paris: Gallimard, 1969): "*L'affirmation et la passion de la pensée négative*," 300–13; see the translation by Susan Hanson in *The Infinite Conversation* (Minneapolis: University of Minnesota Press, 1993), 202–10. Subsequent citations of *L'entretien infini* will be preceded by the abbreviation "EI."

4   "*And yet, when the event itself comes, it brings this change: not the deepening of the separation but its effacement; not the widening of the caesura but its levelling out and the dissipation of the void between us where formerly there developed the frankness of a relation without history*" (A 329/292). In subsequent remarks on effacement (in a passage from *L'écriture du désastre* to which I will return), Blanchot indicates the possibility of this use of the term "effacement" for the death that he refers to as "organic." See, *L'écriture du désastre* (Paris: Gallimard, 1980, 114–15, translated by Anne Smock, *The Writing of the Disaster* (Lincoln: University of Nebraska Press, 1986), 69–70. Subsequent citations will be preceded by the abbreviation "ED."

5   A striking instance is to be found in the letter Blanchot sent to Roger Laporte (ultimately destined to Philippe Lacoue-Labarthe). The phrase appears (in quotation marks, thus as a citation) almost at the beginning of this important letter in a summary response to hostile critical remarks by Tzvetan Todorov: "Neither the analysis nor the critical judgment of Todorov touch me. For the judgment judges him as well. And whether or not I should belong to the past is truly without importance. '*Tout s'efface, tout doit s'effacer*'" (in *Maurice Blanchot, Passion Politique*, ed. Jean-Luc Nancy [Paris: Galilée, 2011], p. 47). Blanchot's statement could be understood by an ungenerous or hasty reader as suggesting that his pre-war positions, like the current debate in which Blanchot found himself ensnared, were ultimately of negligible significance (this judgment would extend, undoubtedly, to all of his work). But Blanchot's intent is surely quite different. He would be suggesting that Todorov has missed where the

real meaning of the history he has traversed (what Blanchot sometimes calls "the meaning of meaning") is to be found, namely in the movement of effacement – thus beyond any "historical" meaning or truth – to which Blanchot had devoted himself in his post-war thought and writing. The point I am suggesting here will only emerge in the course of this discussion. But in anticipation of my conclusions, let me suggest that Antelme gives to Blanchot a relation to an experience of history that is not available to the domain of "history." In other words, he gives, in a saying of effacement, an opening onto disaster, which Blanchot draws forth in writing *"Dans la nuit surveillée"* and in reciting the names of the camps he associates with Antelme's own name. Antelme gives to Blanchot a way of relating to the "immemorial" that would not foreclose it, as do appeals to history like that of Todorov or even Nancy himself. Unfortunately, Nancy fails to grasp this point and brings his astonishingly ungenerous judgment on Blanchot back onto himself in his preface to this volume.

The notion of "effacement" itself requires a study on its own (which I must now acknowledge as a welcome obligation). It is quite noticeable in *L'espace littéraire* ([Paris: Gallimard, 1955], translated by Anne Smock as *The Space of Literature* [Lincoln: University of Nebraska Press, 1992]; henceforth abbreviated as "EL"), where it serves to describe the writer's experience of losing himself in his writing. ("In the effacement toward which he is summoned, the 'great writer' still holds back; what speaks is no longer he himself, but neither is it the sheer slipping away of no one's word. For he maintains the authoritative though silent affirmation of the effaced 'I'" (EL 17-18/27). But it is also given a striking ontological import when Blanchot describes the disintegration of place in his famous meditation on the image and the non-presence of the corpse. This essay, "The Two Versions of the Imaginary," begins with a statement on the image that is already pertinent for this discussion: "When there is nothing, the image finds in this nothing its necessary condition, but there it disappears. The image needs the neutrality and the fading [*effacement*] of the world; it wants everything to return to the indifferent deep where nothing is affirmed" (EL 345/254). The becoming-image of the thing, like the becoming-image of language, as Blanchot describes it in these pages, is itself a form of effacement. But this becoming-image points into a featureless void: "It is as though … the monotony of an infinite disintegration were at work to efface the living truth proper to every place and make it equivalent to the absolute neutrality of death" (EL 353/259). In both of these last sentences, we glimpse the meaning of the *"tout"* in *"tout s'efface"*: it is the order of truth or that of the "day," what Blanchot calls in the second sentence "the world" (I will return to this point). I would add that every time Blanchot brings into the play the term *"sans,"* "without" (*"x sans x"*), we have to do with a form of effacement. We will see further uses of this critically important term as we proceed.

6   Blanchot's developing thought of fragmentation is in fact inseparable from his turn to the notion of *"le neutre."* For the link between these terms, see *L'entretien infini* (447–458/298–313). Leslie Hill's *Maurice Blanchot and Fragmentary Writing* (London: Continuum, 2012) is particularly valuable for this topic.

7   "It remains, however, that if death, murder, suicide are put to work, and if death loses its sting by becoming powerless power and then negativity, there is, each time one advances with the help of *possible* death, the necessity of not disregarding or simply passing over the unphrased death, the death without name, without concept, *impossibility* itself" (ED, 112/66).

8   This sentence is drawn from Blanchot's essay, *"N'oubliez pas,"* in *Maurice Blanchot: Écrits politiques 1953–1993* (Paris: Gallimard, 2008), 242. The full passage reads as follows: "Must we say once again (yes, we must) that Auschwitz, an event that makes a ceaseless appeal to us, demands, through the testimonies, the inexhaustible duty not to forget: Remember, beware of forgetting and yet, in this faithful Memory, *never will you know*. I underline this because what

is said here sends us back to that for which there is no memory, to the unrepresentable, to unspeakable horror, which, however, is always, in one way or another, and always in anguish, the immemorial" (translated by Zakir Paul in *Maurice Blanchot: Political Writings, 1953–1993* [New York: Fordham University Press, 2010]). I have restored the plural to Blanchot's reference to "*les témoignages*" in view of the import of the text on Antelme we are reading here. It is quite significant, I believe, that the exigency presented by the Shoah passes by way of the singular voice.

9 I address Blanchot's two essays and their pairing in *Last Steps: Blanchot's Exilic Writing* (New York: Fordham University Press, 2013), 34–56.

10 *Robert Antelme: Textes inédits sur L'espèce humaine, Essais et témoignages* (Paris: Gallimard, 1996).

11 See *L'entretien infini* (Paris: Gallimard, 1969), 196, 197. In the translation by Susan Hanson, *The Infinite Conversation* (Minneapolis: University of Minnesota Press, 1993), see p. 134.

12 See Robert Antelme, *Textes inédits*, 75.

13 I am referring to the encounter with the young woman on the street which plays a role I hesitate to call "central" in *Le pas au-delà* (86–87). My commentary on this episode and its meaning for Blanchot appears in *Last Steps*, 130–36.

14 The term would appear to take up something from Blanchot's previous description of Antelme: "he was so simple and at the same time so rich." But it remains challenging to think "plenitude" together with the exposure to the void to which Blanchot refers in this text.

15 I am proceeding here from a very rich passage in the pages on fragmentation from *L'entretien infini* to which I referred earlier. There, Blanchot writes the following: "*Will you, as a self, accept taking this self as problematic, as fictive, and nonetheless more necessary in this way than if you were able to close up around yourself like a circle sure of its center? Then, perhaps, in writing, you will accept as the secret of writing this premature yet already belated conclusion that is in accord with forgetting:* that others write in *my* place, this place without occupant that is my sole identity; this is what makes death for an instant joyful, aleatory" (EI 458/313). See my commentary on this passage in *Last Steps*, 140–42.

16 The phrase I have cited ends with the words, "*supposez-le.*" It is conceivable that the "*le*" refers to the child named in the immediately succeeding phrase.

17 In *La part du feu* (Paris: Gallimard, 1949). A translation of this essay by Lydia Davis appears in *The Station Hill Blanchot Reader*, ed. George Quasha (Barrytown: Station Hill Press, 1999), 359–400.

Danish Yearbook of Philosophy, Vol. **48–49** (2013–2014), 37–51

LA TRANSCENDANCE DE L'HISTOIRE

Søren Gosvig Olesen

Ce sont les vainqueurs qui écrivent l'histoire : On le dit et le répète souvent, mais ce n'en est pas moins faux. Staline, Bismarck, Napoléon n'étaient-ils point vainqueurs ? Ce n'est pas leur version de l'histoire que l'on raconte aujourd'hui. L'histoire s'écrit certes par les vainqueurs, mais leur histoire est sujette à révision. Autant dire que l'histoire ne s'écrit pas une fois pour toutes ou ne s'écrit pas simplement, et jusqu'à nouvel ordre aucun vainqueur n'aura vaincu pour toujours. Une réécriture peut même s'imposer assez vite : se présente aux Italiens un homme d'affaires, nouveau dans la vie politique et sans tâches de la corruption ayant sévi dans le pays, mais il suffit d'un peu de temps pour qu'il s'avère que Berlusconi est le pire de tous.

Tout se passe comme si l'histoire menait sa propre vie en marge des individus, fussent-ils vainqueurs ou vaincus. Histoire sans sujet, comme disait Louis Althusser, ou bien histoire à la place du sujet, histoire devenant sujet ? Mais s'il est vrai que l'on ne saurait faire dériver l'histoire du sujet, ou de la somme des sujets, de la soi-disant « intersubjectivité », il est vrai également qu'un sujet ne se constitue jamais par une histoire dont il est exclu.

Considérons l'affaire sous un autre aspect. Nous pouvons nous dire, nous qui sommes présents ici aujourd'hui, « hommes du XXI° siècle ». Et ce sans doute de plein droit. Supposons toutefois qu'un nouveau-né fût présent à cet endroit en même temps que nous. Quiconque dirait alors d'un tel enfant qu'il est « homme du XXI° siècle » ou « fils de son temps » nous semblerait sans doute avoir mauvais esprit. Pourquoi ? Le nouveau-né n'est-il pas présent au même titre que nous ? ne fait-il pas partie de l'histoire du simple fait d'avoir fait son entrée au monde ? n'est-il pas en plein dedans ? Il n'y a pas d'être plus *présent* que l'enfant, cela est certain. Mais d'un autre côté sa présence est telle (nous pouvons dire peut-être : d'une telle intensité ou densité) qu'elle échappe au temps – comme si d'une certaine façon l'enfant ne fût pas de ce monde. Etant déjà dans le monde il y est comme s'il n'en faisait pas encore partie.

Nous avons considéré jusqu'ici l'histoire en un sens qu'il conviendrait d'appeler simplement empirique (ou encore factuelle ou chronologique), et sous cette forme déjà elle nous est apparue comme ne se suffisant pas à elle-même, soit en ceci qu'elle ne s'écrit pas une fois pour toutes, soit parce que l'être humain ne semble pas d'emblée y avoir sa place. C'est en ce sens, c'est-à-dire envisagée dans son dépassement d'elle-même, que l'histoire est dite ici, au moins dans un premier temps, *transcendantale*.

On entendra ainsi par « histoire transcendantale » cette histoire qui ne se passe pas ici et cependant ne se passe pas non plus ailleurs, cette histoire qui, si elle n'est pas présente, n'est pourtant pas non plus passée ou à venir, puisqu'elle est en un seul moment indivis: cette histoire ne se situe pas, sauf dans le mouvement de son dépassement, processus ou passage.

C'est à cette histoire que je me suis proposé d'introduire, et c'est à propos de cette histoire que j'entends discuter, en fin de compte, quelques difficultés ou ce qu'il est convenu d'appeler des problèmes.

I

En vous invitant à parcourir ce bout d'itinéraire avec moi aujourd'hui, je ne fais que vous proposer de reprendre le sentier déjà battu depuis des siècles par les philosophes. Plus ou moins grands, la plupart des philosophes depuis Descartes l'ont au moins croisé. A vouloir en citer on n'a que l'embarras du choix. De sorte qu'à celui qui voudrait savoir comment je vais former mon équipe je dirai : patience ! Ils vont y être tous, ou presque.

Balisons notre chemin à l'aide d'un mot que j'ai trouvé à la dernière page de *La philosophie du non* de Gaston Bachelard et qui a l'air parfaitement simple : « Avant de savoir compter, je ne savais guère ce qu'était la raison »[1].

Voilà bien une de ces petites phrases qui a de quoi conforter ceux des lecteurs de Bachelard qui ont coutume de prendre celui-ci pour un écrivain qui avait la plume légère. Que Bachelard enfant ait dû apprendre l'arithmétique avant de s'attaquer aux grands principes de la logique, quel intérêt finalement – puisque cela est bien normal ! Mais à y regarder de plus près, on découvre un sens tout autre qu'autobiographique et qui renverse complètement les évidences de la normalité. Si l'ordre de l'apprentissage du petit Gaston est « bien normal », c'est qu'il vaut pour tout le monde. Ce qui nous amène à dire que la raison est toujours à l'œuvre avant d'avoir prise sur elle-même, et qu'il ne saurait en être autrement. On découvre la possibilité de la raison après l'avoir réalisée. Et même, c'est beaucoup dire.

Apprenant à compter, en effet, on n'apprend *guère* ce qu'est la raison. C'est à peine si l'on apprend ce qu'est le nombre. Tout au plus apprend-on à manier ce qu'on nous *dit être* le nombre ou *les* nombres. Mais ce qu'est le nombre – on sait combien de théories se sont aventurées à nous le dire. Peut-on dire que l'écolier *sait* ce qu'est le nombre pour peu qu'il sache compter ? Non, c'est l'inverse qui est vrai : nul ne peut savoir ce qu'est le nombre qui ne s'est familiarisé avec les nombres et leur « traitement ». Nous sommes ici à un niveau du savoir que Husserl nommerait « pré-constitué » et Heidegger « pré-ontologique », deux discours différents, certes, mais qui se rejoignent ici, où nous devons pourtant les laisser en suspens encore un moment, sauf pour autant que nous voudrions signifier par cette terminologie que l'enjeu est philosophique, c'est-à-dire que n'entre ici en jeu le mathématicien, pas plus en somme que l'écolier.

J'apprends à compter, soit, mais comment ? et qu'est-ce que j'apprends par là ? Prenons un exemple qui ne le cède en rien en simplicité au *dictum* de Bachelard : « 7 + 5 = 12 ». Pour être toute simple, la proposition ne s'exempte pas néanmoins de toute lecture. Il faut en effet lire, non pas « sept plus cinq égale douze », mais bien « sept plus cinq font douze ». Afin de savoir que 7 + 5 égale 12, il faut avoir vu que 7 + 5 *font* 12 : il faut avoir compté. L'identité n'est établie qu'après coup, nous comprenons que 7 + 5 dit la même chose que 12, qu'il y a là deux manières différentes de mettre ensemble douze unités. Mais une fois établie, l'identité est tellement établie que nous ne nous apercevons plus de l'avoir établie. C'est pourtant ce qu'il faut voir.

Sinon pourquoi Kant – en qui l'on aura reconnu l'auteur de l'exemple 7 + 5 = 12 – persisterait-il à citer un problème d'arithmétique aussi facile à résoudre ? On le trouve aussi bien dans sa *Critique de la raison pure* que dans ses *Prolégomènes*. Et à chaque fois il ajoute : Cela deviendrait plus clair si l'on prenait comme exemples des chiffres plus grands[2]. Alors que justement il ne choisit pas de chiffres plus grands. C'est qu'il faut faire comme si nous ne savions pas encore comment résoudre un problème d'arithmétique, pour facile qu'il soit. C'est qu'il faut nous transposer dans un temps *d'avant* notre apprentissage (des nombres), ce qui nous est difficile lorsque nous nous trouvons d'ores et déjà dans son *après*. Eût-on choisi un exemple plus compliqué (des chiffres plus grands), un problème difficile à résoudre par simple « calcul mental », et nous ne nous serions aperçu, ni du passage de l'avant à l'après, ni de son importance fondamentale.

Lorsque j'apprends à compter, on ne peut pas dire que j'apprends la possibilité du nombre ; j'en fais seulement l'expérience, je m'engage dans cette histoire de fait qu'est un apprentissage. Passer de l'expérience du nombre à sa possibilité revient à faire un pas de plus. C'est une autre histoire, ou en tout cas : cela va nous entraîner dans une autre histoire. Ayant appris à compter, je peux m'apercevoir que ce avec quoi je m'étais familiarisé n'était autre que la possibilité du nombre. Toujours est-il que cette possibilité ne saurait apparaître qu'après coup. Jusqu'alors, c'est-à-dire « de prime abord et la plupart du temps », n'étaient apparus que les nombres sans qu'apparaisse le nombre en tant que nombre. Il n'empêche que, rétrospectivement, et de la sorte seulement, je suis en mesure d'établir que la possibilité du nombre était déjà là, en jeu.

C'est ainsi que Bachelard nous dit, dans l'ouvrage qu'il nomma *Le rationalisme appliqué*, que « l'épistémologie nous enseigne l'histoire *telle qu'elle aurait dû être* » et nous situe dans un « temps logique » scandé en « périodes intemporelles »[3]. A-t-on seulement mesuré l'audace de ces formules ? S'est-on posé la question de savoir ce que peut bien être une histoire qui est « telle qu'elle aurait dû être » ?

Bachelard propose sa formule de l'histoire dans un chapitre de son livre où il explique comment le théorème de Pythagore se laisse démontrer à partir de toutes les figures possibles imaginables. Le carré jouit d'un privilège immérité dans la démonstration usuelle : N'importe quelle figure construite sur l'hypoténuse est égale aux deux figures de même sorte construites sur les cathètes. Il n'est même pas besoin de figures annexes, le théorème se laisse aussi bien démontrer par des figures construites au-dedans du triangle, à savoir les triangles des deux côtés de la hauteur. Et Bachelard de conclure : On aurait dû le prévoir…

L'exemple se retrouve un peu partout dans l'histoire de la philosophie. Entre autres chez Hegel qui nous dit, dans sa « Préface » à la *Phénoménologie de l'esprit*, que le triangle rectangle ne nous apparaît en tant que tel qu'après la construction des figures annexes, après que nous l'ayons perdu de vue, affairés comme nous étions à comparer les carrés sur ses côtés : « C'est seulement à la fin que le triangle est rétabli, le triangle auquel nous avions proprement affaire… »[4] Le résultat n'est résultat que pour autant qu'il résume en lui le processus qui y amène. Le résultat est « ein als wahr eingesehenes »[5]. C'est en quoi la phénoménologie de Hegel, d'après ce que nous lisons dans l'Introduction au même ouvrage, veut rendre compte du savoir en tant seulement que celui-ci doit parvenir à sa manifestation[6]. En lui-même, le triangle rectangle ne saurait faire épanouir le théorème de Pythagore, seule la construction prescrite par le théorème en fait montre. De même, le nombre 12 à lui seul ne nous dit rien ; pour savoir qu'il est égal à 7 + 5 il faut avoir fait le compte. En règle générale, disons même que *A*, pris isolément, ne saurait nous dire ce que dit *A* = *A*. L'identité (A) ne nous apparaît que rétrospectivement, c'est-à-dire une fois que nous avons posé sa différence d'avec un autre (A) pour dépasser ensuite cette différence en posant l'identité des deux (A = A). C'est ce passage ou processus que Hegel appelle « le pur mouvement de la réflexion »[7].

Ce qui doit ici retenir notre intérêt n'est pas tant le principe d'identité que le mouvement par lequel on arrive à celui-ci, et plus précisément la pureté de ce « pur » mouvement. Il est vrai qu'un tel mouvement implique et le temps et l'espace. Mais il s'agit toutefois d'un mouvement sans lieu ni date. Peu importe que Pythagore ait été le premier à prouver le théorème concernant le triangle rectangle, peu importe que la possibilité de la géométrie se soit éclose en Egypte, et peu importe la chronologie, le temps de la montre, lorsqu'il s'agit d'apprendre, d'enseigner, voire de découvrir. Ce que nous visons ici est l'histoire « telle qu'elle aurait dû être », puisque c'est cette histoire seule qui saurait établir le véritable écart de l'avant et de l'après, de même que seule cette histoire saurait s'établir dans cet écart qui s'ouvre dans notre histoire de fait.

Il est vrai que la philosophie ancienne avait déjà vu comment, suite à la progression de notre connaissance, le rapport de l'avant et de l'après s'inverse, et préconisé qu'en toute recherche nous devons partir de ce qui est « premier pour nous » (προτερον προς ημας) pour arriver ensuite seulement à ce qui est « premier par nature » (προτερον φυσει). Telle est la terminologie que l'on trouve partout chez Aristote[8]. Il n'empêche qu'il reviendra aux philosophes modernes de s'interroger précisément sur l'inversion de ce rapport de l'avant et de l'après. Car si tant est que ce qui est premier ne se trouve qu'à la fin, en quel sens devons-nous le dire premier ? Et quel statut accorder à ce chemin que nous devons parcourir afin de trouver ce qui est premier ? Le moins qu'on puisse dire d'un tel chemin ou mouvement, c'est qu'il est incontournable « für uns Menschen wenigstens ». Mais je crois qu'il faut se risquer à dire plus. Je crois qu'il faut dire que ce chemin ou mouvement est ce que *nous nous découvrons être*.

Je m'explique : C'est seulement après avoir établi que A = A que je puis considérer comme établie l'identité de A, et c'est seulement après avoir suivi la démonstration du théorème de Pythagore que je puis revenir sur le triangle rectangle et reconnaître en lui le triangle pour lequel vaut ce théorème. Et qui plus est : C'est seulement *après* avoir établi de telles vérités que je suis en mesure d'affirmer que l'état de choses dont elles parlent était tel qu'elles disent *avant* leur découverte. Autrement dit, la vérité même de ce qui fut le cas avant notre découverte ne se laisse affirmer qu'après notre découverte. Pour le dire autrement encore : La connaissance humaine n'est autre chose que le mouvement de cet avant à cet après.

C'est là le sens de l'exemple des lois de Newton dans le paragraphe 44c de

Sein und Zeit sur la vérité, où Heidegger se demande si en conséquence de sa conception de la vérité il faut dire que ces lois étaient fausses avant leur découverte, pour répondre que non, mais que d'autre part elles n'étaient pas non plus vraies. La distinction même du vrai d'avec le faux suppose le mouvement jusqu'à cette distinction. Nier ce mouvement revient à réduire à rien la connaissance humaine. Il faut constater qu'à cet égard Husserl va plus loin encore, puisqu'il fait entrer l'histoire dans la définition même de la philosophie et des sciences. Philosophie et science, selon sa *Krisis*, ne sont autre chose que « *le mouvement historique de manifestation de la raison universelle, innée dans l'humanité comme telle* »[9]. Il faut attendre Merleau-Ponty et Derrida pour trouver une élucidation des questions que pose une telle définition. Je vous prie de bien vouloir les attendre un peu ici aussi.

Nous étions partis d'une petite phrase de Bachelard : « Avant de savoir compter, je ne savais guère ce qu'était la raison ». Il me semble que pour exprimer brièvement notre lecture de Bachelard, nous pouvons transcrire cette phrase comme suit : La pratique du λογος nombre amène à la possibilité du λογος nombre et par suite à la possibilité du λογος raison. Il n'y a pas d'autre chemin. Et c'est au bout de ce chemin que nos perspectives se trouvent renversées ; nous ne nous trouvons pas d'emblée dans le « temps logique ». De même que nous n'avons jamais commencé par la logique : Il faut découvrir la logique à l'œuvre afin de résumer ses lois ; il faut qu'existe une logique matérielle avant que nous ne puissions établir une logique formelle capable de subsumer ses lois. Résumer, subsumer : On aura reconnu par cette terminologie le projet de la logique transcendantale.

Il me semble toutefois que l'on peut remonter plus loin. Après tout, Bachelard n'est pas le premier à observer la raison à l'œuvre avant de se tourner directement vers elle (encore qu'il ait trouvé une formule particulièrement heureuse pour cet ordre de progression). Le même mouvement est lisible chez Descartes déjà. Celui-ci se pose la question de l'*avant* et de l'*après* à propos du morceau de cire que, au jour de la Seconde Méditation, on fait fondre tandis qu'il l'observe. Il s'agit, ici encore, de l'identité. On se souvient que cette identité s'établit à l'aide du concept ; en l'espèce le concept *extensio, extensum*, « qui réside en mon esprit », pour parler comme Descartes. Par là, toute *res extensa* dépend d'ailleurs de la *res cogitans*. Mais n'importe ; ce dont il s'agit pour nous, c'est que *et* la *res extensa* *et* la *res cogitans* dépendent du processus, du mouvement. Descartes ne commence pas par le *cogito*. Tout comme Gaston, René a commencé par la pratique des sciences, pour ensuite les mettre en doute. Ce petit itinéraire, du doute au *cogito*, de la Première à la Seconde Méditation, est précurseur par rapport aux longs voyages sur la mer que seront la *Critique de la raison pure* et la *Phénoménologie de l'esprit*.

II

Dans ce qui précède, l'être humain a été décrit comme s'il ne fût que raison. Il convient maintenant de mettre l'accent sur son accès à la raison pour autant que celui-ci fasse partie de son accès au statut même d'*humain*. Quel est ce passage qui demeure et pourtant, c'est-à-dire justement pour autant qu'il doit être passage, ne demeure pas ? Difficile à dire, puisque nous tournons alors le regard vers quelque chose qui ne « subsiste » pas. Loin de la substance... Remplaçons, dans un premier temps, notre question sur le passage par cette autre, plus simple : Eu égard à ce passage que nous avons dit passage d'un *avant* à un *après*, quelle est la différence entre l'homme d'*avant* et l'homme d'*après* ?

Déjà le sujet de la connaissance de Kant, je veux dire le sujet qui s'exerce à son exemple « 7 + 5 font 12 », n'est pas n'importe quel sujet. Avant de savoir compter, qui étais-je ? Quelqu'un qui ne savait pas encore que 7 + 5 font 12. C'est-à-dire, et je le dirais prudemment : *par exemple* un enfant. Mais par ailleurs un enfant, ce n'est pas seulement quelqu'un qui ne sait pas compter ou calculer. Ne nous viendrait-il pas plutôt à l'esprit de caractériser l'enfant comme celui qui ne sait pas encore *parler* ? Avant de savoir parler, donc...

C'est ainsi qu'Agamben nous rappelle l'acception originaire du latin *infantia*, mot qui désigne, non seulement ce que nous appelons « enfance » ou « infanzia », mais aussi ce que l'on nomme *aphasie*. L'enfant est un être muet au moins en ce sens qu'il n'a pas encore acquis l'usage de la parole. L'enfant est quelqu'un qui se trouve *en avant de* la langue. Et après, lorsqu'il aura appris ? Y a-t-il même un tel *après* ? Nous apprenons toujours, et la langue ne cesse d'apparaître, de naître lorsque nous parlons. Le passage de l'avant à l'après aura toujours lieu, tant que notre langue ne sera pas une langue morte. Nous la mettons au monde, et avec elle nous-mêmes, et le monde même... En d'autres termes, qu'est-ce que l'enfant acquiert en acquérant l'usage de la parole ? qu'est-ce qu'il apprend en apprenant à parler ?

Il faut bien admettre que l'enfant apprend plus et autre chose que la langue, si du moins on se restreint à entendre par celle-ci seulement des mots et des phrases. L'*usage* de la parole, cette formule le dit déjà : Apprenant à manier la langue, on apprend à situer les choses, y compris à trouver la situation de celui

qui dit : « je ». Mot difficile s'il en fût. Il suffit de penser au jeune enfant à qui
l'on dit par exemple : « Tu ne dois pas crier ! » L'enfant, s'il est encore à ses
débuts dans la langue, peut croire répéter la leçon en rétorquant sur le champ:
« Tu ne dois pas crier ! » Ce qui, à y regarder de près, n'a rien d'étonnant. Ce
qui devrait nous étonner est plutôt que « tu » soit « je ». Tout comme nous nous
étonnerions, pour peu que nous puissions nous transposer dans un état de prime
enfance, que « ici » soit « là », que « maintenant » soit « alors », etc.

Si l'on peut de la sorte expliquer, comme le fait Agamben sur les traces de
Benveniste, la fonction du *je* à partir de ce que la linguistique nomme les *shifters*, il faut sans doute conclure que « je » ne désigne pas autre chose que celui
qui dit « je » dans l'acte du discours où il est dit. Conclusion qui peut aussi
s'énoncer négativement : « Le transcendantal ne saurait être le subjectif »[10]. En
effet, c'est ce qui s'ensuit. On pourrait même ajouter que la philosophie a tiré
cette conséquence depuis bien longtemps. Le transcendantal n'est plus le subjectif. Mais il n'est pas non plus un effet de langage.

Car en effet, nous ne *savons* pas que « ici » soit « là », que « maintenant »
soit « alors », etc., mais nous *apprenons* qu'il en est ainsi et que la langue procède de la sorte. Par où je ne vise nullement à « réfuter » Agamben qui en a
parfaitement conscience. C'est même par le biais de ce raisonnement que l'on
trouve chez lui en toutes lettres une définition de l'histoire au sens transcendantal du terme. Selon Agamben, l' « histoire transcendantale » constitue « la
limite et la structure a priori de toute conscience historique »[11].

Il faut bien admettre que le mot « histoire » est pris dans cette définition en
plusieurs sens, tant il est vrai que nous devons entendre par histoire transcendantale la condition de l'histoire empirique (dont nous prenons conscience). Si
l'on devait s'en tenir au thème de la langue, on dirait : Le fonctionnement de la
langue est un fait, certes, mais que la langue arrive à fonctionner ne l'est pas.
Cela veut dire encore une fois que nous ne pouvons décrire un *avant* qu'à partir de son *après*. L'origine de la langue n'est pas dans l'indescriptible mutisme
d'un stade pré-langagier. Pas plus que l'origine de l'histoire n'est dans le préhistorique ou l'anhistorique tout aussi indescriptibles. L'origine que nous cherchons à décrire est tout à fait dans son devenir, dans un *originarsi*. Quelque peu
comme une source qui, elle, n'est que son jaillissement.

En posant et en déplaçant ainsi la question de l'origine nous visons toujours
ce passage qu'il faut bien oser nommer passage de l'être humain à son statut
d'humain. A ce propos c'est encore Agamben que je citerai : l'homme est cet
être qui est toujours au-dessous ou au-dessus de lui-même. Certes, on pourrait

citer tant d'autres, Hegel, Nietzsche, Heidegger, ou même Arendt ou Sartre. Mais le mot d'Agamben a l'avantage de rendre audibles les connotations ethico-politiques ou même religieuses jusque dans la détermination ontologique : sous-hommes, surhommes – connotations qui font entendre encore la condition de l'homme comme un être donné toujours au pluriel, c'est-à-dire dont le statut dépend sans cesse des autres et de la reconnaissance.

Cependant, ne retenons pour cette occasion que la détermination de l'homme comme l'être qui n'est pas d'emblée ce qu'il est. Si le transcendantal ne saurait être le subjectif, c'est, comme l'explique Jean-Luc Nancy en quelques pages denses de *La communauté désœuvrée*, que le sujet « est ce qui devient ce qu'il est », et par là même que « l'histoire est la constitution ontologique du sujet lui-même »[12]. Ne considérons pour l'instant que ce passage, cette origine de l'homme qu'est la transition du pré-humain à l'humain. Transition historique s'il en fût : A une époque donnée, l'être que nous nommons humain s'est dressé sur ses pieds de derrière et s'est levé ainsi au-dessus du stade animal.

Epoque immémoriale, certes. Mais en quel sens immémoriale ? Car il ne s'agit pas d'un fait – et surtout pas de ce genre de fait qu'on a coutume de nommer accompli. A un moment donné de sa préhistoire, l'homme s'est levé, il est arrivé à la station debout, à la verticalité, condition humaine. Mais on sait que cela ne veut pas dire que depuis, il est donné à chacun de nous de naître de la sorte. Je ne fais ici que répéter la leçon des *Notes de travail* du dernier Merleau-Ponty : l'époque immémoriale dont il est question n'appartient pas plus à *L'espèce humaine* qu'il n'appartient à l'être humain au singulier. Nous naissons à, plutôt que *dans* la condition humaine.

Si l'époque d'*avant* notre condition est immémoriale une fois que nous avons atteint l'*après*, c'est qu'elle appartient à la prime enfance, autant celle de *L'espèce humaine* que celle de chaque individu de l'espèce. Il semble que nous ayons là, finalement, sinon déterminé, alors au moins cerné le passage dont nous n'avons cessé d'interroger la nature. Les différentes variantes du passage, de l'*avant* à l'*après* de la raison – « Avant de savoir compter... », de l'*avant* à l'*après* du langage – « Avant d'avoir acquis l'usage de la parole... », de l'*avant* à l'*après* de la station debout – « Avant d'avoir appris à marcher... », ont dépeint le passage lui-même comme la plus fondamentale *differentia specifica* humaine. Quel que soit le passage à l'humanité, il semble bien que ce soit le passage lui-même qui finit par définir celle-ci. En dernière analyse, il faut donc élaborer la définition de l'histoire transcendantale en disant qu'elle n'est autre chose que le passage du préhistorique à l'histoire, en ajoutant bien entendu que nous laissons dans cette définition aux mots « préhistorique » et « histoire » leur sens ordinaire, empirique.

En jouant encore sur le double sens (empirique et transcendantal) du mot histoire on pourrait résumer cette définition en la faisant valoir pour l'être humain, non pas en tant que sujet ou substance, mais en tant qu'existence. On entendra alors par être humain cet être qui est historique du fait de son devenir historique. C'est ainsi que l'homme se définit chez Kierkegaard par sa répétition ou véritablement sa reprise de la condition humaine.

III

Mais cessons de procéder comme si nous étions sur terrain ferme, examinant et la tradition, et l'état de la question, au sujet de l'histoire au sens transcendantal du terme, et en posant quasiment que cette histoire constitue un mot d'ordre, voire une solution aux problèmes philosophiques de la connaissance et de l'existence humaines. On sait bien que ce n'est jamais avec une telle assurance que nous pouvons avancer en philosophie, et vous êtes bien en droit d'attendre de moi au moins un aperçu des réserves à faire, quitte à voire percer enfin l'histoire transcendantale comme problème plutôt que comme solution.

Puisque nous en étions à Kierkegaard, retenons pour ce qui suit sa définition de l'existence humaine comme reprise de toute la condition humaine. Nous sommes tous Adam, comme le résumait un jour Jean-Paul Sartre[13]. Chez Kierkegaard, cela est l'histoire de la chute, de ce péché originel qui n'est originel que s'il tire son origine, non seulement d'Adam, mais aussi bien de ce singulier qu'est chacun de nous[14]. Qui plus est, cette histoire, comme vous savez, est tout instant. C'est l'instant de l'angoisse.

Il peut sembler étrange, certes, que l'histoire se définisse par l'instant plutôt que par la durée. Mais il faut dire au moins que ce n'est là nullement une particularité de Kierkegaard. Il en va de même chez Heidegger, notamment chez ce « später Heidegger » qui entreprend d'écrire l'histoire de l'être et qui définit l'histoire à partir de cet avènement ou événement qu'il nomme *Ereignis* ou (plus proche en cela à Kierkegaard) *Eräugnis*[15]. Et même chez le premier Heidegger, resserrant son thème de la relation de l'être et du temps dans le rapport de l'être humain au temps, l'existence humaine est définie comme histoire sans qu'il ne soit question d'une quelconque étendue de celle-ci[16]. Le temps qui s'étend ou s'étire et qui a une durée, cette histoire n'est que la trace de l'authentique histoire que Heidegger nomme parfois histoire « ontologique ».

L'histoire qui est *eigentliche Geschichte* n'*est* pas, mais arrive, advient ou surgit : *ereignet sich*. La durée de ce que d'ordinaire l'on nomme histoire, c'est-à-dire l'histoire nommée empirique, factuelle et chronologique dans ce qui précède, cette durée n'est que la trace de l'histoire événement.

Chez les penseurs d'aujourd'hui il n'en va guère autrement. Le chef-d'œuvre d'Agamben déjà cité, *Infanzia e storia*, qui ne cesse de scruter la notion de l'histoire transcendantale, définit lui aussi cette histoire à partir de l'instant dont l'instance est toute transition[17]. Derrida, introduisant à *L'origine de la géometrie* de Husserl, dit avoir trouvé la désignation « histoire transcendantale » chez Husserl lui-même (quoiqu'en une occurrence seulement[18]), et propose une définition de l'histoire qui ne fait que retourner une remarque de Husserl. Cette remarque, une formule que lâche Husserl à un moment donné de ses *Leçons sur la conscience intime du temps* : « Im absoluten Übergehen », et qui peut certes sembler fortuite, va fournir toute la leçon que tire Derrida de Husserl : c'est le passage qui est absolu[19]. Et Nancy, pour qui « l'histoire finie » est « l'arrivée du temps de l'existence, ou de l'existence comme temps », désigne comme « sens minimum » de cette histoire, non pas « la succession des événements », mais « leur dimension commune »[20].

Or, ce nouvel absolu de la philosophie, combien il est transitoire ! Voilà qui va désormais faire question. A vrai dire, ayant poussé la définition de l'histoire jusqu'à ce point, c'est à peine si l'on en aperçoit l'absoluité. Car le transitoire absolutisé, que recèle-t-il de transitoire ?

A ce qu'il semble, c'est à cause de tels problèmes que l'histoire transcendantale va avoir assez mauvaise presse, à partir d'une certaine époque, au moins en France. Michel Foucault notamment n'a de cesse d'en finir avec cette histoire qui n'est, selon lui, que « l'Histoire pour philosophes ». Ce qu'il reproche surtout aux philosophes champions d'une telle histoire, de Hegel à Sartre, c'est leur tendance à la totalisation de l'expérience humaine. Reproche qui marque le chapitre conclusif de *L'archéologie du savoir* par un assaut à ce que Foucault choisit de baptiser « la grande destinée historico-transcendantale de l'Occident »[21].

On reconnaît là le thème depuis lors galvaudée de « la fin de l'histoire », thème que l'on peut trouver dans un premier temps par exemple chez Jean-François Lyotard, selon qui il n'y a plus depuis Kant de place pour une philosophie de l'histoire[22], et chez Michel Haar, qui proclame hardiment : « l'Histoire transcendantale est achevée »[23]. Prises de position qui ne sont pas à négliger ici, eu égard aux définitions que l'on vient de donner, et qui impliquent justement qu'il ne saurait y avoir de fin de l'histoire – sauf à adopter un ton apocalyptique en philosophie, puisqu'une telle fin équivaudrait à la fin de l'existence humaine.

Si l'on relit aujourd'hui le dernier chapitre du livre de Foucault, on s'aperçoit que la cible de sa critique n'est autre que la subjectivité qui se masque sous le thème de l'histoire pour autant que le rôle de celle-ci revient à être révélateur du moment transcendantal. L'histoire des philosophes d'hier est « notre » histoire, c'est l'histoire de l'humanité, la ruse de la raison dont elle gouverne et l'origine et la téléologie. Il se peut que Foucault ait été motivé par la critique jadis à lui-même adressée par ceux qui avaient pris la parole au nom de cette histoire, Lucien Goldmann, Henri Lefebvre, ou Alfred Schmidt en Allemagne. On dit que Foucault avait étudié à fond la *Critique de la raison dialectique* de Sartre ; et Dieu sait que quiconque a eu cette patience demeure sous le coup d'une pesante entreprise de totalisation encore sous l'influence de Hegel. La critique foucaldienne de la philosophie de l'histoire est-elle en vérité anti-critique ? Mais Foucault n'aurait-il pas pu se contenter alors de reconduire l'argument de Roman Jakobson précisant le statut des perspectives synchronique et diachronique pour signaler que – n'en déplaise aux philosophes défenseurs de l'histoire « vivante » ! – l'une n'est pas plus historique que l'autre[24] ? Et n'est-ce pas dépasser le but que de mentionner, comme le fait en effet Foucault, non pas Goldmann, Lefebvre et les autres, mais bien Kant, Husserl et Merleau-Ponty[25] ? Et lorsque Foucault déclare que son but est « d'affranchir l'histoire de la pensée de sa sujétion transcendantale », ne suffirait-il pas, à nous lecteurs d'aujourd'hui du moins, de rappeler le mot d'Agamben selon lequel « le transcendantal ne saurait être le subjectif »[26] ?

Le dialogue final de *L'archéologie du savoir* ressemble à un dialogue platonicien, ou en tout cas à bon nombre des dialogues platoniciens, en ceci que cette finale est aporétique. Foucault avoue être sérieusement embarrassé par la question de savoir si son archéologie, si son analyse discursive qui est « discours sur les discours », est plutôt histoire ou plutôt philosophie[27]. Et en effet, on ne saurait résoudre ou dissoudre un problème philosophique par l'histoire, pas plus que l'inverse. Cela ne ferait évidemment qu'ajourner le problème. Reprenons pour le moment la formule de ce problème en termes foucaldiens : en quoi un *a priori* historique est-il historique et en quoi *a priori* ? si un tel *a priori* doit bien être *historique*, ne doit-il pas être chaque fois de la même façon *a priori* et de la même façon *historique* ? mais en quoi un tel *a priori* est-il alors historique ? et ne finit-on pas par construire de la sorte une histoire *a priori* ?

Si cependant Foucault n'a su démêler son archéologie des entrelacements de la philosophie et de l'histoire, si enfin lui non plus n'a su esquiver le problème de la totalisation hégélienne, il n'en demeure pas moins qu'il a entamé le dialogue avec le problème et qu'il en a avoué la survivance embarrassante. Totalisation hégélienne, style de pensée qui nous hante encore : la pensée qui vise le *tout* en réduisant à chaque fois le différent à l'identique. Totalisation qui peut fort bien avancer masquée sous le nom de l'histoire. Car enfin, qui ne voit pas que l'histoire, fût-elle conçue de façon transcendantale, pour être histoire doit être à tout moment histoire. Par où même l'histoire finit par avoir une forte ressemblance avec n'importe quel autre *ens supremum* ayant posé sa candidature en tant que dernière instance tout au long de l'histoire de la philosophie.

Faut-il cependant attribuer une telle acception et une telle tradition au mot histoire ? C'est ce qu'il semble aux philosophes, c'est au moins ce qu'il a semblé à certains philosophes à une certaine époque. Jacques Derrida, à qui l'on doit d'avoir comme exhumé la notion d'histoire transcendantale et de l'avoir développée dans toute son ampleur dans l'Introduction à *L'Origine de la géométrie* de Husserl dont il fait paraître la traduction en 1962, va lui-même abandonner le terme peu après. Son geste est motivé dans la communication sur « La différance » qu'il prononce à La société française de philosophie en janvier 1968, et ce plus précisément dans un passage où il est dit que : « Si le mot « histoire » ne comportait en lui le motif d'une répression finale de la différence, on pourrait dire que seules des différences peuvent être d'entrée de jeu et de part en part « historiques ». »[28] D'où il ressort que le mot qu'est censé remplacer la « différance » n'est autre que celui de l' »histoire ». Mais encore : Faut-il admettre que ce dernier mot véhicule forcément la répression finale des différences ? Cela est vrai sans doute de la pensée hégélienne, cela vaut sans doute pour nombre des figures sous lesquelles cette pensée a su se travestir. Mais n'avons-nous pas appris à penser autrement le motif de l'histoire, et Derrida n'est-il pas sur ce point justement notre maître à penser ? Force est d'admettre en tout cas que si le seul mot d'histoire risque de figer en son nom, c'est-à-dire par l'effet de *nommer*, ce mouvement différant qu'est l'histoire, il n'en va guère autrement du mot « différance ». Et ce de l'aveu même de Derrida : « car il n'y a pas de *nom* pour cela, pas même celui d'essence ou d'être, pas même celui de « différance ». »[29]. Notre auteur a beau ajouter immédiatement après que la différance « n'est pas un nom » – il se trouve lui aussi, malgré son inventivité, capturé par la grammaire, par la grammato-logique du nom de *la* différance, faisant de son désaveu une dénégation, et, non sans s'en apercevoir, il est amené à déclarer son invention nulle et non avenue. Il n'y a de nom pour cela – même pas celui de « différance » : or, si ce mot est vain ou fortuit, l'est-il moins que celui d'histoire ? en d'autre mots, pourquoi la différance ? ou même « l'archi-écriture » ?

En d'autres mots encore, ou en un mot : pourquoi pas l'histoire… La « différance » derridienne, l' »Ereignis » heideggerien ne disent-ils pas ce que dit, dans une terminologie plus traditionnelle, j'en conviens, le mot *histoire* tel qu'il vient d'être motivé ? C'est ce que n'hésite pas à supposer Jean-Luc Nancy dans *La communauté désœuvrée*[30]. Reprendre cette supposition à mon compte – voilà ce que j'ai trouvé de mieux : c'est même ce que j'ai trouvé de mieux à faire en vous présentant la notion de l'histoire transcendantale et ses péripéties jusqu'aujourd'hui. Autant dire que je n'ai pas trouvé mieux. Il m'a semblé que, jusqu'à nouvel ordre, nous aurons besoin d'un mot pour nommer ce mouvement du *transcendere* qui est en jeu dans toute transcendance. Il est vrai qu'un problème nous est apparu avec le mot, avec la notion d'histoire, et qui est sans arrêt d'éviter que ce mot mette fin au *transcendere* en figeant, de la façon la plus traditionnelle qui soit, la transcendance en quelque chose de transcendant, en quelque chose de subsistant par lui-même, c'est-à-dire en tout autre chose que l'histoire. Car l'histoire n'a pas de fin, le *transcendere* ne s'arrête pas.

Limité par l'horaire de ma conférence, je dois cependant m'arrêter ici et maintenant. Ce que je fais en vous remerciant de votre attention.

Notes

1   Gaston Bachelard: *La philosophie du non*, Presses universitaires de France, Paris 1940, p. 144.
2   Immanuel Kant: *Kritik der reinen Vernunft*, B16; *Prolegomena zu einer jeden künftigen Metaphysik*, A 29. Benno Erdmann, un des éditeurs de Kant, avait raison lorsqu'il proposa d'inverser l'ordre des chiffres dans la phrase (*KdrV*, B16) de Kant : « Daß 7 zu 5 hinzugetan werden sollten, habe ich zwar in dem Begriffe einer Summe = 7 + 5 gedacht », de sorte qu'on lira: « Daß 5 zu 7 hinzugetan werden sollte, etc. » Kant veut parler d'une tâche: Ajoutez cinq à sept ! A placer 7 devant 5 dans la phrase expliquant le problème d'arithmétique chez Kant on ne lit que l'expression du résultat. Cf. le résumé succinct que l'on doit à Koyré : « 1 + 1 n'*est* pas deux. Cela *fait* deux, ainsi que l'avaient vu déjà Bradley et Kant » (Alexandre Koyré : « Emile Meyerson : *Du cheminement de la pensée* », p. 651, in *Journal de psychologie normale et pathologique*, 1933, pp. 649–655.)
3   Voir *Le rationalisme appliqué*, Paris, PUF 1986 (1949), p. 96 et p. 26, italiques du texte.
4   G.W.F. Hegel: *La phénoménologie de l'esprit*, trad. J. Hyppolite, Aubier, Paris 1941, p. 37 (Erst am Ende wird das Dreyeck wieder hergestellt, um das es eigentlich zu thun ist…, *Phänomenologie des Geistes*, *Gesammelte Werke*, Felix Meiner, Hambourg 1980, Band 9, « Vorrede », p. 32)

5   Hegel, « Vorrede », op. cit., p. 32 (en italiques dans le texte).

6   La phénoménologie de l'esprit est « die Darstellung des erscheinenden Wissens »; Hegel, *Phänomenologie des Geistes*, « Einleitung », p. 55.

7   Voir Hegel: *Wissenschaft der Logik, Gesammelte Werke*, Felix Meiner, Hambourg 1978, Band 11, p. 264.

8   Voir l'article classique de Hans Reiner: « Die Entstehung und ursprüngliche Bedeutung des Namens Metaphysik », in *Zeitschrift für philosophische Forschung*, 8 (1954), pp. 210–237, particulièrement son chapitre 2, p. 214 et suiv.

9   Husserl: *La crise des sciences européennes et la phénoménologie transcendantale*, trad. G. Granel, Gallimard, Paris 1976, p. 21 (« Philosophie, Wissenschaft, wäre demnach *die historische Bewegung der Offenbarung der universalen, dem Menschentum als solchen « eingeborenen » Vernunft.* » dit le texte allemand. Voir: *Die Krisis der europäischen Wissenschaften und die transzendentale Phänomenologie, Husserliana VI*, Martinus Nijhoff, Hague 1976, pp. 13–14).

10   G. Agamben: *Infanzia e storia*, Einaudi, Turin 2001 (nouvelle édition), p. 44.

11   Agamben, *op.cit.*, p. 48.

12   Jean-Luc Nancy: *La communauté désœuvrée*, Bourgois, Paris 2004 (nouvelle édition revue et augmentée), p. 246.

13   J.-P. Sartre: « L'Universel singulier », pp. 20–63 in *Kierkegaard vivant*, ouvrage collectif, Gallimard, Paris 1966, p. 49 et p. 50.

14   Sur tout ceci, cfr. Søren Kierkegaard: *Le concept d'angoisse*, chapitre 1, §2 sur la notion du premier péché (*Begrebet Angest*, Caput I, §2, Begrebet den første Synd).

15   Le terme heideggerien *Eräugnis* a trait au mot *Auge* qui désigne l'œil en allemand, comme le terme kierkegaardien Øieblik se rapporte au mot danois pour l'œil (øje aujourd'hui, Øie du temps de Kierkegaard).

16   C'est parce que le *Dasein* est foncièrement *Bewegtheit* et *Geschehen* qu'il est *Bewegung* et *Geschichte*. Voir en particulier §72 de *Sein und Zeit* (et plus particulièrement les pages 374–375 de l'édition Niemeyer).

17   Agamben, *Infanzia e storia*, p. 55: « ma questo transito, questo istante è la storia. »

18   Derrida: « Introduction » à Husserl: *L'origine de la géométrie*, Presses universitaires de France, Paris 1962, pp. 129–130 (en note).

19   Voir Derrida, op. cit., p. 165: « *l'Absolu est le Passage* » (en majuscules et en italiques dans le texte).

20   Nancy, *La communauté désœuvrée*, pp. 261–262 et p. 261.

21   Foucault: *L'archéologie du savoir*, Gallimard, Paris 1969, p. 273. Pour l'expression citée: « l'Histoire pour philosophes », voir aussi l'entretien « Foucault répond à Sartre » dans *La Quinzaine littéraire*, N° 46, 1967, pp. 20–22, reproduit comme texte N° 55 dans Foucault: *Dits et Écrits*, I, Gallimard, Paris 1994.

22   J.-F. Lyotard: *L'enthousiasme. La critique kantienne de l'histoire*, Galilée, Paris 1986, p. 77.

23   M. Haar: *La fracture de l'histoire*, Millon, Grenoble 1994, p. 9: « *l'Histoire transcendantale est achevée* » (majuscule et italiques du texte).

24   Voir R. Jakobson: *Essais de linguistique*, Minuit, Paris 1963, pp. 36–37.

25   Foucault, *L'archéologie du savoir*, p. 265.

26   Agamben, *Infanzia e storia*, p. 44, cf. supra, p. 8.

27   Foucault, op. cit., p. 267.

28   Derrida: « La différance », in *Marges de la philosophie*, Minuit, Paris 1972, p. 12.

29   Derrida, « La différance », in op. cit., p. 28.

30   Nancy, op. cit., pp. 273–274.

Danish Yearbook of Philosophy, Vol. 48–49 (2013–2014), 53–72

L'AMBIVALENCE D'UNE HISTORICISATION RADICALE DE LA PHÉNOMÉNOLOGIE CHEZ HEIDEGGER

SERVANNE JOLLIVET

Ressaisissant le chemin parcouru dans un court texte daté de 1936, Heidegger ne manque de rappeler combien il est redevable à Husserl de l'avoir initié, converti au « voir phénoménologique », soulignant à quel point le travail accompli dans son sillage s'est avéré décisif. Comme il le ressaisit en quelques lignes, ce rapport n'est pas moins, dès l'initiale, emprunt d'ambivalences, comme en témoigne la distance prise avec une approche qu'il juge encore insuffisamment radicale :

> La phénoménologie restait en effet dès le départ rivée à une position philosophique fondamentale, qui est celle du cartésianisme et du postkantisme – à laquelle je n'ai moi-même jamais adhéré ; mon propre chemin me conduisait davantage à une réflexion sur l'histoire – ce qui m'a amené à me confronter avec Dilthey et à prendre pour point de départ la vie comme réalité fondamentale. Mais c'est bien par la "phénoménologie" que je suis parvenu à m'assurer de la démarche et du questionnement de mon travail, ce qui fut également fructueux pour me permettre d'interpréter l'histoire[1].

Force est de constater que c'est bien sur ce terrain de l'histoire que s'opère la rupture. Dès le début des années vingt, c'est en effet à une radicalisation du geste phénoménologique que Heidegger en appelle, qui doit permettre, en déconstruisant ses présupposés encore objectivants et théoriques, de « regagner une relation véritable et originaire avec l'histoire, élucidée *à partir de notre propre situation et facticité historique* »[2]. A travers le projet de « science originaire » (*Urwissenschaft*) mis en œuvre dès 1919, orienté sur ce qu'il nomme « l'expérience de la vie facticielle », il va alors s'agir de dépasser les limites d'une perspective encore *constituante*, telle qu'elle empêche précisément la prise en vue de l'histoire, initialement évacuée par Husserl. Replacer l'histoire au cœur du projet phénoménologique présuppose donc un infléchissement décisif, pour ne pas dire un remaniement total, un « complet renversement » comme Husserl pourra lui-même en juger. Ce sont sur quelques-uns de ces déplacements que j'aimerais ici revenir, ainsi que sur les conséquences que cela entraîne sur un plan méthodologique, mais également au regard d'une refondation qui s'expose à relativiser son propre geste, voire à l'écueil relativiste qui menace une telle historicisation.

Le projet d'une phénoménologie de l'expérience de la vie facticielle

Le premier point sur lequel Heidegger fait porter sa critique vise tout d'abord le caractère absolu, présupposé par Husserl, de l'évidence de ce qui serait donné « phénoménalement » dans l'intuition ou perception pure. Certes il ne manque de reconnaître qu'en recourant à l'*intuition catégoriale*, celui-ci a bien contribué à « libérer l'être de sa fixation dans le jugement »[3] et, ce faisant, à rétrocéder à un niveau plus originaire, antéprédicatif. Il ne peut néanmoins suffire de mettre entre parenthèses l'expérience « naturelle et mondaine », comme il le fait en la soumettant à l'*epokhè*, autrement dit de suspendre notre rapport au vécu sous prétexte d'en saisir de manière plus adéquate le sens. Si la réduction husserlienne vise à mettre « hors jeu » l'historicité contingente de ce vécu sous prétexte d'accéder à un niveau d'évidence absolu, le geste est bien ici inverse. C'est désormais d'« en bas », de la conscience naturelle et de ses expériences vécues et singulières dont il faut partir pour accéder au domaine phénoménologique originaire, qui n'est autre que cette sphère immanente du vécu mise entre parenthèses par Husserl.

Comme l'a bien vu Dilthey, parce qu'elle s'ancre dans un faisceau de motivations, de désirs et tendances qui échappent le plus souvent à toute appréhension rationnelle, il serait de vain de vouloir appréhender cette expérience de manière purement théorique ou objectivante. Car ce n'est pas tant le « sens de contenu » ou la « teneur de sens » (*Gehaltssinn*) du vécu – ce dont il est fait l'expérience – qui doit être ici visé (le *was*), que *la manière* (*wie*) dont nous pouvons en faire intentionnellement l'expérience. Assurément Heidegger ne manque de reconnaître l'avancée décisive que constitue la théorie de l'intentionnalité husserlienne, qui permet d'appréhender les phénomènes non plus en termes de « contenus » de conscience, mais à travers leurs seuls modes d'apparition. En découvrant le « fait primaire » de l'expérience intentionnelle, lieu de corrélation originaire du sens dans la conscience, Husserl aurait bien tenté d'accéder, sans préjuger du contenu de l'expérience historique, au « sens relationnel » ou référentiel (*Bezugssinn*). Il n'en serait pas moins resté au « seul *rapport* de telle sorte que celui qui considère ne relève pas du questionnement »[4], s'empêchant ainsi de prendre en vue le sens en son entier, « sens d'accomplissement » (*Vollzugssinn*) compris en sa dimension purement événementielle. Car l'enjeu n'est pas seulement de voir comment l'intentionnalité se concrétise à travers une expérience vécue, mais bien de la penser sous les traits d'un « souci » en situation, ce qui présuppose de prendre en vue « comment je vis moi-même dans l'expérience concrète, *comment j'y prends part* (sous le mode de l'"accomplissement") »[5].

Ce présupposé d'une immanence à soi de tout vécu – la vie faisant pour ainsi dire toujours, comme il le souligne, « retour à soi par le biais d'elle-même »[6] – exclut donc tout recours à une norme de jugement transcendante ou à un quelconque critère de valeur extrinsèque. Pour autant qu'elle « est liée en tant que telle à l'existence personnelle, et non pas à telle ou telle signifiance historique [mais] à un ici et maintenant [*Jetzt-Hier*] facticiel et concret »[7], il n'est possible d'en pré-supposer le sens, sorte d'en soi « extra- ou supra-historique » dont l'originarité ou l'évidence pourrait être ressaisie. Car le vécu historique n'est jamais prédonné et ne peut être réduit à un « fait » dont on pourrait dégager la « signification » une fois pour toutes. Accessible dans la compréhension que nous en avons, chaque fois *reconstruit*, différemment interprété à la lumière d'une situation donnée, son sens demeure résolument ouvert, sorte d'horizon, de « contexte de sens » (*Sinnszusammenhang*) marqué par une multiplicité d'orientations et de « rapports signifiants ». Accéder à ce domaine originaire exclut donc d'emblée, à moins d'en tronquer la portée, toute possibilité de réduction ou suspension (*Ausschaltung*) quant à la manière dont nous appréhendons naturellement les choses. Focalisée sur ces « rapports signifiants », la démarche est ici éminemment *compréhensive* et doit permettre de les interpréter et expliciter comme autant de « formes expressives »[8] (*Ausdrucksformen*) par lesquelles la vie se comprend toujours déjà en situation.

Comme Heidegger le souligne, cette explicitation n'a pour autant rien d'évident, puisqu'il va précisément s'agir d'éliminer tout ce qui en entrave l'accès (conceptualité inadéquate, rigidifications, « sédimentations » théoriques, etc.). L'interprétation étant toujours fruit d'une compréhension dont les conditions de possibilité doivent être élucidées, ce qui était pensé par Husserl comme l'intuition « catégoriale » s'avère donc intrinsèquement « herméneutique »[9], en tant qu'elle est elle-même amenée à prendre en vue ses propres présupposés pour s'assurer de l'originarité et légitimité de sa démarche. Ce sera là tout l'intérêt du projet de *destruction* (*Destruktion*) ou *déconstruction* (*Abbau*), mis en œuvre dès les années vingt et principalement dans les cours de Marbourg, que de préparer le sol à une telle libération de la sphère d'expérience originaire en en déconstruisant les préjugés et préacquis (*Vorbegriffe*). Pour le phénoménologue, cela présuppose de déconstruire ses propres outils théoriques (concepts fondamentaux) et présupposés ontologiques – ce qui débouchera sur une déconstruction de l'histoire même de l'ontologie – mais également de mettre au jour sa propre « situation herméneutique », à savoir la compréhension implicite qui sous-tend sa prise en vue des phénomènes. Cela ne signifie aucunement qu'il soit possible d'en épuiser la compréhension, sorte d'élucidation intégrale qui permettrait d'en finir « une fois pour toutes » avec les présupposés qui le déterminent et le conditionnent. Parce qu'« *il n'y a d'histoire qu'à partir d'un présent* », c'est l'idée même d'objectivité qui n'est plus de mise, qui pouvait permettre de surplomber ou de mettre à distance, d'objectiver les phénomènes en présupposant la pureté d'une démarche libre de présupposés. Comme Heidegger le souligne, cette historicisation fait donc bien partie intégrante du projet phénoménologique :

> La phénoménologie ne veut pas se placer en dehors de l'histoire comme si elle n'en était pas affectée. C'est impossible dans la mesure où toute découverte s'insère dans une continuité historique, où elle est co-déterminée par l'histoire. Dans la phénoménologie elle-même vivent des motifs historiques qui, partiellement, conditionnent des questionnements et des coups d'envoi traditionnels et recouvrent l'accès véritable aux choses [10].

S'il s'agit bien de remonter aux expériences originaires dont les concepts fondamentaux sont dérivés, dès le début, Heidegger ne manque donc de souligner l'irréductible relativité de ce geste. Le critère même qui nous permet de juger « de l'originarité ou de la non-originarité »[11] des concepts qui nous ont été légué n'est en effet « jamais absolu [mais] avant tout relatif, surtout à considérer que nous ne visons nullement une origine (absolue), mais bien le concret et l'unique »[12]. Toute interprétation reposant sur une décision préalable qui nous permet de trancher – ce qu'il désigne en 1921 sous le terme de « dijudication » (*Dijudikation*) – il n'est alors aucun critère préexistant, autre que celui qui est requis au vu de la situation de l'interprète. La dijudication, on le voit, joue ici un rôle pour ainsi dire analogue à celui de l'*epokhè* chez Husserl. L'usage de l'*epokhè* permettait en effet, en suspendant l'adhésion spontanée propre à l'attitude naturelle, de neutraliser ou de mettre hors circuit ce qui est objectivé au profit d'une perception plus 'adéquate'. C'est ce qui permettait, dans la perspective husserlienne, tout en reconnaissant la relativité phénoménale de toute donation de sens, d'accorder au vécu de conscience une évidence indubitable. En décidant à son tour de ne se fier qu'à l'évidence de l'expérience vécue, Heidegger reprend ici le geste husserlien en le radicalisant. Car la dijudication n'est pas elle-même suivie d'une réduction : elle doit au contraire permettre de réintégrer dans l'analyse ce qui était justement exclu par Husserl, qui n'est autre que cette dimension « historique concrète et individuelle » du vécu dans lequel s'ancre toute expérience facticielle.

La relativité radicale du geste phénoménologique

A l'évidence, Heidegger semble avoir sapé tous les garde-fous qui permettaient encore à Husserl de se prémunir contre les risques de relativisation induits par une telle historicisation. Historicisation de son objet tout d'abord, dans la mesure où l'expérience facticielle est toujours « située », dépendant d'un ancrage *hic et nunc* lui-même soumis à l'interprétation. Historicisation du geste lui-même, marquée par la circularité de l'analyse, garante de « l'authenticité » du problème en tant qu'il est pris à sa source. Concèdant qu'il a définitivement renoncé à l'illusion d'accéder à une quelconque validité 'objective', Heidegger ne manque de le reconnaître : « *Le relativisme est en ce sens inévitable* »[13].

Faut-il alors en conclure qu'une telle relativisation viendrait saper et ruiner le projet initial visant à radicaliser la phénoménologie husserlienne en direction d'une « archi-science » ou « science originaire » (*Urwissenschaft*) susceptible de saisir « *l'originarité de l'historique en son absoluité* [c'est-à-dire] en sa non répétabilité absolue »[14] ? Très tôt, Heidegger est soucieux de ne pas s'enferrer dans une telle impasse. Comme il le souligne lui-même dès 1920, une telle position « est tout à fait éloignée de la thèse selon laquelle la philosophie ne serait elle-même que le fruit de sa propre situation spirituelle facticielle et comme telle nécessairement et d'emblée *relative* »[15]. Que la philosophie prenne en vue sa situation et son propre ancrage historique ne signifie renoncer ni à la portée principielle de la démarche phénoménologique, « l'originarité de sa position spirituelle (*Geisteshaltung*), irréductible aux autres sciences », ni à la radicalité de cette refondation. Dans une lettre adressée à Karl Löwith en 1921, c'est en ces termes qu'il explicite ce qu'il entend par « relativisme » :

> J'impose ma "position" – et je suis "injuste" vis-à-vis des autres dans la connaissance que je suis moi-même "*relatif*" [...] Je travaille concrètement, facticiellement à partir de mon "je suis" – à partir de ma provenance spirituelle et facticielle comme telle [...] et c'est avec cette facticité de l'être tel, l'historique, que l'existence se démène[16].

Reconnaître l'absolue unicité de cet ancrage – qu'il thématisera à travers la notion de « *Jemeinigkeit* », qui marque l'irréductible ipséité de tout vécu, en tant qu'il toujours déjà *mien*, vécu en propre – c'est bien admettre son indéniable relativité. Que cet « être-'absolu' » n'ait rien d'universel que l'on pourrait objectiver, mais soit de l'ordre d'« un être-unique (*der-Einzelne-Sein*) radicalement concret et historique »[17] ne signifie pas pour autant que le geste phénoménologique doive se dissoudre dans un pur phénoménisme, réduit à ne décrire que ce qui se donnerait dans l'expérience. Partant du vécu, il ne s'y épuise pas, pas plus qu'il ne débouche, même partant de notre radicale ipséité, sur une forme de solipsisme ou de « "monisme" de l'existence »[18]. Ce que Heidegger nomme « expérience facticielle » ne se réduit pas davantage à un vécu de conscience, pensable en termes psychologiques, ce qui amènerait de fait à relativiser les acquis de l'analyse et à considérer qu'une telle herméneutique tombe elle-même « à la merci de la contingence ». Comme il le souligne dans un passage décisif, ce qui est proprement visé dans l'analyse, ce n'est pas « ce dont il est effectivement fait l'expérience *en un tel sens* ni même ce qui est toujours appréhendé sur le mode d'un vécu »[19].

S'il part bien de la concrétude de l'existence, c'est en effet toujours en vue d'accéder à son « sens d'être ». Et c'est précisément en repensant cette « absolue relativité » de l'expérience historique comme une caractéristique *fondamentale* de l'existence que le défi peut être relevé, visant à ériger la phénoménologie en « science pré-théorique » ou « théorie universelle » de ce qui n'est pas tant *objet* de connaissance qu'un *champ d'expérience* singulier. Comme il s'y attelle les années suivantes dans son herméneutique de la facticité, ce sont en effet les structures « existentiales », conditions de possibilité au fondement même de toute expérience, qu'il s'agit de dégager. Il ne s'agit alors plus tant de rendre compte d'une expérience, singulière et concrète, que de parvenir à reconduire l'existence, initialement pensée comme « relativité » foncière, « mobilité » (*Bewegtheit*), puis comme « rapport » (*Bezug*), transcendance (*Überstieg*), à ce qui la rend possible, jusqu'à la mise au jour de ce fondement paradoxal qu'est « l'historicité » (*Geschichtlichkeit*). L'ambivalence est certes encore très nette au début des années vingt, Heidegger oscillant perpétuellement entre des déterminations en apparence contradictoires, qualifiant tour à tour l'expérience d'absolue ou d'éminemment relative. Comme il le montrera, la contradiction n'en est pas une : ce sont justement les présupposés sur lesquels cet apparent paradoxe est sis qu'il va s'agir de déconstruire, d'où la nécessité d'abandonner ces qualificatifs, jugés peu adéquats, et de s'extraire d'un tel cadre théorique.

Les présupposés de la critique husserlienne

L'interprétation que donne Heidegger du débat qui oppose Husserl à Dilthey sur cette question du relativisme, à laquelle il consacre une partie du cours de 1923/24 (GA 17), analyse qui sera ensuite reprise dans ses grandes lignes dans les conférences de Cassel l'année suivante, est sur ce point des plus éclairantes. Dans le texte désormais célèbre paru en 1910 dans la revue *Logos*, sous le titre « Historicisme et philosophie des visions du monde »[20], Husserl prend en effet à parti la philosophie diltheyenne en l'accusant d'avoir sapé toute possibilité de refondation rigoureuse de la philosophie, réduite à une « vision du monde » purement contingente et relative. En sacrifiant toute « universalité de principe » au profit d'une attention portée à « *la sphère concrète de la vie empirique* », l'historisme diltheyen aurait selon lui cédé à une forme de « subjectivisme radical »[21], ravalant la *quaestio juris* à une question purement factuelle, absolutisant la vie jusqu'à se fourvoyer dans un « relativisme qui n'est pas sans parenté avec le psychologisme naturaliste en prise aux mêmes apories »[22].

Plus que de prendre parti pour l'une ou l'autre position – absolutisme *versus* relativisme – ce sont précisément les présupposés qui sous-tendent cette critique et réfutation de l'historisme que Heidegger entend déconstruire. Visant à offrir une « légitimité normative » (*Normgesetzlichkeit*) au geste phénoménologique, garantie par l'anhistoricité de sa démarche, le cœur de la critique husserlienne consisterait en effet « à opposer manière purement formelle de ce qui vaut et le sens réel et temporel »[23]. C'est ce qui lui permettait d'accéder par sa « science eidétique » à des « valeurs absolues, atemporelles », et d'invalider en retour la scientificité de toute approche dite « historisante », telle celle de Dilthey. Or, comme Heidegger entend le montrer, « la tendance qui consiste à vouloir expliquer (l'historisme diltheyen) à la lumière d'une quelconque philosophie normative pour ensuite le faire passer pour un relativiste, lui est absolument étrangère »[24]. Non seulement la critique husserlienne porte à faux mais c'est la spécificité même du projet diltheyen qui est ici manquée, « la possibilité même de comprendre en quelque sens que ce soit *de manière positive* son travail »[25].

Dans la brève correspondance échangée à la même époque avec Husserl, Dilthey s'offusque par ailleurs ouvertement de cette méprise, se défendant « d'être considéré comme un sceptique »[26]. S'il admet bien « *la finitude de tout phénomène historique (...), et par suite la relativité de toute appréhension humaine* », c'est précisément afin de trouver un « point de vue surélevé » et stable lui permettant de dépasser « cette contradiction insoluble (qui) surgit quand la conscience historique est poussée jusqu'à ses dernières conséquences »[27] et de se prémunir contre un tel écueil relativiste. Comme il le rappelle, jamais il n'a en effet été question de mettre en cause l'indépendance de « ce qui est signifié dans le jugement, [...] état de choses qui (demeure) *transcendant par rapport à l'expérience vécue* et qui renvoie à une configuration psychique sur le mode d'une détermination d'essence »[28]. Preuve en serait la distinction qu'il introduit entre l'expérience vécue et ce qu'il nomme « expérience transcendantale [29] ou encore « autoréflexion » (*Selbstbesinnung*), réflexivité permettant de suspendre méthodologiquement cette relation naturelle liant la conscience à ses objets. Loin d'être purement descriptive, à savoir focalisée sur le seul vécu, état de réceptivité à l'égard d'un dehors, la psychologie « *analytique* » qu'il met lui-même en œuvre vise donc bien, tout comme le projet husserlien, à expliciter les conditions et associations internes au fondement de l'expérience.

Comme on le voit, le véritable point d'achoppement n'est donc pas tant ici la question du scepticisme, et la mise en cause du statut transcendant de la philosophie qui ruinerait la possibilité même d'une connaissance objective, que le statut accordé par Husserl à l'historique. Reliquat d'un « platonisme tout à fait banal »[30] reposant sur la prééminence du monde idéel au détriment des phénomènes changeants du monde sensible, Husserl présupposerait en effet une scission là où, pour Dilthey, il ne s'agit que d'un rapport de dérivation. Pour reprendre ici l'image du 'fleuve', instable et contingent, que serait le vécu historique, « la typique qui peut être décrite de cet écoulement » dépend bien, pour Husserl, d'une normativité préexistante et c'est en vertu même des « idées, saisies et fixées dans le regard » qu'est rendue possible une « connaissance absolue »[31]. Ce qui est historique, purement factuel, ne prendrait ainsi sens *en sa totalité* qu'à travers cette « unité idéale » préétablie. Comme Dilthey lui-même le fait remarquer, Husserl ne ferait que « consolider les choses qui s'écoulent dans le devenir pour ensuite venir lui adjoindre un concept d'écoulement qui porte sur sa totalité »[32], alors qu'il s'agit précisément, à ses yeux, du sol premier à partir duquel toute objectivation ou ressaisie théorique est elle-même dérivée. Certes il reconnaît bien lui-même que la totalité historique ne peut être comprise sans en dégager la 'cohérence' ou 'cohésion' (*Zusammen-hang*) intrinsèque. Etant toujours déjà inhérente à la réalité historique, il serait cependant vain de vouloir la rapporter à une « unité idéale », « établie à partir de la seule cohérence [formelle] de concepts valant universellement »[33]. Aux yeux de Heidegger, son projet reste assurément encore scientiste, au point qu'il pourra lui reprocher de ne pas avoir suffisamment détaché le problème de l'histoire de considérations épistémologiques. En reconduisant toute objectivation aux « faits de conscience » et à l'« expérience interne », Dilthey n'en aurait pas moins accompli une avancée décisive, préparant ainsi le sol à cette genèse théorique à laquelle il entend lui-même s'atteler dès le début des années vingt.

A la source de l'opposition absolu/relatif

Comme on le voit, il ne s'agit ce faisant pas tant de défendre ici le soi-disant « historicisme » de Dilthey que de déconstruire le postulat fondamental qui sous-tend la critique husserlienne, à commencer par ce que Heidegger juge être un véritable « ratage » de l'historique, dégradé au rang de *fait*, de matériau positif, couplé selon lui à une totale méconnaissance de notre historicité fondamentale. Visant à accéder à une *certitude* à toute épreuve susceptible de doter son projet d'une rigueur comparable à celle de la science mathématique, ce n'est en effet qu'« en éliminant purement et simplement l'histoire »[34] qu'il parviendrait à sauver ce présupposé d'une absolue validité. Non seulement l'argumentation de Husserl contre « l'historisme sceptique » de Dilthey porterait à faux mais, comble du paradoxe, elle se révélerait en son fond « non phénoménologique ».

> L'histoire est ainsi de manière négative rendue inoffensive. Ce qui la menace n'est rien d'autre que le souci visant à sauver la validité absolue et à exclure l'histoire comme quelque chose d'insignifiant pour la philosophie[35].

La critique du relativisme – que cristallise, sur un plan épistémologique, le spectre du scepticisme – ne serait ainsi que l'envers réactif et défensif d'une position purement dogmatique qui ne trouverait sa légitimité qu'en excluant ce qui semble la menacer. Si Husserl pensait réfuter le scepticisme diltheyen en pointant l'incohérence et l'autocontradiction formelle auxquelles aboutit toute conception relativiste, Heidegger entend donc en retourner l'argument. Car, à ses yeux, ce n'est pas tant le relativiste qui se contredit en prétendant donner valeur de vérité à sa propre position que celui qui s'attelle à sa critique en déplorant l'absence *d'un certain type de vérité*, « vérité absolue » que le relativisme viendrait lui-même ruiner. Au point qu'il faille nous demander, nous dit Heidegger, si le scepticisme n'est finalement pas lui-même « une construction de son adversaire qui voudrait le réfuter afin de s'assurer soi-même de sa propre réfutation »[36]. A l'inverse, affirmer qu'il n'y a pas de vérité valable, ou que toute vérité est relative, c'est toujours présupposer « qu'il y a au moins *une* vérité absolue »[37]. Reposant sur les mêmes présupposés, la position sceptique demeurerait donc « absolument inoffensive », attestant par la négative cela même qu'elle tente de réfuter.

Critiquer l'historisme sous prétexte qu'il aboutit au relativisme ne résout donc rien à ses yeux, c'est bien plutôt se tromper de cible, ne pas voir qu'ainsi posé, le problème demeure purement circulaire, ce qui empêche de s'attaquer à sa source même. Heidegger entend donc renvoyer ici dos à dos les deux positions, pour autant qu'elles présupposent toujours un « critère de validité » qui n'est lui-même jamais remis en cause. Si le relativisme apparaît bel et bien inévitable pour qui se refuse à toute absolutisation, une fois le postulat d'une telle opposition déconstruit, non seulement l'accusation de relativisme n'a plus lieu d'être, mais c'est « le rapprochement même de l'historique avec le relativisme qui perd son sens »[38]. Non seulement l'opposition, « la séparation du scepticisme et de l'absolutisme doit être intégralement rejetée »[39], du fait même qu'ils reposent sur un même postulat. Mais, assimilé au relativisme, c'est l'historique qui est manqué, par là la possibilité même, écrit-il,

> de voir s'il ne repose pas dans l'historicisme *une possibilité de déterminer autrement la vérité*. Cette position est considérée d'emblée selon le sens que la critique se choisit elle-même, de telle sorte que la validité absolue et le fait de tenir pour valable sont alors opposés l'un à l'autre […] Il se pourrait pourtant que l'idée d'une validité absolue soit dépourvue de sens […] Une autre possibilité au sein de cette alternative ne vient pas même au regard[40].

S'il n'examine pas encore, en 1924 dans le cours qu'il consacre à Husserl, le fondement de cette opposition – qu'il déconstruira à mesure dans ses cours de Marbourg – il n'entend pas moins déjà découvrir la motivation originaire qui sous-tend un tel geste et dont la philosophie grecque serait dès ses débuts porteuse : « l'idée d'une certitude absolue, portée par la tendance à surmonter la contingence même de notre *Dasein* »[41]. Si la science est parvenue à une objectivité à toutes épreuves, talonnée par la philosophie dans ses tentatives successives de refondation, ce serait toujours au prix d'une oblitération de notre historicité fondamentale. Certes il ne manque de reconnaître à l'historisme le mérite d'avoir replacé l'histoire au cœur du questionnement. Remettant en cause tout présupposé absolutiste, il participerait lui-même de cette « rébellion fertile contre l'aliénation de la philosophie », voyant dans la conscience historique ce qui aurait contribué à « libérer l'esprit humain de [ses] dernières chaînes »[42]. Cette tentative n'en serait pas moins « *demeurée à mi-course* », participant à sa façon du même « ratage », cette « déshistorisation » (*Entgeschichtlichung*) fondamentale qui marquerait toute objectivation et démarche théorique. Car l'histoire, prise pour objet par la science historique – et *a fortiori* l'historisme – demeure bien, aux yeux de Heidegger, éminemment superficielle au regard de l'historicité vivante qu'il s'agit d'appréhender. L'assimilation de ce qui est historique (*geschichtlich*) avec ce qui est seulement historicisé (*historisch*), dit-il, aurait ainsi « pour conséquence de *dégrader intégralement le Dasein historique*. L'histoire n'entre ainsi dans le champ du regard qu'en tant qu'objet de science, ce qui barre tout accès à ce qui est véritablement historique »[43]. D'où la nécessité, comme il le souligne dès le milieu des années vingt, de mettre au jour cette « origine existentiale de la science historique » en montrant qu'elle prend bien sa source dans une historicité qui nous est constitutive.

Se refuser de trancher comme le fait Heidegger face à ce débat, voire contester « l'horizon même au sein duquel parler de relativité a un sens » ne revient donc pas, loin de là, à renoncer à toute prétention visant à constituer la phénoménologie en « connaissance 'historique' en un sens radical »[44]. C'est en effet seulement en se libérant de « la crainte d'un tel fantôme », qu'il est possible d'aller droit « aux choses mêmes » et de renouveler intégralement l'approche phénoménologique en « *se confrontant à l'histoire qui provient du sens de ce que nous sommes facticiellement* »[45]. Comme il s'en explique dans le cours suivant, *Logik. Die Frage nach der Wahrheit* (GA 21), c'est seulement en découvrant les motivations profondes qui sous-tendent une telle critique que le débat est amené à révéler ses propres contradictions. Il ne peut en effet suffire de déconstruire le postulat substantialiste sur lequel repose une telle opposition pour le dépasser, comme il s'y attelle lui-même dès les années vingt, puis dans les cours de Marbourg en prenant pour cible le moment fondateur « platonico-aristotélicien ». Car une telle « omission » prend elle-même sa source dans une tendance qui nous est propre, « tendance sécurisante » ou « tendance à l'occultation » – qui nous permet de nous « libérer de l'inquiétude suscitée par l'historique »[46]. Véritable « fatalité », celle-ci serait en effet indissociable de l'ambivalence fondamentale de l'existence, tiraillée entre sa propre finitude et sa quête de stabilité, qui témoigne non seulement d'un « besoin de sécurité » mais, à ses yeux, d'une véritable « peur du *Dasein* »[47], véritable fuite en avant qui nous amène à occulter notre être. Si la déconstruction vise bien à lever les obstacles qui entravent l'accès aux « expériences originaires », c'est donc bien *in fine* à l'herméneutique qu'il revient d'en découvrir le fondement structurel, pour ainsi dire ontologique, initialement pensé sous les traits de la « ruinance » (*Ruinanz*), et que l'on retrouvera ensuite dans *Être et Temps* à travers l'existential du dévalement (*Verfallenheit*).

L'ambivalence de l'historicité comme fondement ontologique

En repensant l'histoire à partir de son enracinement facticiel, et en l'éclairant à la lumière de la « question *ontologique* » de l'historicité, Heidegger entend ainsi sortir du faux débat dans lequel l'historisme demeurait pris. Car avant même de pouvoir être envisagé comme une détermination factuelle ou empirique, l'historique est d'abord d'ordre *existential*. Cela lui permet ainsi de défaire le lien indéfectible qui rive traditionnellement l'historique à ce qui *est* (étant), pour le penser désormais en sa dimension proprement 'possibilisante', à savoir non plus tant au regard de réalisations factuelles que de l'ouverture originaire qui les rend possibles. Certes Heidegger ne manque de reconnaître que Dilthey avait lui-même, comme il le souligne dans les conférences de Cassel, une conscience aiguë de « la vitalité de la force agissante du passé »[48]. S'il est l'un des premiers à découvrir son enracinement dans l'historicité humaine, il ne serait néanmoins pas allé jusqu'au bout, ni ne serait parvenu à « interroger l'historicité elle-même (qui n'est autre que) la question relative au sens de être, à l'être de l'étant »[49]. Car il s'agit bien, comme il l'écrit, « d'élaborer l'être de l'historicité, *l'historicité et non l'historique*, l'être et non l'étant, l'effectivité et non l'effectif », question qui ne relève précisément pas « de la recherche historique empirique »[50]. Il n'en faut pas moins, comme il le souligne dans *Etre et Temps*, radicaliser ce geste, ce qui implique de remonter à une unité plus originaire, qui n'est autre, en dernière analyse, que notre constitution fondamentale, foncièrement temporelle. C'est ce qui va lui permettre, sans renoncer à notre ipséité la plus radicale, d'éclairer à sa source le phénomène de l'histoire en remontant au « fondement celé (*verborgene Grund*) de l'historicité du *Dasein* »[51], qui n'est autre que la « *possibilité la plus propre, non relative (unbezüglich*) et indépassable »[52] qu'est notre « être-vers-la-mort ».

En le reconduisant à son fondement ontologique, Heidegger parvient ainsi à en assumer et radicaliser les postulats de l'historisme, tout en se gardant, par la perspective transcendantale, voire 'fondamentale' qu'il met encore en œuvre à la fin des années vingt, de ses conséquences relativistes. Avec ceci de paradoxal que ce « fondement » n'en est pas un, et bien plutôt à penser comme « hors-fond » (*Abgrund*). Car il ne s'agit pas ici de céder à l'illusion fondamentale de pouvoir accéder à un fond dernier, encore moins, comme le lui reprochera Löwith, d'assurer – en suspendant son analyse à une condition prétendument « naturelle » (le pouvoir-mourir du *Sein-zum-Tode*) – à son analyse une sorte de « stabilité préhistorique » (*vorgeschichtliche Standfestigkeit*)[53] qui le prémunirait des conséquences relativistes d'un tel geste. Face au risque encouru d'un tel contresens, ne rappelle-t-il pas d'ailleurs dans l'ouvrage qu'il consacre à Kant deux ans plus tard que « *l'élaboration de ce qui constitue essentiellement la finitude doit elle-même toujours être principiellement finie et ne peut jamais être absolue* »[54] *? Assurément, même si une telle interprétation fondamentale ou* « *naturaliste* » *ne tient pas, le geste qui consiste à reconduire l'histoire à une* « *possibilité dernière* » *(Grundmöglichkeit)*, sorte de fondement ou d'invariant ultime, lui-même « non relatif » et soustrait à toute historicisation, demeure éminemment ambiguë. Il semble que ce soit précisément là toute la difficulté d'une pensée qui, tentant d'assumer à plein sa finitude, peut difficilement échapper au risque d'absolutiser sa propre position finie. Heidegger ne parviendrait ainsi à dépasser les conséquences relativistes de son propre historisme qu'en *ontologisant* ce qui rend possible cette relativité même de l'existence. Si cela lui permet de « régler d'un geste le problème de l'histoire »[55], comme il le reconnaîtra lui-même, force est de constater que le problème du relativisme n'est pas réglé pour autant. Même à la hisser au rang de structure indépassable, d'existential, à travers ce qui peut être considéré comme une forme d'« ontologie anhistorique », l'historicité continue bien de constituer un véritable talon d'Achille pour une analyse qui demeure encore en 1927, quoi qu'il en dise, encore « fondamentale ».

Relativité de la vérité dans Etre et Temps

Hisser l'histoire au rang de « phénomène » présuppose donc de l'appréhender, non plus de manière factuelle ou empirique, mais bien de manière *existentiale*, sur le mode d'une *expérience* facticielle qui n'est autre que la réappropriation vivante de possibilités qui nous sont transmises. Rapportée à l'être-au-monde dans lequel cette expérience s'enracine, elle-même sise sur la temporalité foncièrement finie de mon existence, une telle conception implique alors de repenser la vérité non plus sur le mode d'une adéquation à ce qui est ou ce qui a « réellement été », pour reprendre ici l'expression rankéenne, mais bien d'une répétition créatrice qui dépend toujours d'une ouverture préalable. S'il n'est de vérité qu'à travers la compréhension que je peux en avoir, c'est donc ultimement cette question, liée à celle de l'être (*Seinsfrage*) qui lui est co-originaire, qui doit être reprise à neuf, « questionnée dans la mesure où elle est au cœur de cette capacité que nous avons de la comprendre »[56].

Les conséquences d'une telle thèse sont considérables. Si l'être est traditionnellement pensé sur le modèle d'une essence, « fond porteur » permettant de rendre compte de l'étant, c'est désormais selon le « sens » qu'il a pour l'être qui le comprend qu'il doit être repensé (*Seinssinn*), ce qui présuppose de « libérer » « l'*apriori* facticiel » qui le sous-tend. Foncièrement « relative à l'être du *Dasein* »[57], la vérité dépend donc toujours d'une ouverture (*Erschlossenheit*) première, qui sous-tend la possibilité même de son découvrement. C'est en effet parce que je suis toujours déjà, par le fait même d'être *au* monde, « dans la vérité »[58], que je peux en énoncer le vrai ou le faux. Comme il le souligne lui-même

> De vérité *"il n'y a"* que dans la mesure où et aussi longtemps que le Dasein est. L'étant n'est découvert qu'*au moment où* et n'est ouvert qu'*aussi longtemps* en général que le *Dasein est*. Les lois de *Newton*, le principe de contradiction, toute vérité en général ne sont vrais qu'aussi longtemps que le *Dasein est*. (Sans) le *Dasein*, il n'y a donc pas de vérité (…) Avant qu'elles ne fussent découvertes, les lois de *Newton* n'étaient pas "vraies" ; il ne s'ensuit pas qu'elles étaient fausses, pas davantage qu'elles le deviendraient si aucun découvrement n'était plus ontiquement possible[59].

Naturellement il ne s'agit pas ici de considérer que l'étant que ces lois « mettent au jour en le découvrant n'étaient pas avant elles », *a fortiori* ici la gravitation à laquelle étaient déjà soumises les planètes avant la venue de Newton. Ni vraies ni fausses avant leur découvrement (*Entdecktheit*), ces lois « devinrent ainsi *vraies* grâce à Newton » au sens où l'étant qu'elles découvrent est soudainement rendu accessible, découvert de manière inédite. Cela coupe court à toute conception progressiste permettant de juger de la supériorité d'une théorie sur une autre, de même que cela n'aurait aucun sens, comme il s'en explique plus tard, de « mesurer, du point de vue de ses seuls résultats, la théorie du mouvement aristotélicienne à l'aune de celle de *Galilée* et de la juger arriérée par opposition à une conception qui serait plus avancée »[60].

Reconnaître ce caractère éminemment relatif de toute vérité ne signifie donc aucunement dévaloriser toute prétention à la vérité d'autant plus, précise Heidegger, qu'une fois ses propres postulats relativisés, « il n'y a pas dans cette « restriction » [ou relativité] de diminution de l'être-vrai des vérités »[61]. A l'inverse, il ne s'agit pas davantage de l'absolutiser et de considérer, comme le fait Husserl, la loi de la gravité comme vraie de tout temps. Pour ce dernier, prétendre en effet « que le jugement dans lequel s'exprime la loi de la gravité n'aurait pas été vrai avant Newton est complètement contradictoire et en général faux : car la validité inconditionnée appartient pleinement, pour toute époque, *à l'intention même de cette affirmation* »[62]. Qu'il soit possible d'en retracer la genèse n'exclut ainsi en rien selon lui la possibilité de reconnaître « l'éternité » de ce sens, alors prémuni contre toute relativisation. Tandis que

Husserl se réfère ici à une conception sinon absolue, tout du moins *omnitempo-relle* de la vérité, Heidegger entend ici reconduire cette prétention à l'ouverture préalable qui la rend possible. Le fait de reconnaître que même la prétention la plus universelle « a pour seule racine le fait que le *Dasein* peut dévoiler l'étant en lui-même et l'offrir à la vue »[63] a assurément pour effet de la relativiser. Dire que la vérité est toujours, comme il l'écrit lui-même, « sur le mode du *Dasein* », ne signifie pourtant pas qu'elle serait soumise à notre bon vouloir, ou à nos caprices changeants. Assurément,

> quand il n'y a aucun « sujet » – au sens strict de *Dasein* existant –, il n'y a ni vérité ni faus-seté. Mais dans ce cas, la vérité n'est-elle pas fonction du « sujet » ? N'est-elle pas subjec-tivisée alors que nous savons bien pourtant qu'elle est quelque chose d'objectif qui ne saurait être soumis au seul sujet ? […] S'il n'y a de vérité que dans la mesure où le *Dasein* existe, toute vérité n'est-elle pas soumise au bon plaisir et à l'arbitraire de l'ego ?[64]

Se refuser de voir la vérité « comme quelque chose « "en dehors de" et "au-dessus de" nous » ne peut suffire à l'invalider. Si elle n'est « n'est ontiquement possible qu'en un "sujet" et que son sort dépend entièrement de l'être de celui-ci », c'est au contraire l'idée même de « validité universelle » qui doit être déconstruite, de même que l'idée d'une « vérité éternelle », « affirmation fan-taisiste » dont la seule légitimité aurait d'avoir « été communément "crue" par les philosophes »[65]. La réponse donnée par Heidegger deux ans plus tard à Davos, face à Cassirer qui l'accuse de céder au relativisme, est sur ce point on ne peut plus claire :

> Lorsque je dis : la vérité est relative au *Dasein*, ce n'est pas là un énoncé ontique dont le sens serait : n'est jamais vrai que ce que pense l'homme individuel. *La proposition est métaphysique* : la vérité comme vérité ne peut être que si le *Dasein* existe. C'est avec l'existence de quelque chose comme un *Dasein* et seulement ainsi que vient la vérité […] La vérité est relative au *Dasein*. La supra-subjectivité de la vérité, cette percée de la vérité au-delà du particulier veut dire : *être-dans-la-vérité c'est être livré à l'étant*[66].

Ainsi repensée comme ouverture primordiale, la vérité n'est plus tant ici recon-duite à cette capacité découvrante qu'au fait d'« être livré à l'étant », jeté dans un monde qui nous précède et nous excède. Si parler de vérité n'est possible « qu'aussi longtemps que le *Dasein* est », c'est en effet que *nous* la présuppo-sons, que *nous* sommes 'dans la vérité', ou plutôt « ce n'est pas *nous* qui pré-supposons la "vérité", mais au contraire c'est *elle* qui rend ontologiquement possible en général que *nous* puissions *être* tels que *nous* "présupposions" quelque chose »[67].

Le passage à la figure plurielle du « nous » est ici absolument décisif dans la mesure où il préfigure déjà le tournant qui l'amènera à sortir de la perspective qui est celle de *Etre et Temps*, jusqu'à juger de son « échec » ou, tout du moins, des limites de la perspective encore transcendantale et formelle qui est encore la sienne en 1927. Car ce n'est jamais de manière solipsiste que nous en venons à découvrir l'étant, mais cela présuppose toujours une ouverture commune face à des possibilités partagées et transmises à l'échelle de notre génération, cette « expérience fondamentale » du sens partagé dont il parlait déjà en 1925 et qu'il pensera ensuite comme « communauté de destin » (*Geschick*). Loin d'y voir un horizon clos, imposé une fois pour toutes, c'est bien plutôt sur le mode d'une ouverture commune qu'il est amené à repenser la vérité, qui scelle à la fois les limites mêmes de notre monde, mais requiert toujours une réappropriation, reprise ou répétition créatrice, voire « refondation » intégrale, comme ce peut être le cas dans l'œuvre d'art. Comme il le souligne dans le cours qui suit, *Les problèmes fondamentaux de la phénoménologie* :

> ce n'est pas nous qui avons à présupposer qu'il y a quelque part une vérité "en soi", une valeur transcendante flottant pour nous je ne sais où, ou un sens valide par soi, mais c'est la vérité elle-même, c'est-à-dire la constitution de fond du *Dasein*, qui *nous* présuppose, qui est *la présupposition de notre propre existence*[68].

Si « la vérité appartient à la constitution ontologique du Dasein »[69], c'est donc qu'elle présuppose elle-même un « être-ensemble » qui constitue mon ipséité à titre de « *Mitsein* », « *Mitdasein* » qui n'est autre que le partage d'un même monde, d'une même ouverture. Purement "déduite" de la temporalité originaire du *Dasein*, l'historicité est ainsi d'emblée présupposée pour autant que nous ne sommes jamais ni au « fondement de notre être » ni ne pouvons jamais « remonter en deçà ». Loin de dépendre de l'arbitraire de chacun, le découvrement de l'étant ne dépend plus seulement de notre seule capacité d'ouverture, mais s'effectue bien « toujours dans les limites d'un être-jeté »[70], à partir d'une donne première. Cet élargissement de la perspective formelle préfigure, on le voit, déjà le futur « tournant » qui l'amènera à reprendre la question de l'être « *comme une question de part en part historique* »[71]. Il ne s'agira plus alors seulement, comme il l'écrira quelques années plus tard, de « cheminer *au seuil* de la question mais bien de s'y mouvoir *de l'intérieur* »[72], ce qui entraînera un remaniement intégral de la perspective encore existentiale développée dans les années précédentes. C'est à cette radicalisation, par lequel le questionnement est lui-même amené à « rejaillir sur le questionner »[73], qu'il s'attellera dès la décennie suivante à travers le projet d'une « pensée d'une histoire de l'être » (*Seyngeschichtliches Denken*). Quant à la notion même d'historicité – à laquelle était jusque là suspendue l'analyse – elle ne tardera à être abandonnée, n'apparaissant rétrospectivement, n'avoir finalement été « *qu'un chemin* »[74], un questionnement au « caractère transitoire »[75], voire une « fausse piste »[76].

Aussi radicale soit-elle, cette tentative menée par Heidegger dès le début des années vingt visant à prendre en vue l'expérience historique, semble ainsi toucher aux limites mêmes du geste phénoménologique. Si ce premier projet lui apparaît par la suite devoir être radicalisé, force est de reconnaître qu'il n'a pas moins permis de poser des jalons décisif pour les philosophies et théories de l'histoire qui se développeront ultérieurement, de Gadamer à Koselleck, sur le sol d'une herméneutique historique. Husserl lui-même ne manquera d'ailleurs de nuancer son projet, à mesure qu'il l'infléchira de manière génétique, allant jusqu'à reconnaître que toute formation de sens est indissociable d'un « questionnement relatif à son *histoire* »[77]. C'est ce qui l'amènera, non seulement à réévaluer « l'historique-factuel » et à reconnaître à cette sphère idéale une certaine historicité, mais à infléchir à terme l'analyse transcendantale en direction d'une « herméneutique de la vie de la conscience »[78], comme il envisage lui-même de le faire sur le tard. Comme en jugera Heidegger, cette tentative peut certes paraître inaboutie et encore insuffisamment radicale, restant encore rivée à une perspective idéale et téléologique[79]. Elle n'atteste pas moins de l'acquis décisif que constitue cette historicisation et de la nécessité d'intégrer l'herméneutique comme part intégrante du projet phénoménologique.

Notes

1   M. Heidegger, « Rückblick auf den Weg » (1936), in *Besinnung* [GA 66], Francfort/Main, Klostermann, 1997, p. 413.
2   M. Heidegger, *Phänomenologie des religiösen Lebens* [GA 60], Francfort/Main, Klostermann, 1995, p. 125, nous soulignons. Voir également *Prolegomena zur Geschichte des Zeitbegriffs* [GA 20], Francfort/Main, Klostermann, 1979, p. 416.
3   M. Heidegger, *Questions IV*, Paris, Gallimard, 1976, p. 315.
4   GA 60, p. 82.
5   M. Heidegger, *Grundprobleme der Phänomenologie* [GA 58], Francfort/Main, Klostermann, 1993, p. 250.
6   M. Heidegger, *Phänomenologische Interpretationen zu Aristoteles: Einführung in die phänomenologische Forschung* [GA 61], Francfort/Main, Klostermann, 1985, p. 160.

7 *Phänomenologie der Anschauung und des Ausdrucks. Theorie der philosophischen Begriffs-bildung* [GA 59], p. 197.
8 GA 58, p. 147–148.
9 La notion d'« intuition herméneutique » apparaît en effet dès le tout premier cours, in *Zur Bestimmung der Philosophie* [GA 56/57], Francfort/Main, Klostermann, 1987, p. 117.
10 M. Heidegger, *Les conférences de Cassel*, trad. J.-C. Gens, Paris, Vrin, 2003, p. 173.
11 M. Heidegger, *Phänomenologie der Anschauung und des Ausdrucks: Theorie der philoso-phischen Begriffsbildung* [GA 59], Francfort/Main, Klostermann, 1993, p. 180.
12 GA 59, p. 74.
13 GA 59, p. 190, nous soulignons.
14 GA 60, p. 88, nous soulignons.
15 GA 59, p. 38.
16 Martin Heidegger, « Drei Briefe Martin Heideggers an Karl Löwith », in D. Papenfuss, O. Pöggeler, *Zur philosophischen Aktualität Martin Heideggers, Im Gespräch der Zeit*, T. 2, Francfort/M., Klostermann, 1990, p. 31, nous soulignons.
17 GA 60, p. 260.
18 GA 58, p. 199.
19 GA 58, p. 162.
20 E. Husserl, « Historizismus und Weltanschauungsphilosophie », in *Logos. Internationale Zeitschrift für Philosophie der Kultur*, vol. I, Mohr, 1910/11, p. 289–341, repris in *Aufsätze und Vorträge* (1911–1921) [Hua XXV], Den Haag, Nijhoff, 1987, p. 3–62, trad. fr. M. de Launay, in *La philosophie comme science rigoureuse*, « Historicisme et philosophie comme « vision du monde », Paris, PUF, Epiméthée, 1989.
21 Hua XXV, p. 43, trad. p. 64.
22 Hua XXV, p. 41, trad. p. 61. Voir également la critique qu'il en donne, in « Die Idee der reinen Logik », in *Einleitung in die Logik und Erkenntnistheorie. Vorlesungen 1906-1907* [Hua XXIV], Berlin, Springer, 1985, p. 32–45.
23 M. Heidegger, *Einführung in die phänomenologische Forschung* [GA 17], Francfort/Main, Klostermann, 1994, p. 96.
24 GA 17, p. 92.
25 GA 17, p. 91.
26 GA 17, p. 113–115.
27 Cf. Notamment W. Dilthey, *Abhandlungen zur Grundlegung der Geisteswissenschaften* [GS V], Leipzig, Teubner, 1957, p. 9, trad. *Critique de la raison historique, op. cit.*, p. 35–36.
28 W. Dilthey, *Der Aufbau der geschichtlichen Welt in den Geisteswissenschaften* [GS VII], Leipzig, Teubner, 1958, p. 30, nous soulignons.
29 GS V, p. 246.
30 GA 17, p. 94.
31 Hua XXV, p. 30.
32 GS V, p. CXII.
33 Lettre de Dilthey à Husserl du 29 juin 1911, in *Les Conférences de Cassel, op. cit.*, p. 113.
34 GA 17, p. 89.
35 GA 17, p. 300.
36 *Logik. Die Frage nach der Wahrheit* [GA 21], Francfort/Main, Klostermann, 1995, p. 21.
37 GA 21, p. 21. C'est à ce titre que le sceptique est dit, plus encore que le dogmatique, « le véritable absolutiste », in GA 61, p. 196.
38 GA 60, p. 165.
39 GA 17, p. 98–99, nous soulignons. Voir également le cours de 1934 : Si toute vérité absolue

est niée, « cela ne signifie pas que nous posons la thèse d'une vérité qui ne serait que relative, relativité qui ne serait qu'arbitraire. Rejeter le point de vue d'une vérité absolue signifie également rejeter toute la relation qui lie l'absolu au relatif. Si l'on peut ne pas parler en ce sens de vérité absolue, il n'est alors pas plus possible de parler d'une vérité relative. *C'est la relation tout entière qui est erronée* », in M. Heidegger, *Logik als die Frage nach dem Wesen der Sprache* [GA 38], Francfort/Main, Klostermann, 1998, p. 80.

40 GA 17, p. 95–96, nous soulignons.

41 GA 17, p. 43.

42 W. Dilthey, GS V, p. 9, trad. p. 35–36.

43 GA 17, p. 93. Dès le même cours, Heidegger reliait déjà le « souci visant à sauver l'absolue validité » avec l'omission (*Versäumnis*), la pure et simple « élimination [*Ausschaltung*] de l'histoire », in GA 17, p. 89.

44 M. Heidegger, *Interprétations phénoménologiques d'Aristote*, trad. J.-F. Courtine, Mauvezin, T.E.R., 1992, p. 31.

45 GA 59, p. 53.

46 A ces « tendances sécurisantes » ou « reposantes » qui caractérisent la philosophie occidentale depuis Platon, Heidegger oppose la détresse exacerbée par le christianisme primitif. Comme il le souligne, le refoulement de l'historique provient bien de ce que « la mutabilité historique apporte une insécurité principielle qui va à l'encontre de la tendance au confort (*Bequemlichkeit*) et de la recherche de la sécurité à tout prix (*Sorglosigkeit – securitas*) », in GA 61, p. 109.

47 GA 17, p. 97–98.

48 M. Heidegger, *Les conférences de Cassel*, op. cit., p. 151.

49 *Ibid.*, p. 171. Heidegger nuancera ensuite son propos, écrivant en 1925 : « J'aimerais ici présupposer selon la conception que je m'en fais que Dilthey n'a certes pas posé la question de l'être et n'avait pas non plus les moyens de le faire mais que cette tendance était pourtant en lui bien vivante », in GA 20, p. 173.

50 *Les conférences de Cassel*, op. cit., p. 171.

51 M. Heidegger, *Sein und Zeit*, Tübingen, Niemeyer, 1993, p. 386.

52 *Sein und Zeit*, op. cit., p. 251.

53 *Ibid.*, p. 188.

54 M. Heidegger, *Kant und das Problem der Metaphysik*, Francfort/Main, Klostermann, 1951, p. 213.

55 *Sein und Zeit*, op. cit., p. 377.

56 *Ibid.*, p. 152.

57 *Ibid.*, p. 227.

58 *Ibid.*, p. 220–221.

59 *Ibid.*, p. 226–227, ainsi que pour les citations suivantes.

60 M. Heidegger, *Grundfragen der Philosophie: Ausgewählte „Probleme" der „Logik"* [GA 45], Francfort/Main, Klostermann, 1984, p. 52–53.

61 *Sein und Zeit*, op. cit., p. 227.

62 E. Husserl, *Logische Untersuchungen*, vol. 1 [Hua XVIII], Den Haag, Nijhoff, 1975, p. 134.

63 *Sein und Zeit*, op. cit., p. 227.

64 M. Heidegger, *Die Grundprobleme der Phänomenologie* [GA 24], Francfort/Main, Klostermann, 1975, p. 313, trad. J.-F. Courtine, *Les problèmes fondamentaux de la phénoménologie*, Paris, Gallimard, 1985, p. 264.

65 *Ibid.* Heidegger précisera un peu plus loin que « l'affirmation de « vérités éternelles » de même que l'amalgame de l'« idéalité » phénoménalement fondée du *Dasein* avec un sujet

absolu idéalisé appartiennent aux résidus de théologie chrétienne qui se sont immiscés dans la problématique philosophique et qui sont encore loin d'en avoir été radicalement évacués ». Voir également GA 24, p. 316, trad. p. 266.

66 *Débat sur le kantisme et la philosophie*, Paris, Beauchesne, 1972, p. 20, nous soulignons.

67 *Sein und Zeit, op. cit.*, p. 227, nous soulignons.

68 GA 24, p. 315, trad. p. 266, nous soulignons.

69 GA 24, p. 314, trad. p. 265.

70 *Sein und Zeit, op. cit.*, p. 366.

71 *Ibid.*, p. 21, nous soulignons.

72 M. Heidegger, *Nietzsche* I [NI], Francfort/Main, Klostermann, 1996, p. 29.

73 M. Heidegger, *Einführung in die Metaphysik* [GA 40], Francfort/Main, Klostermann, 1983, p. 4, trad. p. 17.

74 *Sein und Zeit, op. cit.*, p. 436.

75 GA 66, p. 414.

76 M. Heidegger, *Seminare* [GA 15], Francfort/Main, Klostermann, 1986, p. 344.

77 Hua XVII, p. 215, trad. p. 281.

78 E. Husserl, *Phänomenologie und Anthropologie* (1931), in *Aufsätze und Vorträge (1922-37)* [Hua XXVII], Dordrecht, Kluwer, 1989, p. 177.

79 L'histoire est en effet encore ici pensée comme étant « conforme à l'essence du sens », in Hua XVII, p. 215, trad., p. 281.

*Danish Yearbook of Philosophy, Vol. **48–49*** (2013–2014), 73–90

MATIÈRES DE L'HISTOIRE :
ECRITURE, VOIX, TECHNIQUE

SUSANNA LINDBERG

Aujourd'hui il semblerait vain de chercher un sens de l'histoire, comme on le faisait depuis Kant et Hegel jusqu'à Heidegger. Le retrait du sens de l'histoire ne signifie cependant pas que notre transcendance ne serait pas historiale, mais que, à défaut de son articulation en fonction d'un sens, son historialité se laisse penser comme une dimension inarticulée d'historialité élémentaire. Quelle est la *matière élémentaire de l'historialité* qui se donne à penser aujourd'hui ? Traditionnellement, on a souvent pensé l'historialité comme une dimension de figuration ni spirituelle ni naturelle mais « culturelle » ou « linguistique » – ce qui nomme des problèmes plutôt que cela ne fournit des réponses. Dans cet article, je vais interpréter l'historialité via les notions d'*écriture* pensée par Jacques Derrida, de *Voix* pensée par Giorgio Agamben, et de *technique* pensée par Bernard Stiegler. Bien entendu, ce n'est pas dire que l'historialité consiste- rait en textes, en témoignages oraux ou en objets techniques, mais que ces termes techniques peuvent être interprétés comme matières élémentaires de l'historialité.

Point de départ : le sens de l'historialité chez Heidegger

Il va de soi, pour moi, que notre transcendance est fondamentalement histo- riale, parce que les questions les plus critiques de notre temps ne me semblent pas attachées à la constitution transcendantale de l'expérience *possible* d'un Je ou d'un *ego* pur, mais à la structure de l'expérience *réelle* qui est nécessaire- ment historique, comme l'ont surtout montré Hegel et Heidegger. C'est Heide- gger qui a pensé le plus rigoureusement la transcendance depuis l'expérience de l'être-au-monde, arguant que, comme le monde est la transcendance du *Dasein*, et comme le monde du *Dasein* est toujours historial, la transcendance est historiale.

C'est dans *Être et temps* que Heidegger définit le plus clairement le *Dasein* comme un être fondamentalement historial. Le *Dasein* est être-au-monde, et le monde « natif » dans lequel il se trouve toujours déjà « jeté », est un monde déjà-là, qui consiste en un passé qui est le passé du *Dasein* bien qu'il ne l'ait pas vécu en personne. Comme le résume bien Bernard Stiegler, c'est l'héritage qui, « loin de se perdre avec le vivant lorsqu'il périt, se conserve et se sédimente, se lègue à la survivance et à la descendance comme un don autant que comme une dette ».[1]

Dès le § 74 d'*Être et temps*, Heidegger montrait cependant que l'historialité proprement dite n'est pas l'adaptation tacite à l'héritage, mais l'assomption de l'historialité comme un *destin* lors d'une re-prise résolue, depuis l'avenir, des possibilités d'existence ayant-été. L'historialité requiert ainsi un dépassement de l'héritage de par une confrontation active avec certaines possibilités d'être ayant été, afin de préparer l'avenir. Dans ses travaux ultérieurs, Heidegger a souligné encore davantage que le passé ne *produit* aucunement l'avenir : au contraire, l'avenir reste à venir, comme signe d'un dieu encore inconnu, ou comme un *Ereignis* inattendu, et seule sa venue pourra changer une possibilité simplement historique en une possibilité destinale. Ainsi, dans *Temps et être* Heidegger précisait-il : « L'historique dans l'histoire de l'être se détermine à partir du caractère destinal d'une destination, et non pas à partir d'un «cours de l'histoire» entendu dans un sens indéterminé ».[2]

C'est cette expérience destinale qui nous semble passée : notre expérience de l'être-au-monde est bien plutôt une expérience de l'éclatement ou de l'absence du (sens du) monde[3] qui va de pair avec un certain éclatement ou absence du (sens de) l'histoire, qui n'est certes pas une fin de l'histoire (celle-ci supposant toujours plus ou moins tacitement que cette « fin » est un *telos* enfin réalisé) mais une fin de la fin de l'histoire, une fin, donc, de son sens, de sa raison ou de son objectif.[4] Comme Heidegger associe cette absence de destin à l'époque de la technique, dont l'analyse reste chez lui ambiguë, la question reste ouverte de savoir s'il l'a repoussée de sa pensée ou au contraire mise en son centre.[5] De surcroît, si le *Ge-stell* technique fait signe vers l'*Ereignis*, celui-ci montre-t-il une autre logique que celle du *logos* de l'histoire (par exemple la dimension anhistorique et terrienne de l'être indiquée par Michel Haar[6] ou au contraire la dimension autrement historiale d'un autre commencement) ou bien, l'*Ereignis* reste-t-il encore soumis à la logique du *logos*, du sens, de la fin de l'histoire à nouveaux frais ? Quoi qu'il en soit, avec Heidegger ou contre lui, c'est bien l'historicité de l'absence du sens de l'histoire qu'il s'agit pour nous de saisir.

Je partirai ici de l'hypothèse formulée par Stiegler mais rendue possible par Jacques Derrida, selon laquelle, dans les grandes lectures heideggériennes de l'historialité (*Être et temps*, les cours sur Hölderlin), la recherche du sens ou du *logos* de l'histoire s'accompagne d'une mise à l'écart du déjà-là quotidien.[7] Mais en quoi consiste l'historialité primitive de ce déjà-là, de l'être-au-monde quotidien ? Principalement dans les §§ 78–81 d'*Être et temps*, Heidegger le juge vulgaire et inauthentique, et il envisage sa temporalité seulement comme un temps du monde public et datable, et non pas comme une historialité destinale. Contre son jugement, je pars ici de l'hypothèse selon laquelle le déjà-là inauthentique, notre premier héritage, est le premier phénomène de l'historicité ou, plutôt, la « matière première » qui rend possible le phénomène de l'histoire aussi bien que son retrait. Mais en quoi consiste-t-elle ?

Dans ce qui suit, j'examinerai trois auteurs – Jacques Derrida, Giorgio Agamben et Bernard Stiegler – qui ont pris, chacun à sa manière, pour point de départ la critique du « logocentrisme » de Heidegger, et qui ont développé par la suite des interprétations originales de ce que, en termes heideggériens qu'eux-mêmes n'utilisent pas, on pourrait appeler « l'historialité vulgaire » ou « quotidienne ». Cette façon quelque peu abrupte de présenter la chose vient surtout de Bernard Stiegler, qui a attiré l'attention sur l'« avortement » de l'historialité vulgaire chez Heidegger. Selon sa thèse centrale, « la transmission du déjà-là [heideggérien] n'est possible que parce que la transmission que permettent les sédiments est d'essence absolument technique ».[8] On peut bien dire que la *technique* constitue chez Stiegler le phénomène ou la matière de l'histoire. Comme il le dit lui-même, l'argument de Stiegler doit cependant beaucoup à la pensée derridienne de l'*écriture* ; et la mise en perspective avec Stiegler nous permet d'envisager l'écriture derridienne comme une interprétation du lieu de l'histoire. Giorgio Agamben a quant à lui développé le motif derridien dans un sens différent de Stiegler et avant lui. Pour Agamben, le langage constitue la matière de l'histoire, au sens où il dit : « on ne peut pas historiciser le langage, parce qu'il est déjà lui-même historicisant : c'est lui qui fonde la possibilité de quelque chose comme une «histoire» ».[9] Dans sa polémique avec Derrida, il interprète cependant le langage selon la Voix et non pas selon l'écriture, donnant ainsi encore une autre perspective sur la matière de l'histoire.

Mon propos n'est donc pas d'examiner le phénomène du *logos* ou du *sens* de l'histoire mais sa matière élémentaire, qui fait qu'elle peut tout d'abord devenir phénomène ou se retirer de la phénoménalité. Je propose d'examiner l'écriture selon Derrida, le langage selon Agamben et la technique selon Stiegler comme autant d'interprétations de la matière de l'histoire, que Heidegger aurait ignorée. Ces matières sont autant de traces du retrait du sens de l'histoire – des lambeaux du monde, d'immenses archives désordonnées sans emploi, des restes non-recyclables dans l'économie du sens. Il ne s'agit pas pour moi de les présenter comme occasions de petites histoires de légitimation en l'absence de la Grande, comme dans *La Condition postmoderne* de Lyotard (car il ne s'agit pas ici de légitimer un savoir du monde), mais plus simplement de prêter attention à l'historialité foncière du monde constituée de matières dont la structure fondamentale consiste en ce qu'elles ne sont jamais présentes entièrement ici et maintenant.

Écriture

Contrairement à la théorie agambénienne du langage et de la théorie stieglerienne de la technique, la pensée derridienne de l'écriture n'est pas d'emblée présentée par son auteur comme une interprétation de l'historialité mais plutôt comme une déconstruction des philosophies de l'histoire ou de l'historialité proposées par Hegel, Husserl et Heidegger. Par définition, l'écriture travaille contre l'émergence d'un *logos* (de l'histoire) en montrant la dispersion et la perte qui guettent toute intention inscrite pour la postérité[10]. Cependant, dans la mesure où l'écriture est une structure différentielle espaçante et temporalisante de la significativité, il a aussi été possible de la développer vers une théorie de l'historialité détachée des « fins », comme dans l'idée de l'« histoire transcendantale » d'Agamben[11], ou dans les travaux sur l'historialité quotidienne de Stiegler.

Cette possibilité d'interprétation repose sur la définition par Derrida de l'écriture en termes d'*héritage*. Comme nous venons de le voir, l'historialité quotidienne du *Dasein* consiste en son être-au-monde, qu'il n'a pas fait mais dont il hérite. Or la pensée derridienne de l'écriture est de part en part une pensée de l'héritage : comme il le dit dans *De la Grammatologie*, « tout graphème est d'essence testamentaire »[12].

Dans nombre de ses premiers travaux, Derrida a relevé l'image du signe et de l'écriture comme « testament » ou « tombe » dans des textes classiques concernant le rôle de la mémoire dans la pensée, notamment chez Platon et Hegel[13]. Il a montré comment cette image, loin d'être une « fleur de la rhétorique » purement décorative, fonctionne dans ces textes de manière régulière, à vrai dire systématique, projetant ainsi toute une théorie de l'écriture que les auteurs eux-mêmes ne pensaient peut-être pas composer mais plutôt simplement écarter en tant que risque à la compréhension proprement dite de l'idée ou du concept. C'est ainsi que la « déconstruction » de textes canoniques faisait émerger une théorie marginale, sinon inconsciente, de l'écriture comme « tombe ». Derrida s'est ensuite servi de cette théorie enfouie pour décrire divers aspects de l'écriture qui, selon lui, ne peut pas être entièrement colonisée ou dépassée par la pensée pure, mais demeure au contraire la condition et le destin de toute pensée. Je me contente ici de rappeler les facettes les plus essentielles de cette théorie de l'écriture, que je crois être bien connue.

D'un côté, l'écriture est le « tombeau » du vouloir-dire de l'auteur. Aucun signe, aucune écriture ne fonctionnent en tant que tels s'il n'est pas *possible* que l'auteur soit absent, mort, disparu : le signe est *la présence de l'absence de l'auteur*, comme le pensait déjà Blanchot[14]. Si l'écriture suppose un auteur ou du moins un scribe, elle suppose aussi la possibilité de sa disparition, et en ce sens elle est toujours un « héritage ». D'un autre côté, Derrida approfondit la théorie saussurienne du signe comme lien arbitraire entre le signifiant et le signifié en la rapprochant de la théorie hégélienne du signe comme tombe, en tant que celle-ci est une structure artificielle, telle une pyramide, dans laquelle « une âme étrangère » est déposée. Ici, l'« âme » n'est pas le vouloir-dire d'un auteur mais le concept : le philosophe espère sa « résurrection » dans l'acte de lecture du texte philosophique. Mais comme Blanchot et Derrida n'ont cessé de le souligner, rien dans le signe lui-même ne garantit cette suppression de la matérialité du signe dans l'acte de la compréhension, et ce qui en ressort peut toujours n'être que la répétition machinale du simple signifiant ou le retour insensé d'un sens mort (symbolisé par Lazare, par des fantômes, par des mort-vivants en tout genre. Pour filer la métaphore encore plus loin, il m'est arrivé de me représenter certaines lectures très anachroniques de Hegel comme des gens sans abri qui squattent une tombe, déployant leur propre vie là où la momie a été dépouillée, puis volée, il y a longtemps déjà.)

Ainsi, toute une tradition philosophique représenterait le signe comme la « tombe » de la signification, que celle-ci soit pensée comme vouloir-dire ou comme concept. Or l'objectif de Derrida n'était pas de confirmer cette idée mais de la renverser, en montrant que le signe n'est pas la trace d'une origine absente mais qu'au contraire la trace est elle-même l'origine du sens : « *La trace est en effet l'origine absolue du sens en général. Ce qui revient à dire, encore une fois, qu'il n'y a pas d'origine absolue du sens en général. La trace est la différance qui ouvre l'apparaître et la signification.* »[15] Il n'y a d'origine qu'à partir de la trace qui en montre l'absence, et en ce sens l'écriture précède l'auteur et le concept, le destinateur et le destinataire, le signifié et le signifiant, qui n'ont dès lors jamais de présence pleine et indubitable. L'écriture elle-même ne vient pas combler ce manque de présence : « *La trace (pure) est la différance. Elle ne dépend d'aucune plénitude sensible, audible ou visible,*

phonique ou graphique. Elle en est au contraire la condition. Bien qu'elle
n'existe pas, bien qu'elle ne soit jamais un *étant-présent* hors de toute plénitude, sa possibilité est antérieure en droit à tout ce qu'on appelle le signe… ».[16]
« La trace *n'est rien*, elle n'est pas un étant, elle excède la question *qu'est-ce
que…* »[17], et c'est pourquoi l'écriture, qui en dépend, n'est pas une présence
pleine, n'ayant son sens que depuis la différance qu'elle met en marche. Finalement, le refus de présence et de réalité caractéristiques de l'écriture ressemble
peut-être à la *khôra*[18], qui donne lieu aux idées et aux copies sans pour autant
rien donner, n'étant que le *lieu* ou la matrice imaginaire de leur commune genèse.

Le défi de cette pensée de l'écriture est une sorte d'irréalité extrême qu'elle
demande de prendre au sérieux. Il serait tentant de penser l'écriture comme une
structure (quasi) métaphysique, comme la structure fondamentale du monde.
Mais Derrida insiste pour dire que l'écriture comme trace n'*est* strictement rien
(d'étant, encore moins de *logos*). C'est aussi pourquoi la pensée ne peut pas
l'affronter directement mais doit d'abord confronter une certaine impossibilité
de la penser comme telle. La pensée de l'écriture avance indirectement, par
détours, en dé-pensant et dé-construisant les figures héritées de l'écriture. Une
telle pensée ne peut pas se *construire* en un système mais doit procéder comme
une pratique de dé-construction où elle dé-pense et dé-fait ce qui dès lors apparaît forcément illusoire ou fictif. Pour nombre de lecteurs hâtifs, cette exigence
a semblé bien trop inquiétante car, ne permettant aucune sorte de fondement
ferme, elle a semblé nihiliste. D'autres ont au contraire pensé y trouver un
système caché (ainsi Agamben, comme nous le verrons à l'instant), et d'autres
encore l'ont utilisée comme fondation sur laquelle ils ont développé une
construction plus positive (ainsi Stiegler, comme nous le verrons aussi).

Mais la question de l'écriture ne se réduit pas à « l'irréalité » de la trace, car
elle comporte aussi la « réalité » des textes sans lesquels la trace ne serait
même pas pensable. On comprend mieux cela à la lumière de certains travaux
ultérieurs, dans lesquels Derrida porte son attention sur le « légataire » de
« l'héritage » qu'est l'écriture (car jamais nous ne lisons, n'écrivons ou ne
pensons sans nous servir des signes hérités, que ce soient les mots de la langue
ou les textes de la tradition). Dans *Donner le temps*, Derrida montre, partant
d'une explication de *Temps et Être* de Heidegger, qu'on ne peut pas penser la
donation sans don ni, à fortiori, l'être sans étant.[19] De même, il est impossible
de penser la trace sans l'écriture factuelle. Dans *Spectres de Marx*, il s'est alors

demandé comment recevoir ce « don » : si tant est que « être c'est hériter », « on hérite toujours d'un secret », et c'est pourquoi « l'héritage n'est jamais un *donné*, c'est toujours une tâche ».[20] Mais quelle tâche ? Hegel pensait dans son *Histoire de la philosophie* qu'il fallait hériter du don du passé en se l'appropriant comme un capital à faire fructifier dans de nouveaux projets – et qu'il ne faut pas hériter comme Antigone avait hérité d'une loi ancienne qu'elle avait pieusement conservée telle quelle. Heidegger pensait dans le § 74 d'*Être et temps* que le *Dasein* doit choisir ses héros et les répéter en sorte que l'avenir soit possible. Pour montrer les limites de ces idées d'une appropriation de l'héritage, Derrida a insisté pour dire que rien ne garantissait jamais que nous puissions simplement nous approprier le passé, utiliser son héritage, le soumettre à nos projets, à nos idées ou à notre avenir. Nous héritons toujours de cette chose complexe qu'est la tombe – qui pourra toujours être hantée par des esprits qui nous regardent et nous obsèdent sans que nous puissions savoir pourquoi et en quoi. En disant que nous devons *apprendre* à hériter, Derrida dit au fond que nous devons nous entretenir avec les « esprits », leur offrir l'hospitalité, vivre avec nos fantômes non pas de manière non-critique mais en les jugeant et en étant jugés par eux. Philosopher, ce n'est donc pas construire un système, c'est avant tout s'entretenir avec des « esprits » passés et à venir.

Dans la mesure où l'écriture derridienne a la structure de l'héritage, il est possible de l'interpréter comme une « matière de l'histoire » – à condition de prendre au sérieux la critique de la matérialité et de l'historialité inhérentes à la notion d'écriture. La pensée de l'écriture suscite l'image du monde comme d'énormes archives sédimentées et désordonnées, dans lesquelles aucun *data-mining* ne pourra trouver un sens unitaire. Mais ceci n'est qu'une image. L'écriture ne fait pas un monde car elle est ce qui rend possible les sens du monde tout comme leurs défaites, tout en étant elle-même le domaine de l'*ab-sens*. Parce qu'elle n'apparaît pas, on doit hésiter de l'appeler phénomène ; parce qu'on ne peut pas la soumettre, on doit hésiter de l'appeler matière ; et c'est pourquoi elle n'est peut-être rien de plus qu'un *lieu* d'avant le monde, comme la *khôra*. L'essentiel, dès lors, n'est pas tant de dire *ce qu'est* la matière de l'histoire, mais ce qu'elle nous invite à *faire*. L'écriture derridienne se lègue comme une tâche de la pensée, une exigence de justice à l'égard de l'arrivant, qui peut tout autant être un « fantôme » du « passé » que l'arrivant absolu ouvrant l'avenir.

Voix

Pour Giorgio Agamben, l'élément de l'« histoire transcendantale » est le *langage*, qui « ne peut pas être historicisé parce qu'il est lui-même historicisant : c'est lui qui fonde la possibilité de quelque chose comme une «histoire» »[21]. Le sens qu'il donne alors au « langage » doit être compris à partir de son *Auseinandersetzung* avec Derrida.

Dans un premier temps, Agamben présuppose la grammatologie derridienne mais l'évalue de manière polémique. « Certes, s'il faut rendre hommage à Derrida d'avoir été le philosophe qui a défini avec le plus de rigueur [...] le statut originel du *gramma* et du signifiant [...], il n'en est pas moins vrai qu'il a cru un moment, ce faisant, ouvrir la voie du dépassement de la métaphysique, tandis qu'en vérité [...] la métaphysique est toujours déjà grammatologie et celle-ci est fondamentologie ».[22] Selon Agamben, la pensée de Derrida donne ainsi lieu à un système de l'indécidable.[23] Agamben pense pouvoir inclure Derrida (et Heidegger, et lui-même) dans la métaphysique, parce qu'il définit la métaphysique comme une pensée de la négativité de l'être et non pas comme une doctrine positive. Cela étant, son évaluation de Derrida demeure inexacte dans la mesure où Derrida ne se situe pas lui-même à l'intérieur ni à l'extérieur de la métaphysique mais dit travailler (dans) ses marges, et ne tente certainement pas d'établir un *système* de l'indécidable, mais de repérer des points d'indécidabilité en fonction du *travail* avec des textes, qui montreront, en outre, que c'est justement là où la raison aboutit à l'indécidable qu'*il faut* décider[24].

Cependant, dans un deuxième temps, Agamben propose, au lieu de l'écriture, une pensée de l'avoir-lieu du langage articulée en termes de Voix, et cette contribution personnelle est originale et intéressante. Partant, ayant reproché à la grammatologie un manque de point de vue éthique (qui n'était effectivement pas bien visible chez Derrida à l'époque de la parution de *Il linguaggio e la morte* en 1982), il propose d'y remédier avec sa propre pensée de la Voix. Contrairement à la critique derridienne de la voix comme symbole de la clarté du *s'entendre-parler*, la pensée agambénienne de la Voix doit rendre compte de l'obscurité de l'*avoir-lieu du langage*.[25]

Selon Agamben, tout comme la métaphysique a tendance à examiner seulement la signification de l'être, et non pas l'expérience *qu'il y a l'être*, de même la grammaire et la logique ont tendance à voir dans le *logos* seulement le système de la langue, et non pas la parole. Mais le seul système de la langue ne fait pas un monde. Seul un événement de langage peut ouvrir un monde et, *a fortiori*, déployer son historialité. La Voix est l'expérience de la nécessité de parler qui est présupposée par tout événement de langage. La Voix n'est pas un phénomène acoustique mais l'instance du pur devoir-dire, « non-plus-voix et non-encore-signifié » qui ouvre le lieu du langage.[26] L'origine du langage est cet impératif de parler sans savoir encore quoi dire, impératif qu'Agamben appelle Voix, tout en le rapportant au « dire » défini par Lévinas, et à la « voix de la conscience » ainsi qu'à la « voix silencieuse de l'être » pensées par Heidegger.

Dans *Le Langage et la mort*, Agamben décompose l'expérience de la Voix en expliquant par des moyens linguistiques la négativité au cœur du *Dasein* heideggérien et du *Ceci* de l'analyse hégélienne de la certitude sensible. Dans les termes de Benveniste, le *je*, l'*ici*, le *ceci*, le *là*, etc. sont des *shifters* qui ne se réfèrent pas aux significations des énoncés mais à l'instance de l'énonciation par quoi le langage a lieu. D'une part le *Dasein*, que la « voix silencieuse de la conscience » appelle à s'assumer comme « je », s'explique alors par le « je » qui, selon Benveniste, « se réfère à l'acte de discours individuel où il est prononcé, et il en désigne le locuteur […] instance de discours ».[27] Agamben souligne que le *je*, tout en se trouvant toujours déjà dans le langage, fait véritablement l'expérience du langage lorsqu'il lui faut dire le monde mais que le mot lui manque – expérience qui a été décrite par Heidegger dans ses lectures de la langue poétique mais qu'Agamben décrit aussi via la poésie des troubadours. D'autre part, outre le *je*, *ici* et *maintenant* aussi – qui ne saisissent selon Hegel jamais le *ceci* – sont des indicateurs qui ne révèlent pas la signification mais l'instance et l'avoir-lieu du langage.

Illustrée par les *shifters*, la Voix ne révèle ni le vouloir-dire du locuteur ni la signification de l'énoncé, mais fait paraître le monde auquel les *shifters* renvoient : ainsi le monde et l'être peuvent s'ouvrir à la pensée. La parution du monde est un événement parce que le mot pour dire le sens du monde n'est pas donné et doit être trouvé : les mots de la langue sont bien là, investis d'une puissance de dire et de ne pas dire[28], mais il faut encore les porter au discours. En principe, l'instance de parole est aussi un moment éthique, car elle amène le locuteur devant les autres, bien qu'ils ne soient pas nécessairement là et ne fassent qu'une communauté d'êtres séparés.

Si le langage est, selon Agamben, l'histoire transcendantale, on peut bien dire que les énoncés sont sa « matière » – à condition de penser les énoncés depuis un langage de la *puissance*.[29] La puissance réside d'un côté dans la Voix, qui révèle le *je* comme puissance et impuissance de dire. La puissance réside de l'autre côté dans la langue qui apparaît alors comme possibilité de signifier ou ne pas signifier ceci. Ce langage de la puissance ne contient pas la signification du monde : il rend compte de l'impuissance et de la puissance de porter le monde à la parole.

Technique

Penseur plus tardif que Derrida et Agamben, Bernard Stiegler met au centre de sa pensée « l'historialité du déjà-là » interprétée comme étant « d'essence absolument technique »[30]. En comparaison avec, d'un côté, le caractère abstrait voire « fictif » de l'écriture derridienne, et avec, d'un autre côté, la tendance métaphysique de la Voix selon Agamben, la technique au sens de Stiegler est concrète, sinon matérialiste.[31] La technique appartient à la quotidienneté : comme celle-ci, elle a tendance à disparaître plutôt qu'à apparaître, et c'est pourquoi elle ne constitue pas exactement un *phénomène* de l'histoire. En revanche, la technique est un supplément originaire : « le supplément est élémentaire, supplémentarité élémentaire qui *est* le (rapport au) temps (différ*a*nce) »[32], que j'ai appelé ici la « matière élémentaire de l'histoire ».

Le propre de l'analyse de Stiegler est l'interprétation de la technique comme mémoire. Stiegler distingue en réalité trois types de mémoire.[33] 1. Tous les êtres vivants ont une *mémoire génétique* qui délimite ce qu'ils peuvent devenir (par ex. les représentants d'une espèce donnée). 2. Les individus ont en outre une *mémoire épigénétique*, à savoir une mémoire nerveuse qui modifie l'individu en fonction de ses expériences. La mémoire épigénétique *individue* le vivant. 3. La mémoire technologique, enfin, est la *mémoire épiphylogénétique*. Celle-ci a lieu dans des objets techniques qui « se souviennent » du fonctionnement du monde (et permettent aux utilisateurs de l'oublier). Les objets techniques n'appartiennent pas aux individus mais aux communautés humaines, dont la cohésion n'est par conséquent nullement naturelle mais technique et artificielle. Selon la thèse fondamentale de Stiegler, la mémoire épiphylogénétique fait l'être des objets techniques, et par là elle conditionne également la mémoire épigénétique. Autrement dit, les choses techniques *sont* la mémoire humaine, et non pas seulement ses moyens. La mémoire humaine n'est pas un processus « intérieur » mais un processus « extérieur » : externalisé, matérialisé, aliéné.

Stiegler développe son analyse de la technique en débat avec Heidegger et Derrida. Son point de départ est l'analyse heideggérienne de l'historialité du déjà-là et son extension en *Ge-stell* technique. Dans le contexte d'*Être et temps*,

Stiegler souligne à la fois l'importance et l'insuffisance de l'analyse heideggé-rienne de l'historialité. Stiegler pense que Heidegger vise en dernière instance une pensée égologique de l'être authentique du *Dasein,* négligeant la quoti-dienneté, ainsi que la temporalité vulgaire et la « mondo-historialité » qui y sont rattachées. Heidegger ne verrait donc pas que la temporalité de l'être hu-main a son origine dans la temporalité vulgaire des choses techniques. En outre, Heidegger confondrait la temporalité vulgaire avec le temps de l'hor-loge, qu'il assimilerait à tort à l'idéalité métaphysique qui finit par supprimer le temps – alors que le temps des choses techniques est en réalité le temps du souci, qui essaie, mais en vain, de contrôler l'avenir[34]. Dans le contexte de la pensée heideggérienne de la technique, Stiegler souligne l'ambivalence grâce à laquelle celle-ci s'ouvre vers une pensée du monde technique, mais échoue pourtant à assumer ses conséquences les plus radicales. Essentiellement, l'in-terrogation heideggérienne de la technique reste réglée sur sa critique de l'époque de la technique qui change l'homme et le monde en ressources tout en obscurcissant la pensée de l'être[35]. Ainsi la pensée de la technique reste une fonction de la pensée de l'être, alors que Stiegler voudrait se confronter à la technique comme telle.

La critique derridienne du « logocentrisme » heideggérien a inspiré ces cri-tiques, et sa pensée de l'écriture a motivé chez Stiegler une théorie de la tech-nique comme mémoire. L'écriture est bien une mnémotechnique, dont Derrida montre qu'elle ne conserve pas le *logos* ni ne permet sa constitution, mais fonctionne plutôt comme un principe de répétition machinale qui peut aussi bien faire que défaire du sens. Cependant, Stiegler se démarque de Derrida sur deux points essentiels. D'abord, Derrida construit sa pensée de l'écriture sous le signe de la « fin de l'homme » : elle est une pensée de la trace comme *diffé-rance* qui doit « inquiéter radicalement la frontière séparant l'animalité et l'hu-manité ».[36] Contrairement à cela, Stiegler interprète la technique spécifique-ment comme origine de l'homme (« la technique inventant l'homme, l'homme inventant la technique »[37]), et pose ainsi à nouveau la question anthropologique dans les termes de la technique. Ensuite, Stiegler pense que son concept de mémoire épiphylogénétique ne trouve « aucun équivalent dans les déconstruc-tions grammatologiques »[38] parce que la *différance* s'inscrit selon lui dans l'histoire de la vie en général, mais pas dans des outils en particulier.

Qui est alors l'« homme » (Stiegler utilise toujours ce nom) ? En suivant Heidegger, Stiegler pense que la question de l'homme n'a d'autre réponse que la question elle-même. Stiegler pense en outre que l'origine de l'homme est le *défaut* d'origine auquel la technique doit *suppléer*. L'homme n'a pas d'essence car il est toujours inventé par les techniques qu'il invente, ou en termes rous-seauistes, il n'a pas de nature car sa nature est l'artifice et la technique qui lui permettent aussi de créer sa nature. Partant de cette co-originarité ou de cette production réciproque de l'homme et de la technique, Stiegler explique cependant l'homme comme un *défaut d'origine* qu'il illustre comme un manque, une ignorance ou une idiotie auxquels les techniques suppléent. Si l'origine trans-cendantale de l'homme est ce défaut d'origine, son origine historique est bien entendu dans les techniques déjà-sous-la-main qui proposent de suppléer au manque. Cependant, l'homme selon Stiegler n'est pas mécaniquement et défi-nitivement déterminé par le déjà-là. Il peut rester étourdi à son égard ; s'il veut l'utiliser il doit l'apprendre ; ou, au contraire, il peut trouver une solution plus ingénieuse à un problème pratique que celui proposé par les techniques sous la main, et peut ainsi les détourner ou les dépasser grâce à de nouvelles inven-tions.

Quelle est l'essence de la technique selon Stiegler si elle n'est pas une forme de connaissance du monde, comme chez Heidegger, mais une *pro-thèse* desti-née à suppléer au défaut d'origine de l'homme[39] ? Stiegler pense que dans les « pro-thèses » techniques, l'homme pose son désir, son pouvoir et son savoir dans des choses en-dehors de lui, et s'éloigne ainsi de lui-même dans le temps aussi bien que dans l'espace. L'être humain ne peut avoir le temps que si la technique se souvient de ce qu'il y avait et prévoit ce qu'il y aura ; et il ne peut y avoir une communauté que si la technique le lie à d'autres êtres humains. L'essence de la technique selon Stiegler n'est cependant pas d'être un outil au service des projets humains. Au contraire, car l'homme est originairement dé-fectueux, « idiot », soucieux mais dépourvu de ressources et des projets. Elle n'est pas non plus le support d'une rationalité supérieure, comme dans les cri-tiques de la société par Heidegger, Weber ou Habermas. La *techné* a sa propre manière d'être qui ne revient ni à la *phusis* ni à l'*épistémé*, parce que la tech-nique consiste dans les *processus des êtres organisés inorganiques* qui ne suit ni les *mouvements des êtres inorganiques* ni la *vie des êtres organiques*. Stie-gler s'appuie sur les recherches anthropologiques et « techno-logiques » des techniques pour rendre compte des processus propres du monde technique.[40] En suivant l'historien Bertrand Gille, il pense les techniques comme des sys-tèmes qui s'organisent, se rattachent, se développent ensemble et forment des systèmes. En suivant le paléoanthropologue André Leroi-Gourhan, Stiegler pense que les systèmes techniques sont des quasi-organismes qui évoluent suivant des tendances techniques combinant l'intentionnalité de l'homme et les lois de la matière. Comme les tendances techniques ne reflètent pas les propriétés ethniques mais des tendances plus générales, elles permettent aussi aux humains de s'échapper du conservatisme naturel des communautés ethniques. En suivant, enfin, le philosophe de la technique Gilbert Simondon, qui a étudié le développement technologique dans les sociétés industrielles, Stiegler montre comment les objets techniques ont de plus en plus tendance à évoluer indépendamment des intentions humaines. Les gadgets et les systèmes techniques ont leur dynamique propre, dans laquelle les machines technologiques se développent dans un rapport avec d'autres machines, plutôt que dans un rapport avec les hommes, créant ainsi une sorte d'environnement technologique qu'on peut analyser comme une écologie de la technologie ou comme une « techno-géographie ». Ainsi – comme nombre de grands penseurs modernes de la technique (Simondon, Heidegger, Weber, Habermas) – Stiegler pense que la technologie moderne est caractérisée par le développement autonome de la technique : l'homme est une fonction de la technique plutôt que l'inverse, la technique forme la conscience humaine et selon certains visionnaires va jusqu'à créer de nouvelles formes de conscience.

Chez Stiegler, les techniques concrètes sont la « matière de l'histoire ». Si l'écriture derridienne est une structure abstraite qui n'*existe* peut-être pas au sens propre du mot, et si la Voix agambénienne est une puissance métaphysique, la technique stieglérienne est quant à elle une structure fondamentale du monde se concrétisant dans des technologies matérielles et sociales. Pour Tracy Colony, Stiegler se rend ainsi coupable d'un « positivisme de la différance » qui le pousse à construire une théorie en dernière instance anthropocentrique et métaphysique : par là il ferait fi des critiques de l'anthropocentrisme et de la métaphysique qui étaient le point de départ même de Derrida.[41] Jean-Hugues Barthélémy pense au contraire que Stiegler a raison de dépasser la « rhétorique spéculative » de Derrida et de passer du côté de la « construction conceptuelle ». Sa pensée ne serait pas plus anthropologique que celle de Heidegger, car il part précisément du *défaut* d'essence de l'homme et interprète la technique toujours comme un *supplément*, et non pas comme une essence de l'homme.[42] Cela étant, je trouve la motivation de la critique de Colony importante. Si on définit le déjà-là historicisant comme une altérité qui se distingue de manière temporelle de la conscience, on ne peut pas l'examiner comme n'importe quel objet mais plutôt comme un effet, dont on ne peut approcher les causes sans une sorte de « spéculation ». Bien que l'examen de la machine comme une mémoire nous permette de la comprendre de manière plus riche, l'inverse n'est pas nécessairement vrai, et l'examen de la mémoire comme une machine peut au contraire réduire la mémoire à n'être qu'un objet parmi d'autres.

Éléments de l'historialité

Les développements de l'historialité quotidienne par Derrida, Agamben et Stiegler ont déployé trois versions de ce que j'ai appelé « matières élémentaires » de l'historialité. Nous avons vu comment l'écriture derridienne apparaît le plus manifestement dans ce qu'on appelle ordinairement écriture, mais qu'elle est aussi une pensée plus générale de la *différance* et de la trace comme conditions du sens et de la signification. La *différance* n'est rien, mais elle est postulée afin de pouvoir expliquer la signification comme un effet. Nous avons aussi vu comment Agamben interprète la pensée derridienne de l'écriture dans les termes de sa propre pensée de la puissance. Il y ajoute cependant une idée de la Voix qui est appelée à rendre compte de l'avoir-lieu factuel du langage et non pas seulement de sa possibilité en général, de l'ouverture de tel monde spécifique et non pas seulement de l'être-au-monde en général. La Voix semblerait ainsi détenir la position métaphysique du sens d'un monde. Nous avons vu enfin comment Stiegler fait de l'idée de l'écriture le fondement de son idée de la technique tout en le changeant en un principe positif concret et nullement métaphysique. Sa « technique » est une généralisation de « l'écriture » de Derrida en particulier parce que les deux sont des mémoires extériorisées, mais Stiegler insère les structures révélées par Derrida dans des choses et en fait leur essence.

Dans tous ces cas nous voyons une conception de l'historialité qui ne se rassemble pas en un sens, ni ne devient forcément phénomène, mais se laisse cependant penser comme étant foncièrement historiale : est historial ce qui, tout simplement, n'est jamais entièrement présent sans renvoyer aussi à quelque chose qui fut et quelque chose qui pourrait être.

Cette « matière » est-elle fictive (comme l'écriture selon Derrida), puissance d'événement (comme la Voix selon Agamben) ou matérielle (comme la technique selon Stiegler) ? Ou plutôt un peu tout cela, sachant que seule l'écriture a rendu possible ces théories de la Voix et de la technique, mais que celles-ci l'obligent en retour à évoluer dans le sens de la communauté et du monde matériel ? À savoir, aussi dans le sens de la politique (et les débats qui ont suivi ces positions n'ont pas manqué d'être avant tout politiques[43]).

Je trouve en tout cas précieuses toutes ces pensées dans la mesure où elles ouvrent la dimension d'une pensée élémentaire de l'historialité. Plus obscure que les dimensions de la *phusis* ou du *logos* de l'histoire – qui peuvent se présenter – la dimension élémentaire est une dimension sans présence à laquelle on ne peut pas accéder directement. Cependant elle est une dimension dynamique de figurations qui ne suivent aucune raison donnée mais créent leurs propres raisons étrangères à la *phusis* aussi bien qu'au *logos* : comme les hantises et les voix de l'écriture ou les inventions de la technique. Les pensées élémentaires de l'historialité nous apprennent à suivre ces raisonnements hors de la Raison, et nous apprennent à vivre un peu mieux dans le monde dépourvu de sens de l'histoire.

Notes

1   Martin Heidegger, *Sein und Zeit*, § 75. Tübingen, Max Niemeyer Verlag, 1984. Voir Bernard Stiegler, *La Technique et le temps*, tome 1 : *La Faute d'Épiméthée*. Paris, Galilée, 1994, p. 150.

2   « Das Geschichtliche der Geschichte des Seins bestimmt sich aus dem Geschickhaften eines Schickens, nicht aus einem unbestimmt gemeinten Geschehen. » (Martin Heidegger, *Zeit und Sein*, in *Zur Sache des Denkens*, Tübingen, Max Niemayer Verlag, 1969, p. 8–9. / *Temps et Être*, in *Questions III et IV*, Paris, Gallimard, 1976, p. 203.)

3   L'absence du monde a été articulée par exemple par Jean-Luc Nancy, *Le sens du monde*, Galilée, Paris, 1993, p. 13. Le thème de l'absence du monde était le point de départ de Derrida dans sa lecture du vers de Paul Celan « *Die Welt is fort / ich muß dich tragen* » (Jacques Derrida, *Béliers. Le dialogue interrompu : entre deux infinis, le poème*. Galilée, Paris, 2003, p. 25, p. 46). Dans ce texte il se réfère à la notion heideggérienne d'« absence du monde » (*op. cit.*, 78) qu'il développe dans *Voyous. Deux essais sur la raison*. Galilée, Paris, 2003, p. 213). Les notions derridienne du « monde » et d'« absence du monde » sont examinées avec soin par Rodolphe Gasché dans *Europe, or the Infinite Task. A Study of Philosophical Concept*. Stanford University Press, 2009, chapter 11 « De-closing the horizon ». On trouvera toute une histoire de la notion philosophique de fin de monde dans Michaël Fœssel, *Après la fin du monde. Critique de la raison apocalyptique*. Paris, Seuil, 2012.

4   La fin de l'histoire était bien entendu comprise comme son accomplissement par Alexandre Kojève et plus encore par Francis Fukuyama, dont l'argumentation fut à juste titre critiquée par Jacques Derrida dans *Spectres de Marx*, Paris, Galilée, 1993. La fin des fins de l'histoire avec Hegel et Heidegger est aussi décrite par Giorgio Agamben, *La Puissance de la pensée*, Paris, Rivages, 2006, p. 160. La fin de la grande Histoire était entendue en un autre sens comme la disparition du grand récit de légitimation par Jean-François Lyotard dans *La Condition postmoderne*, Paris, Minuit, 1979, qui voyait l'émergence de petits récits de légitimation à la place. Bien que cette proclamation de la fin de la grande Histoire condense bien une pensée partagée par pratiquement tous les penseurs « continentaux » de l'époque, sa résolution en « petits récits » est problématique, car il ne s'agit pas forcément de passer à d'autres légitimations mais de se défaire de l'idée même de l'histoire comme légitimation.

5   On sait que selon Heidegger, « L'essence de la technique moderne [...] est identique à la métaphysique moderne » (« L'époque des conceptions du monde », *Chemins qui ne mènent nulle part*, Gallimard, Paris, 1990 (1962), p. 100 / « Die Zeit des Weltbildes », *Holzwege*, Vittorio Klostermann, Frankfurt am Main, 1980 (1950), p. 73). Par exemple dans « Contribution à la question de l'être », il analyse cette essence commune en termes d'une transcendance époquale : la technique « se fonde manifestement dans ce renversement de la transcendance dans la rescendance de la forme du travailleur » (« Contribution à la question de l'être », dans *Questions I-II, op. cit.*, p. 217 / « Zur Seinsfrage », in *Wegmarken, op. cit.*, p. 393). Dans « La question de la technique », il analyse la technique comme un « envoi qui rassemble » (*versammelnde Schicken*) ou comme un « destin » (*Gechick*), en sorte que « c'est à partir de lui que la substance (*Wesen*) de toute histoire se détermine » (« La question de la technique », *Essais et conférences*, Gallimard, Paris, 1980 (1958), p. 32 / « Die Frage nach der Technik », *Vorträge und Aufsätze*, Neske, Stuttgart, 1994 (1959), p. 28). Le rapport libre à la technique a été décrit par exemple par Rex Gilliland dans « The Destiny of Technology », *Heidegger Studies* vol. 18, Duncker & Humblot, Berlin, p. 115–128; Miguel de Beistegui dans le chapitre 4 « The Grip of Technology » de son livre *The New Heidegger*, Continuum, New York and London, 2005, p. 97–124 et Hans Ruin dans *Ge-stell* dans « Ge-stell : Enframing as the Essence of Technology », in *Martin Heidegger: Key Concepts*, ed. Bret W. Davis, Acumen 2010.

6   Michel Haar, *La fracture de l'histoire. Douze essais sur Heidegger*. Paris, Jérôme Millon, 1994, p. 9–24.

7   Cette hypothèse est formulée le plus clairement par Bernard Stiegler in *La Technique et le temps*, tome 1, p. 105–152. Il me semble que cette hypothèse présuppose l'analyse par Jacques Derrida du rejet du temps vulgaire dans le § 82 d'*Être et temps* dans « Ousia et grammé. Note sur une note de Sein und Zeit », *Marges de la philosophie*. Paris, Minuit, 1972, p. 31–78. Tracy Colony conteste la pertinence de l'argument de Stiegler dans «A Matter of Time: Stiegler on Heidegger and Being Technological», *Journal of the British Society of Phenomenology* 41, n° 2, May 2010, 17–31. Je ne discuterai pas en détail la thèse de Colony ici – je note seulement que Stiegler n'*ignore* certainement pas la richesse de l'analyse de l'outil et en général du déjà-là quotidien dans *Être et temps* et de la technique dans des textes ultérieurs de Heidegger (voir p. ex. Stiegler, *La technique et le temps I*, p. 255 sqq.). Mais la pensée heideggérienne de la quotidienneté est une pensée de l'oubli du déjà-là, et on se meut ici constamment sur la ligne fine entre une pensée de l'oubli et une pensée oubliée.

8   Bernard Stiegler, *La Technique et le temps*, tome 1, *op. cit.*, p. 151.

9   Giorgio Agamben, *Enfance et histoire. Destruction de l'expérience et origine de l'histoire*, Paris, Petite bibliothèque Payot, 2000 (1. éd. 1978), p. 64. [citation légèrement modifiée]

10   Jacques Derrida développe sa pensée de l'écriture surtout dans *De la grammatologie*, Paris, Minuit, 1967 ; *L'écriture et la différence*, Paris, Seuil, 1967 ; *Marges de la philosophie*. Paris, Minuit, 1972 ; et *La dissémination*, Paris, Seuil, 1972. Pour approfondir le sujet, on consultera, en plus de l'étude classique de Rodolphe Gasché, *The Tain of the Mirror: Derrida and the Philosophy of Reflection*, Harvard (MA), Cambridge University Press, 1986, surtout deux études récentes : Marc Goldschmit, *Une langue à venir. Derrida, l'écriture hyperbolique*. Paris, Leo Scheer, 2006, et Catherine Malabou, *La Plasticité au soir de l'écriture*. Paris, Éditions Léo Scheer, 2004.

11   Agamben énonce son idée de l'« histoire transcendantale » dans *Enfance et histoire*, Paris, Payot et Rivages, 2000 (1. éd. 1978), p. 65. Avec une référence à Agamben, Søren Gosvig Olesen montre plus précisément comment on peut interpréter Derrida en termes d'histoire transcendantale dans son livre *Transcendental History*, Palgrave MacMillan, 2013, p. 120–126.

12   Derrida, *De la grammatologie, op. cit.*, p. 100.

13 La sémiologie de Hegel est surtout étudiée dans « Le puits et la pyramide », dans *Marges de la philosophie, op. cit.*, la théorie platonicienne de l'écriture est étudiée dans « La pharmacie de Platon », dans *La dissémination, op. cit.*

14 Derrida souligne ceci également dans « Signature événement contexte » dans *Marges de la philosophie, op. cit.*

15 Jacques Derrida, *De la grammatologie, op. cit.*, p. 95.

16 *Ibid.*, p. 92.

17 *Ibid.*, p. 110.

18 La *Khôra* imaginée par Platon dans le *Timée* est analysée par Jacques Derrida dans *Khôra*, Paris, Galilée, 1993.

19 Jacques Derrida, *Donner le temps 1. La fausse monnaie.* Paris, Galilée, 1991

20 Jacques Derrida, *Spectres de Marx*, Paris, Galilée, 1993, p. 40, 94.

21 Agamben, *Enfance et histoire, op cit.*, p. 64–65, traduction légèrement modifiée.

22 Agamben, *Le langage et la mort*, Paris, Christian Bourgois, 1991 (orig. 1982), p. 81.

23 Voir Giorgio Agamben, *Stanze*, Paris, Christian Bourgois, 1998 (1. éd. 1981), p. 260–261. Sans toutefois citer son nom, Agamben critique Derrida (ou des derridiens) dans plusieurs articles rassemblés en français dans *La puissance de la pensée*, Paris, Rivages, 2006 (« tradition de l'immémorial », p. 136–137 ; « *Se. L'absolu et L'Ereignis », p. 160–161) ; et en commentant Derrida directement dans « Pardès. L'écriture de la puissance », où Agamben finit par interpréter la trace derridienne comme une matière intelligible (p. 307). Cette interprétation a été contestée par Adam Thurschwell dans « Cutting the Branches for Akiba : Agamben's Critique of Derrida » (in *Politics, Metaphysics, and Death*, ed. by Andrew Norris, Durham and London, Duke University Press, 2005, p. 180 sqq.) – mais la question est épineuse, car Derrida parle lui-même de son objectif comme d'un « matérialisme quasi transcendantal mais aussi obstinément intéressé par un matérialisme sans substance : un matérialisme de la *khôra* pour un «messianisme» désespérant. » (Derrida, *Spectres de Marx*, Paris, Galilée, 1993, p. 267).

24 Jacques Derrida, *Force de Loi*, Paris, Galilée, 1994, p. 34–40.

25 *Ibid.*, p. 58–59. Si la voix chez Derrida appartient à la problématique de la présence à soi, ce n'est pas le cas de la Voix chez Agamben, qui appartient plutôt à la problématique de l'événement. C'est pourquoi l'analyse de Jeffrey Librett me semble erronée, quand celui-ci pense que la Voix décrite par Agamben serait une *pure présence* (Jeffrey Librett, « From the Sacrifice of the Letter to the Voice of Testimony : Giorgio Agamben's Fulfillment of Metaphysics », *Diacritics* 2007, p. 15). Pis encore, Librett se trompe à mon avis ignoblement lorsqu'il prétend que « pour Agamben, dans le témoignage de l'Holocauste, comme conséquence du meurtre ostensiblement non-sacrificiel des Juifs européens, une certaine grâce se sera produit » (*ibid.*, p. 32).

26 Agamben, *Le langage et la mort, op. cit.*, p. 75.

27 Cité in Agamben, *Enfance et histoire, op. cit.*, p. 60 ; cf. *Le langage et la mort, op. cit.*, p. 54 sqq.

28 Agamben décrit la puissance de la parole très bien dans « Pardès. L'écriture de la puissance », in *La puissance de la pensée. op. cit.*, p. 293–308 – indépendamment du fait qu'on a pu le questionner en tant qu'analyse de Derrida.

29 Sur la puissance selon Agamben, voir aussi « La Puissance de la pensée » dans *La Puissance de la pensée, op. cit.*, p. 233–246.

30 Bernard Stiegler, *La Technique et le temps*, tome 1 : *La Faute d'Épiméthée*, Paris, Galilée, 1994, p. 151. Stiegler développe sa théorie philosophique de la technique surtout dans la trilogie *La Technique et le temps*, qui comporte, outre le volume cité, le tome 2 : *La Désorientation*, Paris, Galilée, 1996 ; le tome 3 : *Le Temps du cinéma et la Question du mal-être*, Paris,

Galilée, 2001.

31 À cet égard elle complète la pensée de Catherine Malabou qui a étudié la compatibilité de la pensée derridienne de l'écriture et des études du cerveau par exemple dans *Que faire de notre cerveau ?* (Paris : Bayard, 2004) et *Les Nouveaux Blessés : de Freud à la neurologie : penser les traumatismes contemporains* (Paris : Bayard, 2007).

32 Stiegler, *La Technique et le temps*, tome 1 : *La Faute d'Épiméthée*, p. 191.

33 Résumé dans Stiegler, *La Technique et le temps I*, p. 185.

34 Cf. Stiegler, *La Technique et le temps I*, p. 11, 226–231.

35 Cf. Stiegler, *La Technique et le temps I*, p. 27. Tracy Colony conteste la pertinence de l'analyse de Stiegler dans « A Matter of Time: Stiegler on Heidegger and Being Technological », *Journal of the British Society of Phenomenology* 41, n° 2, May 2010, 17–31). On peut sûrement défendre Heidegger contre Stiegler, mais la proposition de Stiegler concernant la technique reste quand même intéressante.

36 Selon Stiegler, la pensée derridienne de l'écriture est fondamentalement une pensée de la *différance* qui « décrit le *processus de la vie* dont l'homme est un cas singulier, mais seulement un cas. Il ne s'agit pas de vider l'être vivant humain de toute spécificité, mais d'inquiéter radicalement la frontière séparant l'animalité et l'humanité » (Stiegler, *La Technique et le temps I*, p. 147).

37 Stiegler, *La Technique et le temps I*, p. 148.

38 Stiegler, *La Technique et le temps I*, p. 186.

39 Heidegger, « Die Frage nach der Technik », in *Vorträge und Aufsätze*, Frankfurt am Main, Neske, 1994, p. 16–17 ; Stiegler, *La Technique et le temps I*, p. 162.

40 Les caractérisations suivantes viennent de Stiegler, *La Technique et le temps I*, p. 95, et elles ont été justifiées par les chapitres qui précèdent ce résumé.

41 Tracy Colony, «Epimetheus Bound: Stiegler on Derrida, Life, and the Technological Condition». *Research in Phenomenology*, 41 (2011), 72–89, p. 88. Voir aussi Nathan Van Camp, «Bernard Stiegler and the Question of Technics». *Transformations* no 17, 2009, p. 10/13.

42 Jean-Hugues Barthélémy, «De la finitude rétentionnelle (sur la technique et le temps de Bernard Stiegler)». *Phénoménologie et technique(s)*, dir. Pierre-Étienne Schmit et Pierre-Antoine Chardel, Le Cercle Herméneutique éditeur, 2008, p. 199.

43 Si le conflit entre Derrida et Agamben s'est envenimé (voir surtout Derrida, *La Bête et le souverain I*, Paris, Galilée, 2008, 12ème et 13ème séances), alors que la pensée de Stiegler suit désormais un tout autre parcours (via l'association *Ars industrialis*), on pourrait reconstituer un débat politique intéressant à partir de leurs critiques respectives de l'ère de la technique, suivant des jalons qui ont été ébauchés p. ex. dans Derrida & Stiegler, *Échographies de la télévision*, Paris, Galilée, 1996, ou dans Daniel Ross, « Democracy, Authority, Narcissism, From Agamben to Stiegler », *Contretemps* 6, 2006.

HISTORICITY AS EFFECTIVE HISTORY

JAMES RISSER

Regarding the concept of historicity in Hans-Georg Gadamer's *Truth and Method*, it is generally well known that Gadamer takes over this concept for his own project from Martin Heidegger. But Gadamer's project is not the same as Heidegger's, and it is in relation to this difference that the concept of historicity becomes something different for Gadamer. In what follows I want to elucidate this difference through Gadamer's idea of effective history and then provide a further interpretation of this idea through a comparison with a similar idea in the work of Michel Foucault.

The concept of historicity in Heidegger

The importance of the concept of historicity emerges early on in Heidegger's work in conjunction with his attempt at clarifying the very starting point of philosophy. Against Husserl's phenomenology as well as the neo-Kantianism of his day, the needed clarification pertains specifically to the character of the theoretical as the original evidence situation of philosophy. For Heidegger this clarification requires a return to the pre-theoretical dimension of life in relation to which a hermeneutic component within phenomenology will become necessary. In order to then accomplish this new approach to philosophizing, Heidegger will at once insist on the need to contest philosophy's history, that is, to destructure the Greek conceptuality within which philosophy operates.[1] In his "Comments on Karl Jaspers's *Psychology of Worldviews*" from 1919, Heidegger calls this destructuring a "genuine conversation with the history that we ourselves 'are'."[2] Thus, from the outset, philosophizing for Heidegger becomes inseparable from the historical in a double sense. It is an engagement with a historical tradition by way of a distinctive appropriation of historical life (what he will eventually call *Geschichlichkeit*).

The account of historical life that Heidegger first gives in relation to Jaspers own work can be appreciated for its relative simplicity when compared with that in *Being and Time*. In his comments Heidegger sees that Jaspers's account of "psychic life" through its limit situations holds uncritically to the subject-object split and poses the question of the proper access to these situations. For Heidegger this access will require "the method belonging to our interpretive, historically enacted explication of concrete fundamentally experiential modes of having-oneself."[3] Explicating the experience of existence, in other words, will require a distinctive form of interpretation in which one is directed back to the being of one's own existence by way of a particular kind of "how" – an enactment of one's existence that extends historically into the past of the I. And so, for Heidegger the distinctive appropriation of historical life, which will define the precise sense of the hermeneutical, occurs in relation to this "how."

It would appear that Heidegger derives the notion of the "how" from Christian sources, and, while Heidegger makes no direct mention of Kierkegaard in this context, we know that it is Kierkegaard who first makes thematic this "how" in his characterization of existence.[4] The "how" constitutes the manner of relating to oneself as an actualization through repetition. What is different for Heidegger is the overt way in which he links the "how" to historical enactment: "When, in accord with the relational sense of one's experience, one is directed historically to one's self, the context of this experience also has a historical nature in accord with its enactment."[5] What Heidegger is calling here the historical (*Das Historische*) "is the concealed source from which historical experience in the sense of the development of objective historical knowledge (the historical human sciences) arises."[6] And this also means that philosophizing as fundamental knowing is accordingly "nothing other than the radical actualization of the historical of the facticity of life."[7]

In the immediately following years this difference that being historical makes in accessing historical knowledge is at the center of Heidegger's engagement with Dilthey. In his Kassel lectures on Dilthey given in 1925, Heidegger is quick to point out what he considers to be Dilthey's advance over previous theory, namely, that all reflection and inquiry arise from life, that is, from an awareness of the interwoven texture of world and self, and not from introspection. It is this insight that is expressed by the hermeneutic maxim "we understand life from out of life."[8] But for Dilthey the standpoint of life is more than contextualized relations. As Heidegger tells us, "for Dilthey authentic historical being [*geschichliche Sein*] is human Dasein," and in recognizing this, Dilthey had begun to understand the authentic meaning of history in phenomenological terms.[9] He had only begun, though, for he could not free himself from an approach to historical life thought in terms of science and the framework of objectivity. Historical meaning remains a product of an objective historical development, which is not to say that he did not make an advance over the neo-Kantians of his time, who in their theoretical approach de-historicize (*ent-geschichtlich*) our original experience of the world. Dilthey's real failure, Heidegger claims, was that he never really considered the full implications of the being of the historical, a point which Heidegger notes was initially made by Yorck von Wartenburg in correspondence with Dilthey. According to Heidegger, while indeed for Dilthey everything in historical life is historically determined, and this would include the human being itself, the need remains "to work out the being of the historical, i.e., historicity rather than the historical [*Geschichtlichkeit, nicht Geschichliches*], being rather than beings, reality rather than the real."[10]

In drawing this distinction Heidegger underscores the idea that historicity involves more than the historical inquirer being situated in history. Historicity pertains essentially to the experience of temporality, and this means the enactment of the how. In the year earlier, in his lecture on the concept of time given to the theological society in Marburg, Heidegger had already made this decisive formulation on the essence of the historical. Decrying historicism and what he calls pseudo history, Heidegger notes that "the possibility of access to history is grounded in the possibility according to which any specific present understands how to be futural." And to this Heidegger adds: "This is the first principle of all hermeneutics."[11]

When Heidegger completes his early account of historicity in *Being and Time,* we see precisely how this temporal occurrence occurs. In relation to the issue of grasping Dasein's authentically being-a-whole, Heidegger asks about the source from which Dasein draws its factical possibilities. In anticipatory resoluteness whereby Dasein frees itself from the they, Heidegger says that this resoluteness discloses the actual factical possibilities of authentic existing from out of the heritage (*Erbe*) that resoluteness take over. This way of taking over one's facticity is one that "snatches one back from the endless multiplicity of possibilities . . . and brings Dasein into the simplicity of its fate [*Schicksal*]."[12] Heidegger then adds, "This is how we designate Dasein's primordial occurring in an historical way, which lies in authentic resoluteness and in which Dasein hands itself over to itself, free for death, in a possibility which it has inherited and yet has chosen."[13]

Heidegger then expands this determination to include others: because Dasein is always also a being-with-others, its occurrence in a historical way is an occurrence-with and therefore determined as destiny or co-choosing a fate (*Geschick*). Choosing one's fate, which is made possible by temporality, is authentic historicity.

What is most decisive in Heidegger's analysis is his further account of how such resoluteness works as a retrieval or repetition (*Widerholung*), "the handing over explicitly (*ausdrückliche Überlieferung*), i.e., the going back to the possibilities of Dasein's having been there."[14] In handing over possibilities of having been, retrieval does not simply bring again (*Wiederbringen*) what is past, nor does it bind the present back to what is outdated. On the contrary, retrieval makes a *response* to a given possibility in the form of a rejoinder (*Erwiderung*) and a disavowal (*Widerruf*). Clearly, the sense of rejoinder is to problematize the possibility of the continuity of history as progress and development. It suggests that the retrieval of the possibility of that existence which has been there (*dagewesenen Existenz*) is a kind of dialogue with the past. More importantly, retrieval can issue in a disavowal in the sense of a counter-claim. The complete sentence in Heidegger's text reads: "But when such a rejoinder is made to this possibility in a resolution, it is made in a moment of vision; and as such it is at the same time a disavowal of that which in the 'today' is working itself out as the past."[15] The disavowal is the countering of the past in the present. The retrieval of the claimed meaning of the past is thus not an actualization in which what was once known now becomes explicitly known again, but a retrieval through an enactment of meaning that disrupts continuity. In choosing its fate – taking up its finite freedom – Dasein carries out its historicizing self-movement: a "whole" that is subject to difference.

It is interesting to note here, as a reminder, that Heidegger's pursuit of the being of the historical turns the question of the historical into the question of being, and it is in relation to this understanding of being that now prescribes the character of philosophical thinking. Philosophical thinking is to carry out the destruction of the history of being, and, in effect, it abandons the question of history in general. For Heidegger history has a single fateful nature as the history of metaphysics.

Historicity as effective history

What then of Gadamer's hermeneutics and to the way in which he takes over the concept of historicity from Heidegger? It is easy to look at Gadamer's formulation of the concept of historicity as a simple reminder of these prior developments. For the sake of his project concerning the self-understanding of the historical human sciences, he not only restates the same basic criticism that Heidegger gives of Dilthey, he also offers no criticism of Heidegger's account of historicity. His difference from Heidegger then presumably lies in his extension of Heidegger's concept of historicity back into the question of history in general, to Dilthey's concern for the understanding that happens in the connectedness of historical life. This is somewhat evident by Gadamer's explicit mention of Dilthey when noting in his analysis of hermeneutic experience that theories of experience up to now, including Dilthey's, have taken no account of the inner historicity of experience. In effect Gadamer too wants to embrace the questions that Yorck von Wartenburg and subsequently Heidegger posed to Dilthey's hermeneutics of history. Now, in doing so, it has been said by several critics that Gadamer loses the radicality of Heidegger's destruction, that historical understanding, against historicism to be sure, simply assumes the *continuity* of historical life as an unfolding of what is essentially self-same. In this context, it remains to be seen precisely what Gadamer means by describing the historicity of understanding as effective history.

At the point in *Truth and Method* where Gadamer has fully prepared the way to elevate Heidegger's historicity of understanding to the status of a hermeneutic principle by translating the hermeneutic circle in terms of the movement of tradition, he introduces the idea of effective history in the following way:

> True historical thinking must take account of its own historicity. Only then will it not chase the phantom of an historical object which is the object of progressive research, and learn to view the object as the counterpart of itself and hence understand both. The true historical object is not an object at all, but the unity of the one and the other, a relationship that constitutes both the reality of history and the reality of historical understanding. A hermeneutics adequate to the subject matter would have to demonstrate the effectivity [*Wirklichkeit*] of history within understanding itself. I shall refer to this as effective history [*Wirkungsgeschichte*]. Understanding is essentially an effective historical event.[16]

What exactly then is effective history? To say the least, it is the action (*Wirken*) of history upon us such that the reader of history is in some sense in the mode of passivity, being affected. Gadamer insists that in all understanding, whether we are expressly aware of it or not, the efficacy of history is at work.[17] In the consciousness of being affected by history there is an awareness of the hermeneutical situation, an awareness of being within a tradition when attempting to understand the past. And it is precisely because one is affected that the understanding of tradition can never be complete. Understanding – and this means also self-understanding – cannot reach its end, one might say, because the beginning has already begun, necessitating that we always take hold of what we want to understand from a perspective. Stated otherwise, being human is to have only histories, not natures.[18] It is in this context that Gadamer introduces the notion of horizon and describes historical understanding as a fusion of horizons:

> This historical movement of human life consists in the fact that it is never utterly bound to any one standpoint, and hence can never have a truly closed horizon. The horizon is, rather, something in which we move and moves with us. Horizons change for a person who is moving. Thus the horizon of the past, out of which all human life lives, is always in motion.[19]

Thus it is for Gadamer that historically effected consciousness affects all understanding of tradition. I have argued elsewhere that we should be cautious when it comes to interpreting this word "tradition" in Gadamer's hermeneutics.[20] We are easily misled if we think of this as a defined cultural history or as a specific lineage, rather than as simply historical transmission in which the multiple voices of the past can be heard. And more so, it is the happening as event within transmission that interests Gadamer. Insofar as history is operating on historical understanding, Gadamer insists that when we understand we understand differently.

But it is precisely here that we encounter the aporia that is at the heart of effective history. Notwithstanding Gadamer's claim that when we understand we understand differently, effective history, on the one hand, is set within a transmission that involves continuity. The interpretive activity of carrying forward the having been of historical life in its possibilities in relation to effective history rests on a comparative relation which requires a dimension of unity. The fusion of horizons constitutes, in effect, an act of sharing, as if there is a normative invariance in the reading of history:

> When our historical consciousness transposes itself into historical horizons, this does not entail passing into alien worlds unconnected in any way with our own; instead, they together constitute the one great horizon that moves from within and that, beyond the frontiers of the present, embraces the historical depths of our self-consciousness.[21]

This sharing, though, should not be confused with a presumed connectedness of events any more than the life of dialogue connects meaning in a continuous series. Put differently, effective history should not be confused with a dialectic of history in which its beginning is linked to its end. The reading of history is not on the way to a future perfection in any form, but is simply the becoming of historical life in its new meaning. Still, it is precisely this one-sided configuration of the unfolding of historical meaning that raises the question of the possibility of how there can be "another history," as we see not only in Heidegger but also in Foucault.

And this is the aporia that is at the heart of effective history, since there is on the other hand Gadamer's insistence on the emergence of difference in the historical event by virtue of effective history. Gadamer explicitly emphasizes this aspect of the historical event in a late essay where he deals once again with his understanding of the difference between hermeneutics and deconstruction. In this essay, Gadamer once again reminds his readers that he considers Derrida in relation to Heidegger and to himself to have much in common. If for Derrida in every sign there is a transgression, so too for hermeneutics there is always a transgression with respect to the ideality of meaning. For hermeneutics, though, this break, this displacement in the orientation to intelligibility, is the impetus for a thinking further, i.e., it is for the sake of an advancement in meaning that brings "the alterity of the true" to recognition. He tells us that he actually recognizes "in the Derridian formulation of the concepts of *dissémination* and *différance* something similar to my 'effective historical consciousness' or 'fusion of horizons'."[22] Gadamer goes on to say that, despite his use of the term 'consciousness', he was attempting to emphasize with this expression the temporality of being. And this means, as we have learned from Heidegger, that what is understood by a consciousness effected by history can never be unveiled as a being-in-itself. What is understood by a consciousness effected by history is not even an object, but is, as an enactment, the making of "something visible in the *how* of its meaningfulness" (emphasis added).[23]

In the context of Gadamer's remark linking hermeneutics to deconstruction, we can say that effective historical consciousness is "an achievement of the transcendental role of the trace" in hermeneutical experience.[24] Gadamer himself understands the trace to be something like a vestige that announces the absence of the origin and at the same time withholds the intelligibility of life from its end. It is the remainder that has entered the middle of things, deferring mediation in such a way that the mediation remains incomplete as a transfer. And with this idea Gadamer is acknowledging that life and ideality can never come together. This preserving of alterity in repetition is nothing less than the structure of hermeneutic experience itself.

How this relation of continuity and discontinuity plays out in Gadamer's now classical analysis of historical understanding can be seen in the relation between being historically situated and the act of transmission as a fusion of horizons. Recall that for Gadamer historical understanding is limited by virtue of being situated, and it is because of our situatedness (being historical) that every historical understanding proceeds from a horizon. The horizon, in turn, is moving, and thus the fusion of horizons embraces the historical depths of our self-consciousness. As Gadamer notes early on in *Truth and Method*, "our historical consciousness is filled with a multitude [*Vielzahl*] of voices in which the echo of the past is heard [and] only in the plenitude [*Vielfachheit*] of such voices is it there."[25] By virtue of these moving horizons human life stands *between* a god-like grasp that could abolish every horizon and a Nietzschean perspectivism that would only produce incommensurable horizons. What the fusion of horizons then accomplishes is not strictly speaking a simple mediation of the past from the perspective of the present, but a transmission in which historical understanding is subject to the effects of an effective history. This effect, which is affecting my historical situation, constitutes a spacing between historical experience and its meaning – a spacing that is ultimately productive for an experience of historical difference. Perhaps this is why Gadamer says that "it is constantly necessary to guard against over hastily assimilating the past to our own experience of meaning."[26] The historicity of understanding, as the experience of tradition, involves both continuity and discontinuity; it is the experience of being carried along by history in which there is a delay in any attempt to praise or condemn it. Effective history means being at the arrival of the historical as the event of tradition. The aporia turns out to be nothing other than the inherent tension of belonging and distanciation that characterizes factical historical life.

Effective History and Historical Knowledge

As a way of extending this interpretation of effective history, I want to briefly consider how it compares with Foucault's version of another history of history, i.e., with another version of effective history. But to even suggest in the first place that a comparison can be made seems forced at best since Foucault is critical of hermeneutics as a method of historical analysis. In relation to his own approach to the historical in which "the effort to think one's own history can free thought from what it silently thinks, and so enable it to think differently," Foucault regards hermeneutics as the opposing effort seeking only to restore an objectified meaning as the deeper meaning of discourse.[27] Foucault has a suspicion that hermeneutics can't be truly suspicious when it comes to

history, and thus it remains within the discourses of conformity where it con-
structs "discourses about discourses and [where it poses] the task of hearing
what has already been said."[28] Against this understanding of hermeneutics,
Foucault's archaeology of knowledge poses its task of determining how the
rules of formation that govern enunciative facts may be linked to non-discur-
sive practices. Foucault goes so far as to say that the analysis of statements of
historical discursive formations avoids interpretation insofar as "it does not
question things said as to what they are hiding, what they were 'really' saying,
in spite of themselves, the unspoken element that they contain," but only "questions them as to their mode of existence, what it means to them to have come
into existence".[29]

But if one takes a broader perspective on hermeneutics, it does not seem so
easy for Foucault to abandon interpretation, for Foucault is in fact re-interpret-
ing history along the lines of an "interpretive analytics," and Foucault's latter
genealogical investigations can themselves be seen as a deciphering of social
practices.[30] The question, then, is not about the wholesale rejection of hermeneutics, but about the character of hermeneutics in the interpretation of thought,
action, and experience that is historically situated. Put differently, it is the question of Foucault's suspicion, which he of course never explicitly stated as such,
as to whether Gadamer's hermeneutics of history can be suspicious enough for
the reading of history that Foucault is after. It is a question, in yet other words,
whether a quasi-hermeneutics of suspicion that one could attribute to Foucault
in his project of exposing discursive formations to an exteriority that lets us see
things in a new way in any way intersects with Gadamer's hermeneutics of history. That Gadamer's hermeneutics, especially in regards to the event character
of historical understanding, is neither a hermeneutics of deeper meaning nor a
hermeneutics of commentary but simply the encounter and enactment of meanings allows us to at least entertain this possibility. More to the point, in assess-
ing Gadamer's version of hermeneutics one has to start from Gadamer's insistence that the event of understanding is not an act of reproduction but, as the
movement of effective history, a matter of the opening of historical life, which
is produced in language, to its differences. It is easy to overlook the fact that
Gadamer and Foucault both want to displace the foundational function of the
knowing subject, and with it the appropriation of meaning, for the sake of making possible history in its differences. Both want to reject the ambitions of a
constituting consciousness intent on the mastery of meaning. Gadamer's version of hermeneutics in particular, while not a historicism, amounts to a histori-

cizing of historical experience, which means to historicize the transcendental distance between the historian and the object of historical research. If this ontological characterization of Gadamer's hermeneutics is accurate, one can claim that Foucault's own historical investigations are legitimated by this hermeneutic practice.

And what then of Foucault's actual version of another history of history? Wherein lies the comparison that, at least in this preliminary analysis, has now been made possible? In his essay "Nietzsche, Genealogy, and History," Foucault points to what it is in Nietzsche that is fundamental to his, i.e., Foucault's, own work, especially as he moves towards his own genealogical concerns. What he points to is the idea of an effective history (*wirkliche Historie*) that is used by Nietzsche to designate a non-traditional history, i.e., a history that is not a history of development. Unlike traditional history that seeks support outside time, effective history is "without constants," shattering the unity of man's being: "Nothing in man . . . is sufficiently stable to serve as the basis for self-recognition or for understanding other men."[31] This effective history deals with "events in terms of their most unique characteristics"; such events are not treaties and battles but "the reversal of a relationship of forces."[32] Effective history is thus a history that is able to exercise a vigilance and scepticism towards the claims of various philosophies to prescribe the meaning of history;[33] and this effective history fits well with Foucault's own genealogical investigations and the practico-political concerns associated with them. Such a history is then a history for thinking otherwise; it is a history opposed to a history of continuity derived either from the presumed authority of the historian, or from idea measured by their influence on the course of general history.

This emphasis by Foucault on discontinuity makes no use of the operation of understanding precisely because Foucault thinks, to say it here in a different way, that hermeneutic understanding is only oriented to the stabilizing assurance of identity. A genealogy is not supposed to search for an origin (Foucault's presumption about hermeneutics) but to uncover the contingent beginnings of discourse.[34] Effective history is not to call back the silent voices of the past for the sake of damming up the "spontaneous upsurge of discourses," but to have something of the opposite effect by becoming what Foucault calls a "history of the present," that is, a history written in relation to our insertion in a particular present. It is a history that "reads the reflections of our own political and ethical concerns off the behavior and customs of [a particular historical world] the way a perceptive traveler in a foreign land will see his homeland anew in light of the experience."[35] But this, it seems to me, is another version of just what Gadamer means by the fusion of horizons as an enactment in which something is made visible in the how of its meaningfulness.

This claim draws us back to the issue of continuity in Gadamer's hermeneutics. Let us recall that for Gadamer continuity is necessitated by receptivity, which, by virtue of it, requires an element of commonality. And by affirming this continuity, Gadamer would insist that any archeology – the archeology that is opposed to traditionality – cannot break free of a general associative context. But this continuity is *not* the continuity that Foucault assumes all hermeneutics will have, namely, the continuity of history in which there is a "safer, less exposed shelter" for the sovereignty of consciousness.[36] It is not the continuity for sovereignty precisely because there can be no sovereignty in a consciousness effected by history. For a consciousness effected by history there is the efficacy of the past that we undergo (a receptivity) that is coupled with the reception of the past that we bring about. This mediation is not in any way dialectical. It is hermeneutical in the precise sense of the "how" of an actualizing repetition. It is what Gadamer call the living tradition and its interpretation. It is the transmission of meaning.

If for Foucault effective history means that there are events of history that interrupt so as to jeopardize authoritative practices, and thus become the occasion to formulate new questions, then there are certainly parallels with Gadamer's idea of effective history. For Gadamer, the efficacy of history follows the structure of hermeneutic experience. Meaning in history takes place in relation to the intrusion of the other and its possibilities of truth.

Notes

1. See Martin Heidegger, "Phenomenological Interpretations with Respect to Aristotle: Indication of the Hermeneutical Situation," in *Becoming Heidegger*, ed. Theodore Kisiel and Thomas Sheehan, Evanston: Northwestern University Press, 2007, p. 168.
2. Heidegger, "Comments on Karl Jaspers's *Psychology of Worldviews*," in *Pathmarks*, trans. William McNeill, New York: Cambridge University Press, 1998, p. 4. These comments were composed by Heidegger soon after the appearance of Jaspers's book in 1919. They were intended as a review but were never published as such. For an excellent analysis of this text see David Farrell Krell, *Intimations of Mortality*, University Park, PA: The Pennsylvania State University Press, 1986, Chapter One.
3. "Comments on Karl Jaspers's *Psychology of Worldviews*," p. 31.
4. In his "Comments on Karl Jaspers's *Psychology of Worldviews*", Heidegger does remark that "concerning Kierkegaard, we should point out that such a heightened consciousness of meth-

odological rigor as his had rarely been achieved in philosophy or theology." "Comments on Karl Jaspers's *Psychology of Worldviews*," p. 36.

5. "Comments on Karl Jaspers's *Psychology of Worldviews*," p. 28.

6. "Comments on Karl Jaspers's *Psychology of Worldviews*," p. 29.

7. Heidegger, *Phenomenological Interpretations of Aristotle*, trans. Richard Rojcewicz, Bloomington: Indiana University Press, 2001, p. 83. It is in this context that Heidegger notes that in philosophizing there is no history of philosophy.

8. "Thinking cannot go back behind life, for it is an expression of it." Wilhelm Dilthey, *Gesammelte Schriften*, Bd. 19, ed. Helmut Johach and Frithjof Rodi Göttingen: Vanderhoeck & Ruprecht, 1997, p. 347. Elsewhere Dilthey writes: "Thinking cannot go back behind life whose function it is. Life always remains a precondition of knowledge . . . contained in that life. As a precondition of knowing, it is itself not open to analysis through knowledge. Thus the foundation of all knowing in which its preconditions are inextricably contained, is life itself . . . . The character of life is visible in the structure of everything alive. Its meaning arises from this. It is unfathomable [*unergründlich*]." Gesammelte Werke, 19, p. 329.

9. Heidegger, "Wilhelm Dilthey's Research and Struggle for a Historical Worldview," trans. Charles Bambach, in *Supplements*, ed. John van Buren, Albany: SUNY Press, 2002, p.162.

10. "Wilhelm Dilthey's Research and Struggle for a Historical Worldview," p. 159. For an excellent analysis of Yorck von Wartenburg's specific contribution to this issue see, Hans Ruin, "Yorck von Wartenburg and the Problem of Historical Existence," *Journal of the British Society fir Phenomenology*, vol. 25, 2 (May 1994): 111–130.

11. Heidegger, *The Concept of Time*, trans. William McNeill, Oxford: Blackwell Publishers, 1992, p. 20e.

12. Heidegger, *Sein und Zeit,* Tübingen: Niemeyer, 1972, p. 384.

13. *Ibid.*

14. *Sein und Zeit*, p. 385.

15. *Ibid.*

16. Hans Georg Gadamer, *Truth and Method*, trans. Joel Weinsheimer and Donald Marshall, New York: Continuum, 1989, pp. 299–300.

17. *Truth and Method*, p. 301.

18. Joseph Margolis, *The Flux of History and the Flux of Science,* Berkeley: University of California Press, 1993, p. 149.

19. *Truth and Method*, p. 304.

20. See James Risser, "Interpreting Tradition." *The Journal for the British Society for Phenomenology*, vol. 34, 3 (October 2003): 297–308.

21. *Truth and Method*, p. 304.

22. Gadamer, "Hermeneutics Tacking the Trace [On Derrida]," in *The Gadamer Reader*, ed. and trans. Richard Palmer, Evanston: Northwestern University Press, 2007, p. 384.

23. *Truth and Method*, p. 563. Gadamer is referring to language here, which is the precise form in which effective history is accomplished.

24. See Maurizio Ferraris, *The History of Hermeneutics*, trans. Luca Somigli, Atlantic Highlands: Humanities Press, 1966, p. 303.

25. *Truth and Method*, p. 284.

26. *Truth and Method*, p. 305.

27. Michel Foucault, *History of Sexuality, vol. 2, The Use of Pleasure*, trans. Robert Hurley, New York: Vintage Books, 1990, p. 9.

28. Foucault, *The Birth of the Clinic*, trans. A.M. Sheridan Smith, New York: Vintage Books, 1994, p. xvi.

29. Foucault, *The Archaeology of Knowledge and The Discourse on Language*, trans. A.M. Sheridan Smith, New York: Pantheon Books, 1972, p. 109.

30. This phrase is suggested by Dreyfus and Rabinow. See Hubert Dreyfus and Paul Rabinow, *Michel Foucault: Beyond Structuralism and Hermeneutics,* Chicago: University of Chicago Press, 1983.

31. Foucault, "Nietzsche, Genealogy, History," in *Language, Counter-memory, Practice*, ed. Donald Bouchard, New York: Cornell University Press, 1977, p. 153.

32. "Nietzsche, Genealogy, History," p. 154.

33. See Thomas Flynn, *Sartre, Foucault, and Historical Reason*, vol. 2, Chicago: University of Chicago Press, 2005, p. 292.

34. See Jürgen Habermas, *The Philosophical Discourse of Modernity*, trans. Frederick G. Lawrence, Cambridge: The MIT Press, 1987, p. 250.

35. *Sartre, Foucault, and Historical Reason*, p. 293.

36. See Foucault, *Archeology of Knowledge*, p. 14.

HISTOIRE, CROYANCE ET CRISE DU SENS

PIERRE RODRIGO

On ne peut guère contester, à ce qu'il semble, que tous les grands courants de pensée du XX° siècle et du XXI° siècle commençant sont d'orientation historique. On va même désormais jusqu'à *identifier* histoire et existence humaine. Sur un plan plus général, c'est sans conteste la temporalité qui a été et qui est encore survalorisée par la pensée moderne et contemporaine. Sans doute en va-t-il ainsi depuis Kant, mais l'exemple le plus frappant est, bien entendu, celui de Heidegger, qui a insisté tout au long de son œuvre sur le caractère éminemment « époqual » de la vérité et qui a interrompu son maître livre, *Sein und Zeit*, par ces deux questions : « Un chemin conduit-il du *temps* originaire au sens de l'*être* ? Le *temps* lui-même se manifeste-t-il comme horizon de l'*être* ? »[1]. On ne saurait mieux souligner la dimension de l'historialité, de la *Geschichtlichkeit des Seins* à laquelle le *Dasein* humain est ontologiquement ouvert, ce qui fait de lui l'étant dont l'existence est originairement historiale et, par suite, factuellement historique. C'est pourquoi Heidegger a pu écrire au § 76 du même ouvrage que « l'ouverture historique de l'histoire est en elle-même enracinée, de par sa structure ontologique, [...] dans l'historialité du *Dasein* »[2].

Ceci étant admis – c'est-à-dire étant admis que *l'historicité* des sociétés humaines reconduit en dernière analyse à une *historialité* et à une *époqualité* plus originaires parce que plus ontologiques –, il n'en reste pas moins légitime d'analyser les régimes d'historicité en eux-mêmes, comme le font les historiens. Il faudrait même dire que lorsqu'on a reconnu pour ce qu'il est le niveau originaire de l'historialité et de l'époqualité de l'être, il devient encore plus nécessaire de se pencher avec attention sur la dimension de l'historicité humaine. Mais sur l'historicité comprise cette fois, non comme ensemble des faits historiques, mais comme *phénomène de l'histoire* ; un phénomène dont la logique s'entretisse par nécessité, comme celle de tout phénomène apparaissant, d'une part, aux sujets à qui ce phénomène se dévoile, et, d'autre part, à l'horizon de monde à partir duquel ce phénomène est ce qu'il est. Une chose est donc de décrire pour eux-mêmes les différents régimes d'historicité dont la succession factuelle constitue ce qu'on appelle l'histoire humaine, mais une autre chose est de conduire cette description jusqu'à la mise en lumière de la liaison intime entre la phénoménalité de l'histoire et l'historialité de l'être et du monde. C'est un tel parcours allant de l'historicité à l'historialité que je voudrais esquisser ici.

Puisqu'il convient, dans cette optique, de partir de l'histoire elle-même, je commencerai par relever – en reprenant sur ce point les résultats fondamentaux des recherches du grand historien allemand Reinhart Koselleck – que depuis l'événement à tous égards bouleversant que fut, à la fin du XVIII° siècle, la Révolution française, c'est tout un régime d'historicité qui a basculé (et le choix du verbe est important : ce régime n'a pas totalement disparu, il se survit encore par fragments, mais il a globalement basculé). Un régime d'historicité, cela signifie une compréhension d'ensemble de l'histoire, de son sens et de ses acteurs. Le régime d'historicité qui a basculé à partir de 1789 est celui qui se résumait dans la célèbre formule de Cicéron évoquant l'*historia magistra vitae* : l' « histoire institutrice de la vie », autrement dit l'histoire en tant que mémoire vive des expériences passées et trésor de sens déposé pour les générations futures. Selon ce régime d'historicité-là, l'histoire avait valeur de dépôt de sens mis à disposition des hommes à venir pour les instruire sur eux-mêmes, sur le sens de leur présent et de leur futur, à la lumière des événements et des actions du passé. L'histoire était donc tout à la fois, *Res gestae,* comme l'espérait l'empereur Auguste en compilant ses conquêtes, et *Ktèma es aei*, comme le voulait Thucydide en écrivant son *Histoire de la guerre du Péloponnèse*. C'est encore ces deux aspects de l'histoire, le chatoiement des faits du passé et l'enseignement d'un sens, que Pufendorf glorifiait tout ensemble lorsqu'il écrivait, en 1682, qu'elle constitue « la science la plus charmante et la plus utile »[3].

Dans les termes de Koselleck, tels qu'ils ont pu être repris ensuite aussi bien par Paul Ricoeur, dans *Temps et récit*, que par un historien tel que François Hartog, après la césure de l'événement de 1789 un nouveau régime d'historicité se fait donc jour. Cela signifie que, sous la pression croissante des événements et des bouleversements historiques, un abîme se creuse de plus en plus entre les expériences précédemment accumulées et « l'horizon d'attente », tout entier orienté vers l'avenir, que les nouveaux événements laissent entrevoir et permettent d'espérer : « Le perspectivisme temporel est le résultat d'une histoire qui, à une vitesse croissante, paraît s'éloigner des événements l'ayant précédée. Depuis la grande Révolution, on trouve partout des indices témoignant de l'expérience d'une rupture (séparant violemment la dimension du passé de celle du futur) et de la conscience qu'ont les gens de vivre une époque de transition »[4]. Tel est le sens du basculement que j'évoquais tout à l'heure. Il fait globalement passer d'une histoire dans laquelle le passé tient le rôle primordial à une histoire dans laquelle la perspective temporelle est polarisée par le futur et par l'idée de progrès – avec, bien entendu, des points de rebroussement où la nostalgie des leçons du passé peut toujours venir faire retour. Mais évidemment, dans ce balancement entre passé et futur, entre trésor de sens accumulé et sens futur à construire, le *phénomène* d'une l'histoire appréhendée sur fond de sa dimension historiale n'est pas nécessairement perçu, loin s'en faut.

Pour percevoir ce phénomène en tant que tel il ne faut, en fait, pas moins de la double perspicacité historique *et* métaphysique de Hegel, telle qu'on peut la voir à l'œuvre par exemple dans ce bref passage que j'extraie du cours de 1822 sur les différents « types d'historiographie » qui est aujourd'hui publié dans l'ouvrage intitulé *La raison dans l'histoire* – il s'agit en la circonstance d'une analyse de ce que Hegel nomme « l'histoire réfléchie » ou « l'histoire réfléchissante », qui est celle qui prétend, précisément, recueillir les leçons du passé : « On recommande aux rois, aux hommes d'État, aux peuples de s'instruire principalement par l'expérience de l'histoire. Mais l'expérience et l'histoire nous enseignent que peuples et gouvernements n'ont jamais rien appris de l'histoire, qu'ils n'ont jamais agi suivant les maximes qu'on aurait pu en tirer »[5]. Que veut dire exactement Hegel ? Tout d'abord, il ne dit pas que l'ancien régime d'historicité n'a et n'avait aucune valeur, aucune pertinence quant à sa capacité compréhensive. Cela, c'est ce que seule une lecture superficielle pourrait nous laisser croire. En réalité, si Hegel écrit que les peuples et leurs gouvernants n'ont rien appris de l'histoire passée et n'ont pas suivi les maximes, et donc les leçons « qu'on aurait pu en tirer », c'est bien que, selon lui, ces leçons *auraient pu* et *auraient dû* être tirées. L'ancien régime d'historicité n'est donc pas à annuler, car, en un sens, il ne l'a que trop été dans ce qu'il avait de plus profond et de plus méconnu ; il a bien plutôt à être reconduit à sa racine *ontologique* (ou « historiale », dans le langage de Heidegger). C'est précisément ce que proposera Hegel avec son « histoire philosophique », cette histoire pour laquelle « Le fait premier est l'Esprit même des événements, l'Esprit (*Geist*) qui les a produits, car c'est lui qui est l'Hermès, le conducteur des peuples ». « L'individu dont elle parle », ajoutera-t-il, « est l'Esprit du monde (*Weltgeist*) »[6]. Ainsi compris, le processus historique se révèle être une authentique phénoménologie de la raison, une phénoménologie dont l'Esprit est la substance incessamment retravaillée par le sacrifice d'elle-même – autrement dit par ce puissant « travail du négatif » en elle dont une juste interprétation, comme celle que propose l'histoire philosophique, conduit à cette conclusion nécessaire que : « Tout [cela] doit contribuer à *une* œuvre. À la base de cet immense sacrifice de l'Esprit doit se trouver une fin ultime. La question est de savoir si, sous le tumulte qui règne à la surface, ne s'accomplit pas une œuvre silencieuse et secrète dans laquelle sera conservée toute la force des phénomènes »[7].

On voit qu'il s'agit avant tout d'*interprétation* et donc de constitution adéquate du sens des phénomènes historiques de surface. Selon Hegel, leur sens est qu'ils sont en vérité des phénomènes-de-monde, et d'un monde qui est monde de l'Esprit, d'un monde à chaque fois ajointé par un certain *Weltgeist* déterminé et de ce fait même époqual. Que les hommes comprennent ou non ce sens, le monde, lui, n'en poursuit pas moins le développement phénoménal de *son* histoire, en instituant ce que l'*Abrégé de l'Encyclopédie des sciences philosophiques* caractérise ultimement comme « l'*universelle histoire du monde* (Weltgeschichte) dont la dialectique des esprits particuliers des peuples, le *tribunal du monde* (Weltgericht), représente les événements »[8].

Historicité et historialité, ou phénomènes historiques et Esprit du monde sont donc expressément conjoints dans l'approche hégélienne de l'histoire. Cette conjonction l'autorise, dans un premier temps, à prendre acte (comme Kant l'avait déjà fait) de la césure de l'histoire introduite par la Révolution française et de rendre raison, à sa manière, de ce temps qui est encore *le nôtre* et dont Koselleck dit fort bien qu'il est celui « où l'on peut de moins en moins faire coïncider l'espace d'expérience traditionnel avec les attentes nourries quant au futur soudainement apparues »[9]. Cette conjonction l'autorise ensuite à reconnaître au sein même de la discontinuité phénoménale l'attestation de l'unité qui la porte et qui demande à être *interprétée* par le biais de la pensée et du langage spéculatifs. Mouvement de l'Esprit et du monde, d'un côté, et herméneutique du sens historique, de l'autre, doivent ainsi aller de pair pour prendre l'exacte mesure du phénomène de l'histoire et pour, tout simplement, continuer à *croire* dans le sens et la valeur d'une histoire désormais vécue comme « horizon d'attente » et non plus *magistra vitae*.

Il est en effet clair que, si le sens du présent ne s'éclaire plus depuis l'espace d'expériences du passé, mais est, à l'inverse, supposé provenir d'un horizon d'attente dont la discontinuité est pourtant la marque déterminante, alors, *ou bien* la croyance en l'efficace de cet horizon est un acte purement irrationnel, *ou bien* cette croyance doit nécessairement s'appuyer sur l'hypothèse d'une raison supérieure réglant le cours des événements – que cette raison soit Esprit hégélien, Dieu providentiel de Bossuet, ou Nature du type de celle de Kant dans son *Idée d'une histoire universelle du point de vue cosmopolitique*. Du moins en va-t-il forcément ainsi pour la philosophie idéaliste qui ne parvient à recoudre le tissu de l'histoire, dont elle voit bien la rupture de régime dans la modernité, que par un recours au *postulat métaphysique* d'un ultime garant du sens : Dieu, l'Esprit ou la Nature. C'est le recours par lequel elle sauve du non-sens les phénomènes historiques et le phénomène même de l'histoire. Mais c'est aussi la voie par laquelle elle dépossède ce phénomène de sa phénoména-lité et de sa logique propres, puisque son sens réside *ailleurs*, dans une instance suprême. Au fond, ce qui n'est jamais soupçonné dans ce genre d'approche idéaliste de l'histoire c'est que l'existant historique que nous sommes puisse être corrélé au monde bien plus intimement, qu'il soit « au-monde », comme dit Heidegger, et qu'en tant que *Dasein* historique il comprenne toujours-déjà ce monde qu'il *interprète* en y existant, voire même, si l'on peut s'exprimer ainsi, *en l'existant*. C'est ce que posait avec netteté l'extrait du § 76 de *Sein und Zeit* qui a été cité plus haut : « l'ouverture historique de l'histoire est en elle-même enracinée, de par sa structure ontologique, [...] dans l'historialité du *Dasein* ». Autant dire qu'il n'y a de monde historique que *par* la compréhen-sion agissante, par le *Verstehen*, d'un existant historial – et aussi *pour* cette compréhension agissante, dont un nom peut être celui de *praxis*.

Dès lors que l'on accepte de raisonner dans les termes d'une telle phénomé-nologie de l'histoire, on se donne la possibilité d'articuler à nouveaux frais l'histoire de l'existant humain et l'histoire du monde : accéder au phénomène de l'histoire c'est alors parvenir à entrecroiser l'histoire de la manifestation du monde, ou l'historialité de l'être, et l'historicité du sens créé par les sociétés humaines. C'est à ce niveau que se situe, par exemple, la réflexion d'Eugen Fink sur la nature du phénomène historique. Dans une étude intitulée *Welt und Geschichte*, qui a paru en 1959 dans le deuxième volume des *Phaenomenolo-gica*, il demande ainsi à propos de l'histoire : « Sur quoi nous interrogeons-nous ? Sur une chose, une substance, un mouvement, sur un mode d'être, un compor-tement, un "rapport" ? En développant la question qui nous dirige, nous cher-chons à pénétrer jusqu'au point où il apparaîtra que le rapport-au-monde de l'existant humain demeure impensé et incompris aussi longtemps que l'on considère l'historique simplement comme le mouvement d'un étant. La marche de la réflexion commence dans la situation [ontologique] au sein de laquelle nous nous trouvons d'ores et déjà placés »[10]. Cette situation étant reconnue comme celle de l'être-au-monde qui spécifie le mode d'être du *Dasein* dans sa différence par rapport aux autres étants, Fink peut ajouter : « L'homme est la créature la plus finie des créatures finies, puisqu'il connaît sa finitude et qu'en même temps il se rapporte à l'infinité de la totalité du monde. "L'historique" en tant qu'il appartient à l'homme comporte manifestement une certaine dimension cosmique, qu'il est d'ailleurs difficile de déterminer »[11].

Il est clair que lorsqu'on analyse interprète ainsi l'entrecroisement, ou le chiasme, entre l'historicité et l'historialité il n'est plus besoin de faire référence à aucune « relève », à aucune *Aufhebung* de la finitude humaine, pour sauver le sens promis par l'horizon d'attente ouvert par l'histoire moderne. On peut alors, pour reprendre une formule de Paul Ricoeur dans le troisième tome de *Temps et récit*, « Renoncer à Hegel ». On le peut même, selon moi, sans éprouver cette crainte du parricide qui semble encore parcourir les pages dans lesquelles Ricoeur avoue, tout à la fois, la nécessité d'une sortie de l'hégélianisme historique et la réticence que cet acte de la pensée lui inspire néanmoins : « Oui, l'honnêteté intellectuelle exige l'aveu que, pour nous, la perte de crédibilité de la philosophie hégélienne de l'histoire a la signification d'un *événement de pensée*, dont nous ne pouvons dire ni que nous l'avons produit, ni non plus qu'il nous est simplement arrivé – dont nous ne savons s'il marque une catastrophe qui n'a pas fini de nous blesser, ou une délivrance dont nous n'osons tirer gloire »[12]. En fait, nous savons fort bien – et Paul Ricoeur le savait tout aussi bien – que sortir du Grand Récit qui recout le tissu de l'Histoire déchiré entre caducité du passé et attente incertaine de l'avenir, ce n'est une catastrophe ou (ce qui revient effectivement presque au même) une sorte de délivrance extorquée de mauvaise foi, *que* si l'on cherche encore à résoudre positivement le *problème* de la détermination d'un sens – un sens *présupposé* – de l'histoire. En revanche, il n'y a ni catastrophe ni délivrance lorsqu'on considère que le sens phénoménal de l'histoire n'est pas un problème à résoudre mais un *mystère* à endurer, lorsque donc on admet qu'une part du sens de ce phénomène demeure à jamais irréductible aux prestations de sens subjectives qu'elle met, dans cette mesure même, *en crise*.

Husserl, en ramenant dans son dernier grand écrit, la *Krisis*, la question du sens de l'histoire à une détermination phénoménologique du soubassement vécu de ce sens dans le « monde de la vie (*Lebenswelt*) » a assurément cherché, lui aussi, une solution au *problème* posé par la crise du sens dans la modernité. Il a en effet cherché dans les prestations subjectives au sein des diverses *Lebenswelte* le fondement, ou l'origine, des constructions ouvertes sur l'infini qui sont celles de la raison historique et scientifique moderne. Mais ce faisant, Husserl-le-moderne ou, comme il lui est arrivé de le dire lui-même dans ses conférences de Paris, Husserl le « néo-cartésien » a conservé l'idée d'une téléologie rationnelle du sens, qu'il a seulement fait bouger en idée d'un *telos* infini des tâches de la raison. Ce bougé est, bien entendu, décisif en ce qu'il assure l'ancrage de toute prestation de sens subjective, aussi idéalisante soit-elle, dans un « monde de la vie » historique concret, mais au fond, comme Fink l'a fort bien vu, cela n'empêche nullement Husserl de continuer à « affirmer la supériorité sur le monde de la subjectivité transcendantale constituante »[13]. Husserl, en ce sens, en liant l'historicité à la naissance de la rationalité ouverte – ce qui signifie, pour lui, en liant l'historicité à la naissance de la raison philosophique instituée et développée par l'humanité européenne depuis les Grecs – a une fois de plus rabattu la compréhension des différents régimes d'historicité sur celle de l'avènement de la raison, et même sur l'avènement *d'une certaine* raison, qui est elle-même historiquement déterminée. Cette raison est la rationalité européenne considérée comme « figure spirituelle » insigne, à savoir, précisera la conférence de Vienne sur *La crise de l'humanité européenne et la philosophie*, « comme l'irruption et le début du développement d'une nouvelle époque de l'humanité, l'époque de l'humanité comme telle, qui désormais ne veut et ne peut plus vivre que dans la libre formation de son existence, de sa vie historique, par les idées de la raison, par des tâches infinies »[14]. Ainsi la percée de la pensée philosophique grecque constitue-t-elle, pour Husserl, ce qu'il nomme emphatiquement « le proto-phénomène de l'Europe spirituelle »[15] et, par voie de conséquence immédiate, le proto-phénomène de *toute* histoire puisque, selon la formulation bien connue du § 6 de la *Krisis*, « l'humanité européenne porte en soi une idée absolue au lieu d'être un simple type anthropologique comme la Chine ou les Indes »[16].

Au nom du caractère insigne de la raison philosophique européenne, cet européocentrisme historique fait violence, non seulement aux régimes d'historicité *autres* que le nôtre, mais aussi au basculement qui a affecté notre propre régime d'historicité au dix-huitième siècle, et que Reinhart Koselleck caractérise, comme nous l'avons vu, de passage d'un « espace d'expériences » léguées par le passé à un « horizon d'attente » commandé par le futur. Husserl suit encore en cela la voie qu'on peut bien dire 'royale' des philosophies de l'histoire modernes, qui, même si elles en viennent à phénoménaliser l'histoire en l'ancrant dans des prestations de sens pré-philosophiques au sein du « monde de la vie », considèrent ces prestations de sens *à partir de* celles de la philosophie, par une sorte d'« illusion rétrospective du vrai », pour reprendre une formule d'Henri Bergson qui me semble appropriée ici. Qu'est-ce que cela signifie ? Deux choses. Premièrement, que l'altérité *des* monde*s* de la vie, des *Lebenswelte*, relativement à notre *Lebenswelt* n'est prise en vue qu'*à partir du* modèle unique de la raison philosophique grecque, celle qui a institué l'humanité européenne exemplaire de « l'homme des tâches infinies ». Deuxièmement, que dans notre *Lebenswelt* même les donations de sens concrètes ne sont comprises par Husserl qu'*à partir de* la donation de sens théorétique, autrement dit à partir de la connaissance du type de l'*epistèmè* que nous a léguée la philosophie grecque. Bref, que les donations de sens historiques concrètes sont dites relever de la *doxa*.

Il faudra toute la lucidité phénoménologique de Jan Patocka pour reconnaître enfin, dans un manuscrit datant du début des années 1970, inédit de son vivant et intitulé « Réflexion sur l'Europe » (et publié aujourd'hui dans le volume *Liberté et sacrifice*), que : « Au point de vue historique, il n'y a que *des mondes* de la vie, dont chacun renferme une composante insaisissable qui n'est pas la *doxa* […]. Cette composante insaisissable est le mystère du monde qui, en tant que tout, englobe et pénètre tous les mondes historiques »[17].

Par conséquent, pour interpréter correctement le phénomène de l'histoire, il ne suffit pas d'entrecroiser l'historicité conçue comme *doxa* à l'historialité conçue, elle, comme rationalité ultime ou, aussi bien, originaire. Ce que j'ai appelé plus haut le mystère du sens phénoménal de l'histoire est irréductible aux termes de ce problème, qui paraît maintenant être, selon toute vraisemblance, un faux problème. Ce que Eugen Fink appelait, comme on s'en souvient, la « dimension cosmique » de l'historicité humaine, autrement dit l'historialité humaine perçue depuis la dimension de l'être-au-monde, n'est effectivement pas un problème susceptible d'être résolu, parce que c'est le mystère même de l'irréductibilité des phénomènes historiques aux lumières de la raison. On peut nommer ce mystère, avec Patocka dans ses *Essais hérétiques sur la philosophie de l'histoire*, la « Nuit », ou, avec Fink, « cette autre dimension du monde qui est sans figure, nocturne et anonyme »[18]. La dimension de mystère du phénomène historique apparaît, sous cet angle, comme ce que la rationalité européenne a précisément voulu, avec obstination, en particulier dans ses philosophies de l'histoire, transformer en une présence diurne, en une lumière du sens, donc en un sens intuitionnable en droit par l'*epistèmè*, sinon en fait par la *doxa*. « Une telle attitude », note Patocka, conduit à « une exténuation généralisée du mystère du monde », puis il ajoute : « Ce processus est immanent à l'essence de l'Europe moderne. Même des recherches aussi profondes que celles de Husserl en témoignent indirectement »[19].

Dans les sociétés à mythes, au mystère du dévoilement du monde, qui est la forme première de la manifestation de tous les phénomènes, y compris des phénomènes historiques, répondent des systèmes de croyances qui tissent des compromis actifs, sensés et efficaces avec des puissances de la Nuit qu'ils n'oblitèrent en aucune façon. Ce n'est affaire ni de *doxa* ni d'*epistèmè*, ni même d'*Urdoxa*. Mais affaire de quoi alors ? À cette question une seule réponse semble possible : c'est affaire de croyance en une forme de présence-absence irrécusable des principes, donc de croyance en une forme de *latence ontologique* ou en une forme d'être qui serait un être de profondeur et non une pure présence, *ousia, essentia* ou *Anwesenheit*. Heidegger, en méditant sur ces quasi non-Grecs que furent ceux qu'on nomme les Présocratiques, a donné un nom à ce mode d'être d'où la culture grecque et européenne a arraché, par conversion, son idéal de présence et de plénitude : *a-lètheia* – terme dans lequel Heidegger nous apprend à entendre toute la charge négative de l'alpha privatif. C'est cette charge négative qui implique qu'il nous faut en fait préserver l'Oubli, la *lèthè*, cet autre nom du mystère de l'être et de la part irréductible pour nous, humains, du sens du tout de ce qui est ; un sens qui est et surtout qui doit rester à jamais *ouvert*, ou, dans les termes de Patocka, un sens *en crise*, et même un sens *comme crise du sens*.

Le phénomène de l'histoire échappe évidemment moins que tout autre à cette « crise » et à cette part d'opacité dont il faut bien admettre qu'elle lui est *constitutive* et non pas accidentelle. Cette part doit nous rappeler à notre finitude, bien sûr, mais aussi à la véritable nature des phénomènes historiques, qui est d'être nécessairement intotalisables quant à leur sens, sous peine d'illusion et de fiction, donc sous peine d'idéologie. Les grandes utopies historiques du dix-neuvième et du vingtième siècles ont témoigné à profusion de la puissance de ces idéologies du Sens historique total (avec majuscule). Jan Patocka, qui a vécu et qui est mort sous le joug de l'une de ces idéologies, en a pris l'exacte mesure lorsqu'il a écrit : « L'esprit, pris en vue sous l'optique de ce qui est *éclairé*, est essentiellement dénaturé […]. L'esprit, c'est l'être-*ébranlé* »[20]. C'est exactement dans le même ordre d'idée d'une critique radicale de toute espèce de Grand Récit idéaliste sur l'Histoire (avec majuscule) que Fichte avait déjà cru bon de rappeler à son temps que « toute cette réalité [historique] n'est vraiment rien de plus que la tombe du concept qui s'efforçait de vivre à la lumière ».[21]

Notes

1   M. Heidegger, *Sein und Zeit,* Tübingen, M. Niemeyer Vg, 1979 (1929), § 83, p. [437], trad. fr. E. Martineau, 1985, p. 296 (hors commerce).

2   *Ibid.*, p. [392], trad. fr., p. 269.

3   Cité par R. Koselleck dans son article fondamental « Le concept d'histoire » (1975), repris dans l'ouvrage intitulé *L'expérience de l'histoire*, trad. fr. A. Escudier *et alii*, Paris, Seuil/ Gallimard, 1997, p. 33.

4   R. Koselleck, « Le concept d'histoire », *op. cit.*, p. 109.

5   G. W. F. Hegel, *La raison dans l'histoire*, I. « Types d'historiographie » (cours de 1822 et 1828), trad. fr. K. Papaioannou, Paris, Gallimard, coll. « 10/18 », 1965, p. 35.

6   *Ibid.*, p. 52.

7   *Ibid.*, p. 55.

8   G. W. F. Hegel, *Abrégé de l'Encyclopédie des sciences philosophiques*, § 548, trad. fr. M. de Gandillac, Paris, Gallimard, 1970, p. 465 (souligné par l'auteur).

9   R. Koselleck, « Le concept d'histoire », *op. cit.*, p. 112.

10 E. Fink, « Monde et histoire », trad. fr. J. Ladrière et J. Taminiaux, publié dans le recueil collectif *Husserl et la Pensée Moderne / Husserl und das Denken der Neuzeit, Phaenomeno- logica 2*, La Haye / Den Haag, M. Nijhoff, 1959 (ici p. 160).

11 *Ibid.*, p. 164.

12 P. Ricoeur, *Temps et récit*, t. III (1985), chap. 6 : « Renoncer à Hegel », Paris, Seuil, coll. « Points-essais », 2001, p. 365.

13 E. Fink, *op. cit.*, p. 167.

14 Cette conférence a été publiée en « Annexe III » de l'ouvrage E. Husserl, *La crise des sciences européennes et la phénoménologie transcendantale*, trad. fr. G. Granel, Paris, Gallimard, 1976, ici p. 352 (désormais noté *Krisis*).

15 *Ibid.*, p. 355.

16 *Ibid.*, p. 21.

17 J. Patocka, *Liberté et sacrifice,* trad. fr. E. Abrams, Grenoble, Millon, 1990, p. 196.

18 J. Patocka, *Essais hérétiques* (1990), trad. fr. E. Abrams, Lagrasse, Verdier, coll. « Ver- dier-poche », 2007, p. 171.

19 J. Patocka, *liberté et sacrifice, op. cit.*, p. 197.

20 Ce fragment est extrait du manuscrit inachevé du sixième des *Essais hérétiques* qui a été tra- duit et publié dans la revue *Esprit*, n° 352, 2009 (texte cité p. 158).

21 Cité par R. Koselleck dans son allocution prononcée à l'occasion du 85° anniversaire de H.-G. Gadamer, « Théorie de l'histoire et herméneutique », recueillie ensuite dans le recueil *L'expé- rience de l'histoire, op. cit.*, p. 261.

Danish Yearbook of Philosophy, Vol. 48–49 (2013–2014), 115–137

SPEAKING TO THE DEAD

HISTORICITY AND THE ANCESTRAL

HANS RUIN

...allow the claim of the dead...
Teiresias to Chreon, in Sophocles' Antigone

Introduction

After Odysseus is washed ashore in the land of the Faiaecans, he is treated with a feast by the king Alkinoos. During this party, he is asked to recount the story of his adventures. He speaks for several hours about the remarkable and terrible things he has experienced. When he wants to stop, the king begs him to continue. Odysseus then responds that there is a time for storytelling, for *mythos*, but also a time for sleep, for *hypnos*. Yet Alkinoos insists, and the story goes on through the night, with tales from the Trojan War, of its heroes and of their dismal fates. At one point during this feast the king asks the bard Demodocus to sing the stories from the great war which by then have already become folk mythology. In the presence of one of the protagonists who actually experienced it, the story of these dramatic events is thus recounted in poetic form within the framework of the literary narrative itself.

In one of her essays in the collection *Between Past and Future*, Hannah Arendt pointed to this particular scene as the beginning of history, where myth and historical facticity meet in the image of the bard and the factual hero.[1] Toward the end of this essay I will return to the same passages from the *Odyssey*, but in order to make a somewhat different point. I will argue that we do indeed encounter an original sense of the historical in the Homeric epic, but not primarily in the contrast between the actual hero and the mythical account of his journey, but instead in the account of his journey to the land of the dead, of which he gives a powerful and moving account during the same night-long banquet at the court of Alkinoos. In short, my thesis will be that it is in the report from the land of the dead, enabled by a sacrificial passage across this threshold, that we can find an early model for the very *ethos* of historical narrative and also of historical consciousness in early Greek literature. In order to reach this point, I will move along a trajectory that brings together Patočka's remarks on being-with-the-dead with Heidegger's theory of historicity with the problem of the spectral in Derrida. I will then discuss how the claim of the dead is actualized in Hegel's reading of *Antigone*, and from there move to the general problem of burial practices and rituals as a way to understand the emergence of historical consciousness and the writing of history. Finally, I return again to Homer as an original articulation of this simultaneous communication with and separation from the dead in relation to Nietzsche and de Certeau.[2]

I

The task uniting us in this thematic issue is to activate resources from phenomenology to try again to think *history*, to think the *phenomenon history*. But is there such a phenomenon? Is there *History*, as a *something* that we can explore in terms of how it is meant, given and constituted for an experiencing subject? Is not this purported phenomenon, or that which is recognized under its name, already from the start multifaceted and dispersed? The Greeks did not have a specific word for it. Greek *historia*, as is well known, means "inquiry", from the verb *historeo*, to inquire or examine, but also to give an account. It has also been traced by philologians back to the word *istor* as the agent of an archaic perfective form of having *seen, oida*, designating "the one who knows from having seen or learned". In the *Iliad*, in the few places where the *histor* is mentioned, it is as a knowledgeable and authoritative person, translated as the "judge" or "arbiter" (e.g., 18:501). In some cases the *histor* can also designate a "witness", which in later Attic Greek is the *martus*.[3] If we try to create a tentative definition of the historian on the basis of these etymological sources it could be: "an inquiring witness who recounts what has been seen".

This is also more or less how the term appears in the writings of Herodotus, in the first instance of a genre of writing that from that moment onward is recognized as "history". The historian is here an inquirer into that which has taken place, in order "to preserve from decay the remembrance of what men have done", as it is stated in the opening passages of his *Historia*.[4] Its object is not an entity, not history or the past as such, but precisely the *deeds* of men, and with the purpose of preventing them from disappearing into oblivion. It is only later that the term "history" also becomes a name for the *object* of this inquiring narration, and ultimately as equivalent to the totality of past events.

This same inherent ambiguity of the term "history" (*Geschichte*), is addressed by Heidegger, in §73 of *Sein und Zeit*, where he turns toward the general phenomenological problem of the historical. He writes: "The most obvious ambiguity of the term 'history' has often been noted [...] it means 'historical reality' as well as the possibility of a science of it".[5] He also comments on the ambiguity surrounding the *temporal* nature of "the historical". Though generally recognized as having to do with the "past", it is still often also posited as that which somehow is still present, exerting its influence in and on the present. History, as he says in a summarizing definition, is the occurrence of something that is both present and past, as "handed down" while still having an effect.

The historicity of an artefact, its *historical* nature, is not something that it carries in itself as an immanent essence. Everything that exists is present, as is self-evident. But one and the same artefact can both be seen as belonging to this present and yet as also belonging to the past. Whether or not it achieves the index "historical" seems to depend on its current use. The particular sense-layer of the "historical" can only be accounted for, Heidegger concludes, by seeing how artefacts indicate a "world within which they were encountered as things at hand belonging to a context of useful things and used by heedful Dasein existing in-the-world". In other words, it is in virtue of being connected to *Dasein as past*, as *having-been-there*, that something is possible as history.

If, however, "Dasein as past" is simply another way of saying Dasein as no longer here, then the phenomenological definition seems to move in circles. In order to define the meaning of history as the peculiar phenomenon of present-past, we would seem to rely again on the existence of past Dasein, in other words non-present Dasein, and thus on the very notion that the whole investigation was meant to clarify, namely the possibility of something being *historical* and yet being here and now. But what Heidegger through his analysis invites his reader to contemplate is instead the peculiar *lingering on* of the past in the present, that which can mark certain things present as also things past, and that which can thus also open *the historical* as a kind of breach or lacuna in the fabric of the present.

In his continued effort to secure this *phenomenological* sense of the pastness of the past he will develop – over the course of the following sections of *Sein und Zeit* – his analysis of the historicity of Dasein as a structure of authentic "repetition", of *Wiederholung*. The main purpose of this account is to understand how Dasein is historical in virtue of constituting itself as a re-enactment and rehearsal of past possibilities for a future. I will not repeat the details of this analysis here. I just want to make a more general point about its orientation in order to prepare for my main argument.

What the phenomenological imperative calls us to do is to explore and seek to clarify the nature of the phenomenal presence of pastness from within the viewpoint of human existence as lived and experienced in a life directed toward a future, without taking this experiential category as given beforehand. From where does this meaning of "past-ness" emerge? This, Heidegger says, is the real philosophical *enigma* (*Rätsel*) that we are facing.[6] He readily acknowledges that we usually take for granted that "being historical" amounts just to having a tiny part in the great "business of world history". Yet, we can and should still ask the philosophical question "on the basis of what ontological conditions does historicity belong to the subjectivity of the 'historical' subject as its essential condition?"

He suggests that we think of this no-longer-being of human existence as "having-been-there" (*da-gewesen*), in other words as the perfective version of *Da-sein*. He could perhaps have said: Da-sein as *non-living*. Somehow, the dead appear here as the source of the meaning of the historical, precisely by not being simply past, but by lingering on in that strange middle-region of perfective being. Heidegger wants to stay true to the phenomenological imperative to seek the meaning of a phenomenon on the basis of its lived futural projection of understanding. But when it comes to the meaning of the past, he is compelled to recognize that the very meaning of pastness somehow implies the pastness of the other, not as an entity from a presumed objective past preserved in the present, but rather as a peculiar pastness in the present, of which we are somehow a part.

History in this sense is thought as "derivation", as *Herkunft*. It is a form of pastness that somehow seems to carry or drag the past with it while at the same time being present. The term *Herkunft* – in the English translations "derivation" – is notable in this context. Heidegger himself does not explore it further. *Kunft* or *Kumft* is the older German word for *coming*, and thus also for the arrival or simply future. The *Her-kunft* thus means that from which something has come or originated, in other words its *ancestry*.

Heidegger himself does not speak explicitly of *ancestry* or of the *ancestral*, the standard German words for which would be *Abstammung* or *Vorfahren*. His own continued phenomenological analysis of the meaning of the historical will lead him instead to focus on what we could describe as a parallel term, namely that of Dasein as "having-been", as *Da-gewesen*.[7]

My motivation for introducing the term "ancestrality" into the discussion has to do with this positive ambiguity, how it designates an in-between life and death. A challenge for any phenomenology of history is to give an account of the possibility of the historicity of an event or artefact as precisely a present absence in the present. The "ancestral" is then meant to capture the phenomenological quality of that which in the present recalls and reaches back into what presents itself as "past". In that sense it can be said to capture the core problem of a phenomenology of history, namely the meaning of present-past, or in Heidegger's terms *herkunftigkeit*, or *Da-gewesenheit*.

By bringing *Dasein* as *da-gewesene* into the discussion Heidegger has pointed the way toward a deeper exploration of this phenomenology of the non-present other for an understanding of the historical. Yet, it is not a theme that he himself elaborates. His analysis of historicity shows how the circular and projective temporality of existence is a prerequisite for historical understanding and awareness. But more generally and importantly it argues for the need to explore the existential roots of history in its reflective, scientific form, the supposedly true account of *how it really was*. Having an understanding relation to the past, and living meaningfully in relation to the past, is not something that requires or rests on the existence of history as an academic or literary enterprise. On the contrary, the theoretical pursuit to secure the truth about the past is a later and secondary event in the evolution of something like the phenomenon of history.

What I want to suggest here is to take the phenomenological understanding of history one step further by exploring the *a priori* structures of historical existence through an analysis of transgenerationality or ancestrality, in Heidegger's terms of *Da-gewesenheit*, as the phenomenality of the non-present presence of the other. The basic premise is that it is in relation to the dead and to the deceased ancestors that we come across a kind of first or primordial sense of *the historical*, and what we could call an original phenomenological datum. Such an exploration can take its lead from Heidegger's suggestion, namely that the meaning of the historical has to do with the being of *Da-gewesenheit*, with Dasein no longer there. Yet it must go beyond his analysis and its preoccupation with the structure of repetition in the living present of Dasein, and of its possible "authenticity". The distinction between an authentic and an inauthentic mode of historicizing inserts an evaluative dimension into the scheme. In the existential process of historicizing an evaluation is usually operative, in terms of an ethical commitment to this or that ancestral force or point of orientation. However, precisely for this reason it needs to be analysed from a more neutral standpoint as part of the structure of historicizing itself.

II

If we cannot elicit the meaning of pastness only from the historicity of living human beings, and if somehow the no-longer living are co-constitutive of the space of the historical, then we need to develop a phenomenology that can account for this phenomenon. In short, we need a phenomenology of what it means to *be-with-the-dead*. Where can we turn for support for such an exploration?

Among the unpublished papers by Jan Patočka, edited and translated into French by Erica Abrams, there is a short and unfinished but remarkable little piece entitled "Fenomenologie posmrtného života", in French "Phénoménologie de la vie après la mort", ("Phenomenology of life after death"), probably written in the late sixties.[8] In this sketch, Patočka raises the question: how can we speak consistently about life after death without presupposing the existence of some kind of "substantial carrier" and "double" of this life, as "soul" or "spirit"? How can we as phenomenologists, with our strict demand to stay with the things themselves in their immediate givenness, speak of something non-existent and non-evidential without giving way to a "metaphysical fiction"?

The first and preliminary response to such a temptation would be to simply say no, this is a territory on which no meaningful discourse can legitimately be pronounced. As phenomenologists we speak from the viewpoint of the living, of and for the living. The dead are no longer here. They have no presence. They leave no evidence. And yet, *and yet,* Patočka adds, we cannot deny that the dead do not "…entirely disappear, for the other continues to live in us […] it is of course only a precarious life, dependent on us, not immortality, but a simple living on that does not last longer than we live…".[9] The life of the dead other is not an independent self-sustaining life, and still it is not nothing. *Somehow the other remains in me.* So far, he adds, no one has tried to give a phenomenological account of this strange phenomenon of how the dead other somehow continues to live, and thus how, in a certain sense, there is life after death. For this phenomenon of a "life after death" exists, indeed, he says, it exists "without any doubt", *sans nul doute.* Therefore it also deserves to be made the object of a phenomenological analysis.

The reason why it has not been done before is that it is said to provide "so little comfort". But now is the time to do it, through phenomenology, as the unique method available for such an enterprise. Through phenomenological analysis the continued life of the dead shall be made visible in its strange and unique presence. In order to approach this difficult task, he starts in the phenomenon of intersubjectivity. Human existence does not exist on its own and by itself. We are beings for ourselves, but we are also beings for the other. From the viewpoint of original temporality we are in a strict sense "totality private", inaccessible to the other, who reaches us from an "outside". And yet the image we have of ourselves is mediated through the other. Indeed, it is only the other who can see us, as it were, "objectively". In this sense our lives are already from the outset mediated, exteriorized and thus in a sense "alienated". Patočka vacillates in his formulations of how to express this enigma of the self through the other. It is both original and deferred in regard to itself. This is also true of the other, whose existence is dependent on me, through the images and representations I have of the other and vice versa. In this sense we live through each other.

For this reason we can also say that I continue to live through the other, in a kind of "quasi-life" in the other. When the other is dead (s)he continues in me, in what from her/his own viewpoint amounts to a "non-existence", and for me a "non-originarity" and yet somehow as being there. This *somehow* is the crux of the matter: in what form of being does the other continue to be? As long as the other lives, there is a reciprocity where we live and exist through each other. With death this reciprocity is cancelled. The dead do not respond, they do not collaborate, they accomplish nothing at all (*il n'effectue rien du tout…*).

The dead is cut off from its possibility, and now only lives as dependent on us. What, then, remains of the departed? Referring explicitly to the memory of his father, Patočka states that all that remains are certain "characteristics" that somehow retain the "essence of a person", a look, a voice, a gesture, etc. The individual person is gone, and yet in this diluted form he remains in the memory of the son. He even states that those who have been close to a person have the special task of "incorporating the other in some form or other in their lives". In this phenomenon of *incorporation* of the dead in and by the living, we come across what he refers to here as an "original conscience of life with the dead" that guarantees that the non-existence of the other is not just a non-being but also a *positive* continuation of life.

This formulation of a continuation of the dead among the living through incorporation, suggested as in passing rather than systematically explored, marks the speculative peak of this short sketch. The rest of the unfinished article contains a discussion of Kojève and the dialectics of desire and a critical reflection on Sartre and his exaggerated subjectivism. At the very end of the text, he returns again to the experience of death of the other, but now explicitly as also a problem of *grief* and *mourning* that can induce a false consciousness of a continued reciprocity where there in fact is none, which he likens with the phenomenon of "phantom limbs". In response to this pain of loss, human existence must ultimately regain its sense of reality and continue its life without the full reciprocity of the other. Seen from this perspective, the text could be read as a kind of extended philosophical work of mourning, a reflexive attempt to come to terms with personal loss and its reverberations in memory, where the dead other is internalized and somehow maintained after death in and through a truncated reciprocity.

As such, it anticipates Derrida's thoughts on the workings of memory in relation to the dead, which he first articulated in his *Mémoirs for Paul de Man* from 1987, a text written in response to the loss of his friend. There he tries to articulate precisely the peculiar and ultimately paradoxical experience of what it means to preserve someone *in* memory.[10] When we experience painful loss, he writes, we say to ourselves that the departed is not fully departed, but that he or she somehow *lives on in our memory*. Yet at the same time it is clear that memory cannot keep or preserve the other, who is irrevocably gone. Should we then, he asks, look upon this ambition to preserve the dead other as only a narcissistic refusal to recognize inevitable loss? No, he answers, the structure of this relation between subjectivity and the dead other and memory is more complex. The presence of the other in the self is the experience of something that is "greater" than the self, and the possibility of mourning someone is ultimately part of and co-constitutive of what it means to be a self.

"Memory" thus becomes a name for an experience of both the volatility and possibility of the subject. It is precisely in somehow being *outside* itself, in a continued relation to what is other than oneself, that human existence is what it is. From his own experience of the loss of his friend, and from his own attempts to reflect in a phenomenological vein on this experience, Derrida comes to a formulation quite similar to that of Patočka some decades earlier.[11]

By the time of the book *Spectres of Marx*, published in 1993, it had grown and taken on new proportions in Derrida's work. Here he recalls how the existential imperative to *live* also implies an imperative to address *death*.[12] Learning to live is learning to exist between life and death, in the existential stretch constituted by one's own life span, from not yet being born to no longer existing, but also to learn to live in relation to those no longer there. In order to describe this situation, this existential in-between, he here suggests that we think of it in terms of "the phantom" (*le fantôme*). Unlike in Patočka's text, the *phantomatic* is not here just a negative border-concept and the name of an illusion to be overcome by a rational work of mourning. Instead it is presented as a *positive* phenomenological category in its own right, for designating a mode of being on the threshold or middle ground between the living and the dead.

To learn to live would then, according to Derrida, partly amount to learning to live with and among spectres and ghosts, as also – as he writes – a "politics of memory, of inheritance, and of generations". It is a politics, but perhaps even more an *ethics*, since it concerns how we comport ourselves in relation to those who are no longer there. There is a peculiar kind of *responsibility* for and toward the deceased, which marks and constitutes the living in their self-understanding. Or perhaps we should speak of it as *responsiveness*, rather than responsibility, since the latter could be taken to imply that we already know what our obligations are. The point here is precisely that there is no certainty on this ground. We do not know what we owe the dead, neither what they owe us.

In several of Derrida's later writings the "spectral" designates precisely this indeterminate space between the dead and the living. In a footnote to the book on Marx he even indicates the possibility of what he calls a "phenomenology of spectrality", that should be carried out, as he writes, "with good Husserlian logic, cutting out a limited, relative field within a regional discipline", that should explore systematically the "original experience of visitation."[13] With such a radicalization of the phenomenological enterprise, Derrida writes "the possibility of the other and of mourning" would be written into the very phenomenality of the phenomenon. In the book on Marx, all of this remained tentative anticipations of something yet to be developed. Husserl is mentioned in the quoted footnote and Heidegger is recalled only in passing. As it stands, the book leaves open the question how and to what extent the question of the spectral would be possible to develop more closely in phenomenological terms.

A few years after the book on Marx, Derrida returned again to this theme in a book entitled simply *Apories*, a series of mediations on death, partly motivated by a reading of Philipe Ariès monumental anthropological study of the culture of death in the West, *L'homme devant la mort* (from 1977). Here he devotes an explicit critical analysis to Heidegger and the existential analysis of death, concluding that "the existential analytic does not want to have anything to do with the revenant and with grief".[14] The remarks explicitly recall the critical analysis of Heidegger's analysis of death that Levinas had developed in his last lecture course in the mid-seventies, published in 1993.[15] In these lectures he criticized Heidegger precisely for reducing the role and meaning of the death of the other, in favour of the problem of personal finitude.

This short survey shows how both Patočka and Derrida, independently of one another, approach the problem of the dead other as a significant theme for phenomenological exploration. In Patočka it remained an unfulfilled promise, a sketch for something to come, that he was never permitted to carry out. In the case of Derrida, it emerged as a central preoccupation in the later writings, in which he increasingly devoted his thinking to this intermediate space of spectrality, of living-on, of spirits and of ghosts. Patočka considered this theme to have been unexplored by previous phenomenologists. Derrida did pay a critical tribute to Heidegger's analysis of finitude in *Apories*. Yet, in relation to the specific topic of thinking mortality from the viewpoint of mourning and the spectral, and thus of thinking the after-life, he followed Levinas' critique. Neither Derrida nor Patočka seems to have sensed the possibility of linking this topic explicitly to the larger question of history and historicity in Heidegger.

From the viewpoint of what I initially outlined as the problem of ancestrality in *Being and Time,* I think we can see retrospectively how these topics tend to overlap, blend, and combine. In order to see how the problem of the dead other, mourning and history can be said come together also in Heidegger's work, we need to go back again to *Being and Time* and what it says explicitly about death in general, and about the death of the other in particular.

A basic premise in *SZ* is that human existence tends to represent itself through alienating categories, elicited from types of non-human being. It is as a consequence of this self-alienating tendency that the constructive attempt to forge a more adequate existential-ontological terminology must run parallel with a "destruction" of the history of metaphysics and inherited modes of designating life. A more genuine or "authentic" grasping of human existentiality requires that *Dasein* is able to tear itself loose from this tendency of "falling prey" to inherited modes of discourse. *SZ* is an attempt to secure a more appropriate terminology for exploring the being and movement of life. Nowhere is this challenge more acute than in the sections that explicitly try to think the nature of finitude and mortality.[16] After having determined the essence of human *Dasein* in the first part of the book as "being-in-the-world" and as "care", Heidegger poses the question how this presumed totality could be conceptually grasped and articulated. Existence is delimited by birth and death, thus constituting what appears as a finite *stretch* of life. In order to really think its totality, however, we cannot simply rest with an understanding of it as a life-process, delimited by death, as if though death were somehow *outside* life, or simply its outer limit. For death *belongs* to life, and life is a being-toward-death, permanently open to the possibility of its non-possibility. What could a proper and supposedly *authentic* conceptual mastery of death amount to?

We think that we know death, simply because we experience it all around us. But what we experience is really the death of the other, not death as *our* death, or as *my* death. We should not take the medical, biological and social "fact of death" for granted as our source of knowledge and reflection for understanding mortality. For death, he says, is ultimately a phenomenon of "Dasein as possibility".[17] Somehow death should be grasped and conceptualized as a phenomenon of life, from the viewpoint of the living, as the very "possibility of impossibility" as his definition reads.[18] In order for the analysis of authentic being-toward-death to be carried through it needs to address the experience of the dying and dead other, as its phenomenal contrast. This takes places in §47, the only place in Heidegger's work that actually does provide a rudimentary phenomenology of the being of the "dead other", or of the other as dead. The argument goes as follows.

When it has reached its "completion" (its *Gänze*), he writes, the other *Dasein* becomes a "no-longer-being-in-the-world". This is the first phenomenal aspect of its being as dead. But how should we understand this phenomenon of *leaving* the world? In one sense the other *Dasein* is no longer here, but in another sense it is here, but now as the apparent thing of a being no-longer-alive. In the dying of others, Heidegger writes, a "remarkable" phenomenon occurs, the sudden transition or reversal (*Umschlag*) of *Dasein*, or (as he adds in a parenthesis) of *life* – to a "no-longer" *Dasein*. It is as if the end of *Dasein* were suddenly the beginning of another type of being or entity, but now in the order of a purely present entity, namely as *corpse*. But this conventional description of what takes place at the moment of death does not capture the phenomenal character of the event. More precisely, it fails to capture the sense in which this being, as he says, "is still remaining" (*nochverbleibende*), and as such not really represented by the purely corporeal. It is not just lifeless, *leblos*, it is "un-living", *unlebendig*. As such it can be the object of multiple concerns, he writes, as in funeral rites and cults. The mourners are still *with* the other, in the mode of a *care* that is characteristic of being-with others, and not the kind of care we devote to objects. A dead body is not taken care of in the same way that we take care of artefacts. We continue to *be* with them, in a world that continues to give meaning and significance to our peculiar mode of being with those no longer there, even though they have, as it were, "left it behind" (*zurückgelassen*).

These reflections basically sum up what Heidegger has to say concerning the dead other. As already stated, the primary purpose of the analysis is not to provide a separate phenomenology of the being of and with the dead – as in the case of Patočka or Derrida – but rather to serve as a negative contrast for raising the question of the nature of a supposedly more authentic being-toward-death. Still, the sheer force of its phenomenality here leads him up against the irreducible problem of *after-life* or *spectral existence*. The dead are not only possible objects of concern. They have a peculiar mode of being, as "still-remaining" and "un-living".

Heidegger does refer at one point to a "being-with-the-dead" (*Mitsein mit dem Toten,* on p. 238), but only to insist that this is not a genuine being-with, since it lacks a shared world. Yet, although he does not explicitly mention the dead other elsewhere in the book, our reading earlier has shown how this phenomenon does emerge again, but under new labels and in a new setting in precisely the sections on history and historicity. It is notable in this context that in a remark that Patočka jotted down in passing as the very last line of his sketch on the phenomenology of after-life, he writes: "L'historiographie comme explication avec les morts...", "historiography as an explication with the dead...", or perhaps even as a way of coming to terms with the dead. ... This truncated sentence is all we have. But it could be read as a cipher, pointing us in the direction of a theme where the question of the dead other is at the heart of it all; namely the existential ground of history, as precisely a being-with-and-coming-to-terms-with-the-dead.

III

Our discussion so far has led us in two seemingly different directions. The question of the meaning of the historical has indicated that it must somehow be sought in the problem of ancestrality as the living-on of the dead other, and thus as a problem of after-life. On the other hand, our attempt to retrieve earlier attempts to discuss precisely the problem of the afterlife has led us in the direction of the phenomenological problem of memorial practices in general, and burial in particular. Is there a way of phenomenologically bringing these two topics closer to one another? At this stage we need to take a broader look at the problem and leave the specific phenomenological sources and turn to the study of *burial* as an exemplary act for exploring the nature of *being-with-the-dead*. It could first seem to be a detour if the purpose is to the get to the heart of the phenomenon of history in general, but I believe it holds a key to a larger problematic, not least in view of the fact that it already surfaced spontaneously in the writings of both Heidegger, Patočka, and Derrida.

In order to introduce this thematic I first want to recall an analysis that marks the most advanced speculative account of burial in the history of philosophy, namely Hegel's *Phenomenology of Spirit*. In the section on "Spirit" he describes how the human spirit over the course of its historical realization falls apart in two separate ethical substances, *human law* and *divine law*.[19] Human law is embodied in the state, whereas Divine law is concretely manifested in the family. In the state the individual recognizes itself as a universal being under universal obligations, whereas the system of the family binds it to an inner and, as he says, "unconscious" ethical order.

The central obligation of the family members toward one another is described as concentrated in one particular act, namely precisely the proper handling of the family member in death, i.e., in *burial*. When a citizen dies it becomes recognized fully as a fulfilled and completed member of its community. Yet, from the viewpoint of the family, death makes him an "unreal impotent shadow". The universality that we reach in death is from the perspective of the one deceased a non-action, something only undergone and suffered passively by unconscious nature. It is in relation to this passive undergoing of nature's course that the specific obligation of the family manifests itself, or as Hegel writes:

> The duty of the member of a family is on that account to add this aspect, in order that the individual's ultimate being, too, shall not belong solely to nature and remain something irrational, but shall be something done, and the right of consciousness asserted in it.[20]

By providing a propel burial the family is thus seen as carrying out – unconsciously and unaware – the work of the rational universalization of spirit in and through death. What nature takes away from the individual in death, namely the individual's activity and initiative, the family members symbolically restore through a proper burial. They transform a passive destiny into a consecrated act, restoring its member to his full universality as individual, also across the threshold of destruction of his corporeal existence.

Since destruction is inevitable, the work of the family *vis-à-vis* the dead cannot ultimately work against nature. Instead it chooses to fulfill the work of nature, but now *as a conscious and willing act*. By laying the corpse to rest in the ground, and by covering it with earth, the family restores the humanity of the human in the face of blind nature.[21]

In Hegel's account, Human Law is connected to light and sky, whereas the Divine Law speaks from the earth and the netherworld. In being bound by the Divine law the members of a family are somehow also bound to and by the dead, in relation to whom their ethical obligations are articulated. Since these obligations are generally not articulated as such, but rather work as forces in relation to which the individual family member experience and perform their actions, they have the character of a *call* from the underworld, and thus form a kind of unconscious pact between the dead and the living.

The dual ethical inheritance and obligation is described as a potential source of conflict. Divine law holds the truth of the community, since it concerns its very principle of self-preservation. But it is what must suffer defeat in the face of the Human law when it is forced to admit its universal ethical responsibility and guilt. Exposed to the light of day the blind commitment to the dead will lead to its own destruction.

Throughout this argument Hegel is glancing toward one narrative in particular, namely Sophocles' *Antigone*. In and through the destiny of Antigone we have perhaps the most powerful testimony from Greek and ancient literature of the compulsion experienced by family members to bury their dead.

Let us ask the general phenomenological question: What is a grave? If we take it from the a- or trans-historical perspective, we would define it as: the location where a dead body is placed. But the grave is also the place where the memory of the deceased is preserved, concretized in and through artful technology. In other words, the grave appears to us as an original form of memorial, a mnemo-technics dating back to the earliest known traces of human culture. The very birth of "culture" is often identified with precisely the first signs of this practice. The earliest forms of hominids used simple tools, but burial sites are unique to Neolithic homo sapiens, with traces of this practice also found among the Neanderthals. Graves have been found that are at least as old as 90 000 years. With the emergence of a cult of burial we also have the emergence of what is often interpreted as *religious* beliefs.

The grave is a technical artefact created in response to an experience of loss, and in the service of a keeping. As such it provides us with a primary datum of an externalized experience of time and history as passage and continuity at once. In and through the grave, the living demonstrate a care for a life that is no longer, and also the continued presence of the dead among the living. It is an artefact created around bodily remains, but not for them as such, but for what they bear witness to, namely the breath and force of life as life, the *spiritus*, *pneuma, ruach, Seele* etc. Thus the grave is also the site of the spiritual, in all its different forms and interpretations. The grave is a house not for corpses, but for or in the service of the *spirits* of those having lived. From the inception of the grave, the dead are living on among the living, and the earth is shared with them.

In Hegel the analysis of burial rites is connected primarily to the attempt to understand the emergence of ethical life in the sense of living obligations, but also as a step in the gradual universalization of spirit. The dead, and the proper caring for the dead, thus obtain a very special role in his genealogy of mature spirituality. It is by integrating the dead in the overall narrative of life that life itself can succeed in sustaining itself in its universality and communality. Death threatens life not just physically with the destruction of its corporeal existence, but through the proper caring for the dead the finite mortal spirit can also transcend its condition in a triumph over precisely this finitude.

We need not follow through all the implications of this genealogy of the gradual universalization of sprit in Hegel's interpretation of the burial practices. It suffices at this point to note how it complements Heidegger's analysis of *Da-gewesenheit* and how it permits us to begin to think in a somewhat more systematic philosophical way about the inner workings of the caring for the dead and the experience of a call from the dead and a responsibility toward the dead. To gather the dead, to builds memorials, but also to preserve them in memory, in the form of narrative of their deeds, combines a ritual practice with the formation of a culture's inner collective memory.

The reason Antigone enters into conflict with the living represented by Chreon is that she experiences her loyalty to the dead, and to the sacrificial rituals for the dead as a primary ethical demand. Her monologue from this moment in the play is so remarkable that it deserves to be quoted in full:

> Tomb, bridal-chamber, eternal prison in the caverned rock whither I go to find my own, those many who have perished and whom Persephone has received among the dead! Last of all shall I pass thither and far more miserably of all, before the term of my life is spent. But I cherish good hope that my coming will be welcome to my father, and pleasant to you, my mother, and welcome, brother, to you. For when you died, with my own hands I washed and dressed you and poured drink-offerings at your graves; and now Polyneices, it is for tending your corpse that I win such recompense....[22]

At this point in the narrative she is no longer speaking to the living, but to the dead. It is to the voices, ears, and eyes of the dead that she directs her discourse. Her ethical orientation is directed toward the deceased, and toward a *claim* issuing from them. Seen from the perspective of the living, she is mad. Having lost her orientation and commitment to the living she is drifting into a space where she no longer communicates with and hears the living. This comes out in a particularly moving way in the dialogue between her and her sister Ismene. Still, the distinction between madness and reason here is not as clear-cut as it may seem from the view point of Chreon. Even Tireisias eventually sides with her sensibility. He notes that the Gods are displeased, that they do not receive the sacrifices, that somehow the communication is broken. He tries to calm Chreon and convince him that he must consider not just the living but also the dead, indicating that the failure to do so it in itself a form of madness: "self will incurs the charge of folly. *Nay allow the claim of the dead*; do not stab the fallen. What prowess is it to slay the slain anew? I have sought your good and for your good I speak…". As we know, Chreon will not listen, and for this he will be punished cruelly by fate.

In a literary-mythical form this drama and encounter could thus be read as articulating the more general problem, namely how the relation to the dead constitutes a space of meaning within which the living constantly move, and which they must learn to master, through ritual and proper comportment, but also through myth, songs, and accounts.

The drama is written around the same time as Herodotus' *Historia*, and the depiction of the emergence of the Persian wars. In view of this contemporaneity, it is striking to note how Herodotus articulates his own motivation at the outset of the book. As quoted earlier, it is motivated by a concern for the dead, to preserve the memory of the dead, where the historical writing itself constitutes a sacrificial event. In other words, if we are looking for the phenomenological meaning of the historical, we should first locate it at the juncture where the living turn toward the dead, taking responsibility for their afterlife, by building monuments to their lives, and thus internalizing the life that has been. The crypt into which Antigone goes can therefore also be seen as a metonym for the space where history is conceived: it is a crypt which for her means that she moves across the threshold, but as she enters it, she is still alive, speaking to and for the dead, having opened herself to their claims.

This will no doubt sound speculative. In order to underpin the importance of contemplating this threshold-space, I now turn again in my last section to the narrative with which was recalled at the outset, namely the *Odyssey*. In its eleventh book we find the most moving account in world literature of an encounter between the living and dead, and of which Odysseus tells the story to his Faiacean hosts, namely the dramatic account of how he goes to speak with the dead in the underworld.

IV

The background for this famous narrative is that after Odysseus and his men have spent a long time on the island of Circe, she advices them to go and speak to Teiresias to find out about the future prospects. But Teiresias, who in Sophocles' drama was still alive, is here dead, having himself become a member of that underworld to whose claims he gave voice. Therefore they need to go to the end of the world and enter a place where they can speak with him, as the only one among the dead who still has the power of divination. Odysseus sails with his ship to the limit of Oceanos, to the land of the winter people who live in constant darkness. On the spot indicated by Circe, he digs a hole in the ground and performs a sacrificial rite, the culmination of which is the pouring of blood from lambs, which calls forth the spirits who drink the blood which permits them to leave their shadowy existence for a moment, to see and to speak with the living.

The first person to rush forward is Odysseus' own rowing mate Elpenor, whom they thought they had left behind, but who has in fact fallen off Circe's roof and broken his neck. He pledges Odysseus to provide him with a grave, so that he is not forgotten. Then comes Teiresias, for whose counsel they have come. This literary encounter between Odysseus and Teiresias contains a remarkable and concentrated scene where the communication with the dead, blood sacrifice, and foresight come together. In the discourse that follows, Teiresias tells Odysseus of the different possible fates that await him, depending on how he acts. The future is not decided, since it still depends on how they will handle the current situation. During the course of this conversation Odysseus can see the shadow of his own mother roaming around, but apparently she is unaware of his presence. Teiresias then explains to him how it is with the dead: "I shall make it clear in a few words and simply. Any dead man whom you allow to enter where the blood is will speak to you, and speak the truth; but those deprived will grow remote again and fade." These words bear testimony of a basic phenomenological dimension of history. Only by giving of our own life to those no longer here, will they speak back to us. Without it they will remain faint shadows.

The encounter with his mother is a particularly moving moment in the narrative. When he enters the world of the dead Odysseus does not know that she is already a part of it. As she drinks from the sacrificial blood she begins to speak and she tells him how she died from the grief of longing to see him. And when he desperately stretches out to hug her, she disappears into thin air, explaining to him that her body has disintegrated and that her soul is but a dream: "dreamlike the soul flies, insubstantial…" After he has spoken to her, all the other shadows come forward, eager to drink of the blood and to tell their stories. Odysseus wards them off with his sword, disciplining the dead as it were, in order to let them speak and bear witness one at a time. They all speak of who they are, whence they come from, what they have done.

A history is thus retold, and an account is given. In the narrative it is the dead who bear witness to the dead. But in fact it is Odysseus who carries their voices and their stories back to the living, to the court of Alkinoos. In this way we can see how Homer establishes the format of a narrative for the historians whose narratives will emerge in the centuries that follow. Like Odysseus in the fictive narrative they strive to preserve and bear witness from the dead, of their origin and their deeds. The sacrificing storyteller thus emerges in this very particular and formative scene as someone who establishes the genre of history as a narrated recollection of the dead.

Among the stories that Odysseus tells to his hosts, this encounter with the dead is the one that impresses the most. He is the one who has been able to travel across the ultimate threshold over to the dead and to bring back their stories to the living. Alkinoos is spellbound by this tale, he refuses to sleep, and wants to hear more. It is Odysseus who cautions him, saying that there is both a time for stories and a time for sleep, and thus – one could add – also a time for memory and one time for forgetting. But Alkinoos insist, and Odysseus speaks on through the night of his encounters with all the heroes from the great Trojan War.

As the presumed writer, it is Homer who controls this narrative from start to end. Yet we can also see how the literary narrative prepares the way for the historian to come. For it is not the bard and his songs that Alkinoos wants to listen to when he wants to hear more about the heroes from Troy. No, it is the voices of the heroes themselves as they have spoken to the one who has travelled across the threshold into the land of the dead, bringing back not tales, but *truth*, not just *mythoi* but *alethes*. As Odysseus tells him of his encounters with Agamemnon, with Achilleus, and the others, who have all suffered death, he begins every passage with the words: "and I saw", *eidon* or *eiseidon*, interchangably. He is here the exemplary *histor*, the one who has *seen*, and who has come back to bear *witness* to what he saw, and what the dead said to him, a seeing witness for the witnesses.

In an article in the journal *History and Theory* from 2000, Francois Hartog has addressed the relation between Herodotus and Homer.[23] His point is essentially that Herodotus in his writings did seek to rival Homer and the bards, but that in the end he turned out to have created for himself a uniquely new type of voice. Hartog's comparison does not engage with any of the details of the text, it moves instead on a more general comparison between them as two forms of narrative of ancient wars and deeds. But it is when we look at the specific passages that I have recalled here that his argument obtains a deeper meaning. It is not just a question of a certain hypothetical intertextual relation and influence. More important is the existential situation and predicament of Odysseus as the story-teller/historian, and what it can also tell us about the phenomenon of the historical as such. Seen from this perspective the Homeric epic anticipates the very possibility of historical narrative, in its combination of travel, recollection, and sacrificial rites for the dead.

The pathetic and moving account of the initial meeting with the rower Elpenor also obtains a new significance in the light of this interpretation. Elpenor is the first to bear witness, and the first of which Odysseus gives an account. The central point in this narrative is not that he died (which is true of everyone there), but that he was left behind *unburied*. What he demands from Odysseus and his friends is that they provide him with a grave, a memorial mound through which he can be remembered. His last wish from the other side in the land of the dead is that the living should erect for him a sign that he lived. After having finished his story about the land of the dead, Odysseus also adds to the narrative that he did indeed return to erect a grave mound for poor Elpenor, in other words that he fulfilled his *duties* to the dead. The act has a metonymic function in the narrative, where the act of burial and the tale of his life and destiny overlap. By giving his testimony and his account, Odysseus has also performed a burial. The story describes how Elpenor has not been forgotten, how even this insignificant man, has been preserved for a future, and given a life in the memory of the living.[24]

The scene with Odysseus with the dead permits us to reflect on the existential foundations for historical awareness, but also on the prerequisites for historical narratives. Before ending, I want to make one more point in relation to this remarkable account, as also a way of tying together the different dimensions of my argument. It is often said about the Greeks' relation to the dead that unlike in other and later cultural configurations, their relation to the dead is mostly one of pity. The dead live in a land of shadows, deprived of the force of life. In the images from Odysseus' encounter during the sacrificial communication with the dead this is also mostly the case. The dead are miserable creatures. Even the great Agamemnon and Achilleus, so strong in life, appear here as a depressed weaklings, where the latter wishes he was guarding cattle rather than being in this sordid place.

As they come forth to tell their stories, Odysseus can treat them like one would treat little children, asking them to get in line, by holding up his sword. Yet, toward the end of the scene, the atmosphere suddenly changes. The rumour has spread among the dead that there is a place where they can tell their stories, and they begin to crowd. Odysseus is gripped by anxiety that he will not be able to control the situation. At this point he is struck by fear that Persephone will send upon him the Gorgon Head, that gaze from the other side that can transform and ultimately kill. At once the situation is frightening, and he realizes that he is not safe from the dead, that they may engulf him and draw him into their world. He quickly departs leaving their longing voices behind.

Through this end the story also captures the other side of the relation to the past as a relation to the dead. Through proper sacrificial rites humans can come into contact with the underworld and with the testimonies and stories from the dead. But if one stays too long, and if one listens too closely, it is not only the living who looks at the dead but also the dead who looks at the living, transforming them into an object of their fateful gaze.

At the outset of his remarkable collection of essays *The Writing of History* from 1975 Michel de Certeau quotes a short and posthumous manuscript by the great French Historian Jules Michelet entitled "L'Héroisme de l'esprit".[25] In this text, that was prepared as a postscript to his *History of France*, Michelet describes his own journey as into the "graves and sepulchres of the dead". He imagines how the souls of the dead through his own work have now "returned less saddened to their tombs". For Certeau this remarkable testimony from one of the greatest modern historians opens the door to a general understanding of history as precisely operating on the threshold of the living and the dead. He writes: "The other is the phantasm of historiography, the object that it seeks, honors and buries. A labor of separation concerning this uncanny and fascinating proximity is effected". He sees Michelet positioning himself at this border where literature has erected its fictions of journeys to the land of the dead. But in doing so, and in fantasizing about the possibility of bringing them back and saving their voices, he is in fact instituting what for Certeau is the fundamental historical operation: which is not the communication with the dead but the effort to "calm the dead who still haunt the present, and at offering them scriptural tombs".[26] What historiography accomplishes is to create – through writing – a separation between the living and the dead.

Certeau mentions both Virgil and Dante as literary examples of literary fictions of journeys to the land of the dead, but he does not mention Homer. From our reading above we can see how its narrative can be used to illustrate to an even greater degree the birth of the historical, precisely in its description of Odysseus' encounter with the dead. In the end, the hero must use his sword to fend off the spirits of the dead, as they come too close. He is their caretaker, who has sacrificed blood in order to let them speak, and who has carried their testimonies over to the land of the living. In doing so he is however also the one who has had to institute the cut, to forge the separation between the claims of the dead and the needs of the living.

Notes

1   Hannah Arendt, *Between Past and Future,* New York: Viking, 1954, p. 45.
2   The text is part of an ongoing project on history and the problem of the dead. See also my "Spectral Phenomenology – Derrida, Heidegger and the Problem of the Ancestral", in K. Siobhan (ed.), *Companion to Memory Studies,* London: Ashgate, 2014, and "Housing Spirits: The Grave as an Exemplary Site of Memory" *Routledge International Handbook of Memory Studies,* ed. Tota and Hagen, London: Routledge, 2015, and "On the Grave as Original Mnemotechnics", in *Art of Memory,* ed. Arrhenius and Berg, Stockholm: Bonniers, 2014). Certain parts of the present text overlap with sections in these essays.
3   Pierre Chantraine, *Dictionnaire* Étymologique *de la langue Grecque,* Paris: Klincksieck, 1974, p. 779: "Du point de vue fonctionel, le nom d'agent *histor* [...] se rattache à *oida* plus qu'a *idein,* c'est celui qui sait pour avoir vu ou appris".
4   Quoted from *The Portable Greek Historians*, ed. M. Finley, London: Penguin, 1959, p. 29.
5   *Sein und Zeit,* p. 378, trans. Joan Stambaugh.
6   For this and the following argument, see SZ, §74.
7   The word "ancestral" has received a new interest recently through the work of Quentin Meillasoux. In his influential book *After Finitude* he takes both phenomenology and all different kinds of transcendental philosophies to task for having failed to overcome what he calls "correllationism", in other words the idea that the real is only available through a constituting subjectivity. In the context of this critique the word "ancestral" is used to point to that dimension of the past that stretches beyond the reach of present humanity, and thus supposedly beyond what any constituting subjectivity can master. See Quentin Meillasoux, *After Finitude. An Essay on the Necessity of Contingency,* trans. Ray Brassier, London: Continuum, 2008. It

seeks to designate any event that is anterior to the emergence of the human species or life on earth. In the same vein Meillasoux also refers to "arche-fossils" and "fossil-matter" as not just *indicating* traces of past life but also as materials indicating the existence of events anterior to all life. This use of the word "ancestral" is misleading and ultimately confusing on two counts. First of all it seeks to designate that which lies entirely beyond the reach of human subjectivity. Yet, it cannot avoid the simple and straightforward epistemological condition, that any statement concerning such a radical "beyond" must be based on some kind of observable evidence in order to make sense. In other words, it is only through some kind of "correlation" with human subjectivity that we can speak in a sensible and comprehensible way about the world as it was. This is not the same as saying that what we speak of is in itself subjective. These are elementary philosophical remarks. Secondly, and more interesting perhaps, is the inner tension in the very choice of these terms to designate that which is entirely beyond subjectivity and human life. Both "ancestrality" and "fossil" refer precisely to life, in the form of traces, in other words of "remains", and thus to the peculiar temporality of a living-on or lingering. Meillasoux seems unaware of these semantic implications, while still somehow relying on them for his purposes, namely to designate an absolute "before".

8   Jan Patočka, "Phénomenologie de la vie après la mort", trans. E. Abrams, in *Papiers phéno-ménomenologiques*, Grenoble: Jérome Millon, 1995, pp. 145–156. I was made aware of this text by Marcia Sà Cavalcante Schuback who refers to it in a beautiful essay on "The hermeneutics of tradition", published in *Rethinking Time: History, Memory, and Representation*, ed. A. Ers and H. Ruin, Stockholm: Södertörn Academic Studies, 2011. She uses it in the context of formulating a theory of tradition as essentially a life between the dead and the unborn.

9   All translations are my own from Abram's French translation: "…le mort ne s'en va pas tout entier, l'autre continue à vivre en nous […] ce n'est, bien sûr, qu'une vie précaire, dépendante de nous – non pas l'immortalite, mais une simple survie qui ne dure au'aussi longtemp que nous-mêmes vivons". In her editorial comment, Erica Abrams mentions an unverified "rumour" according to which this text was composed following the death of Patočka's wife, which would date it to 1967. Part of the content of the text, would suggest an earlier date. A letter to Walter Biemel, however, indicates that the topic was still on his mind as late as 1976, the year before his untimely death, and that he was planning to write more about it. Whichever is true, it seems clear that his thoughts here are at least partly animated by a personal experience of loss.

10 Derrida (1987), 32.

11 The point here is not to establish intertextual connections or paths of influences. It is known that Derrida read Patočka some years later, as documented in his comments on Patočka's *Heretical Essays* in his book *Donner la Mort* from 1994. What is more interesting is to see how they both, starting from a reading of Husserl and Heidegger, come to this topic through different trajectories.

12 *Spectres of Marx*, trans. P. Kamuff, New York: Routledge, 1994.

13 *Ibid.*, p 237n: "The original experience of haunting."

14 *Apories*, Paris: Seuil, 1996, p. 110.

15 *Dieu, la mort et le temps*, Paris: Grasset, 1993.

16 The relevant sections are §§46 onward.

17 *Ibid.*, p. 250.

18 *Ibid.*, p. 262. In his critical reading of these passages in *Apories* Derrida questions the aspiration behind this whole exercise. The idea of somehow finding an "authentic" sense of death, behind and beyond the "inauthentic" death of the other, ends up, he argues, in an aporia. His point is well argued, and it would deserve a longer comment. Yet here I will bypass this ques-

tion of the viability of articulating *Dasein's* authentic being-toward-death, and focus instead on its negative correlate, the death of the other.

19 *The Phenomenology of Spirit* is here quoted in the English translation by A. V. Miller, Oxford: Oxford University Press, 1977, section 445.

20 Ibid., section 452.

21 The same point is made in an excellent recent article by David Ciavatta "On Burying the Dead: Funerary Rites and the Dialectic of Freedom and Nature in Hegel's Phenomenology of Spirit", in *International Philosophical Quarterly* 47/3 (2007): 278–296.

22 Translation by R. C. Jebb in *Greek Drama*, New York: Bantam Classics, 1962, p. 101.

23 "The Invention of History: The Pre-History of a Concept from Homer to Herodotus", François Hartog *History and Theory* Vol. 39, No. 3 (Oct., 2000), pp. 384–395.

24 Note also that the earliest known historical chronicles were literally written on gravestones, so as to make indistinguishable the very element of burial and historical writing. Burial is the creation of history, and historical writing is a form a burial, at least in Nordic iron age burial culture, from which we have no other texts preserved, apart from engravings on gravestones.

25 Michel de Certeau, *The Writing of History*, trans. T. Conley, New York: Columbia University Press, 1988, pp. 1–2.

26 *Ibid.*, p. 2.

Danish Yearbook of Philosophy, Vol. 48–49 (2013–2014), 139–152

HISTORY AS SOIL AND SEDIMENT

Geological Tropes of Historicity in Heidegger, Husserl, and Merleau-Ponty

Jacob Martin Rump

Many twentieth-century accounts of history have used geological tropes to describe the phenomenon of historical knowledge, and such terms have been of particular importance in the phenomenological tradition. In Heidegger's references in *Being and Time* to the "soil of history," Husserl's account in his later work of "sedimentation" in the lifeworld, and the reformulation of this notion in the phenomenology of Merleau-Ponty, geological tropes are used to illustrate important insights into the relation between contingency, a priority and historicity. This paper seeks to contribute to an understanding of history – understood phenomenologically as *historicity* – through an analysis of these geological tropes.

Our findings can be summarized as follows: such geological tropes help the phenomenologist to describe the way in which history is always determined within a complex interplay between only *temporarily* fixed determining structures – such as riverbanks, insoluble sediment, soil, etc. – and free-flowing praxis, a situation in which historical events are at once determinant *of* and themselves determined *by* human activity. Paradoxically, the *constant* and "grounding" element in such conceptions of history is not the sediment and hard rock of historical fact, but the the constant change and variability – despite the sense-giving continuity – of human experience structured by historicity. We begin with a brief overview of the landscape on the philosophy of history in which these views arose, and then continue to an analysis of the tropes themselves.

I. A Schematic History of Historicity

This conception of history has a history.[1] The philosophy of history in the late nineteenth and twentieth centuries in both Anglo-American and Continental traditions – like other branches of theoretical philosophy – was marked by a characteristic *epistemological turn.*[2] This more "critical" philosophy of history, as the moniker suggests, eschewed the speculative idealist pronouncements of thinkers like Hegel, Croce, and Collingwood, whereby we can inquire into the nature and destiny of history in itself, arriving at timeless truths concerning the historical, and sought instead to focus on the nature and limitations of historical *knowledge* by means of careful methodology. But as this epistemological turn continued on toward the middle of the twentieth century, some philosophers – notably though not exclusively[3] those engaged in self-described *phenomenological projects* – nonetheless felt that, as unanswerable as seemed those timeless and speculative questions concerning the *essence* of history, the fact of *historicity* – that we are and experience the world as historical beings – is not simply present in our everyday lives but indeed definitive of human ways of being in the world. Thus, while sharing in the more general resistance to the speculative conception of history as an autonomous and self-enclosed area of inquiry about which universal and timeless truths can be discovered, these phenomenological thinkers of history also resisted the positivist and neo-positivist views that arose in immediate reaction to it. For the recognition of historicity implies that historical inquiry is not simply continuous with the sciences, and does not consist exclusively of inductive generalizations on the basis of historical *facts,* since historicity is not something that happens but rather a character of the happening or event itself; a characteristic *form* of human experiencing independent – in some sense – from its *content*.

The thinking of history through the phenomenon of *historicity* is further distinguished from other twentieth-century approaches in its insistence, a corollary to the claim above, that the recognition of historicity as a fundamental element of the human condition demands a rethinking of the character epistemological inquiry as such. Because of the centrality of historicity, the problem of historical knowledge can no longer be seen as merely a specialized sub-question within the larger discipline of epistemology, to be left aside for separate treatment; the problem of historical knowledge becomes according to these phenomenological currents of thought not merely one domain of epistemological inquiry among others, but a fundamental problem for *any* account of knowledge, because a fundamental element of human *experience.*[4]

And since the philosophers responsible for the development of the phenomenological conception of historicity all saw themselves working to some degree in the post-Kantian *Critical* tradition, they remained insistent on the ongoing interrogation of historicity and historical knowledge Critically, as phenomena of experiential life manifesting the limiting structure of subjectivity. As Kant recognized, reason – including historical reason – must be kept in check through the insistence that its claims be constantly submitted to the tribunal of experience. Thus – taking the liberty of characterizing their varied methodologies in common terms, though we should not forget that there remain important differences – Heidegger, Husserl, and Merleau-Ponty all proceeded by investigating the distance between *accounts* of historical knowledge and the lived historicity of *actual experience*, which is never a mere account or representation of fact, thereby building into their conceptions of history a recognition of the ways in which the theoretical account ultimately has fallen short of fully doing justice to history as a *phenomenon of experience,* and thus protecting their inquiries not only from the excesses of rational speculation but also from the preconceptions of a neo-positivist history of brute facts.

The phenomenological attempt to grapple with the phenomenon of history qua historicity was thus framed by (varied versions of) two basic and opposed positions: 1) The implicit speculative idealist reliance on a form of determinism, according to which history is understood, roughly, as the series of rational structures which by virtue of their containment determine all historical events in a way that allows – at least sub specie aeternitatis or from the standpoint of "absolute knowing," – complete predictability of all events and historical meanings; and 2), the positivist and neo-positivist's relativism regarding the historical in its own right, according to which, outside of our scientific generalizations on the basis of historical facts, there is no determinant order in history as such, and history does not itself make sense in its unfolding but is made sense of through imposed external forms of explanation. Phenomenological conceptions of history as historicity sought to describe historical knowledge in a way that recognizes the legitimate insights of both extremes while simultaneously avoiding the complete ascription to either of them.[5]

Geological tropes function as a unique means of approaching such a middle ground. They are employed in descriptions that avoid both of these extremes not – as we might expect – by *staking* a substantive middle ground, but by constantly retracing iterations of an intermediary strategy that resists the move to stake any *ground* at all. This strategy is open to the phenomenologist because of her locating of history in historicity, conceived within a schema defined by the temporal difference between subjective and objective manifestations of the historical. These accounts of historical knowledge are best characterized not in terms of a sought after *ground*, but in terms of a formally definable *movement; a constant reassessment of historicity that takes the place of grounding.* The result is thus a peculiar sort of "groundless grounding"[6] based in individual and collective lived experience, understood not as a set of atomic historical facts or partial intuitive givens of a greater whole but as the revelatory and constantly shifting temporal structure of our historical being-in-the-world.

II. Heidegger and the Soil of History: Historicity as Temporal Difference

Heidegger's *Being and Time* presents a sustained phenomenological discussion of historicity in terms of such a structure of temporal difference, revealingly described in terms of "the soil of history." In describing the "stretching" of Dasein through time, the fact that Dasein experiences the world as a series of "nows" but is still a single, continuous being in being-towards death, Heidegger writes, "the question of Dasein's 'connectedness' is the ontological problem of Dasein's historizing. To lay bare the *structure of historizing*, and the existential-temporal conditions of its possibility, signifies that one has achieved an *ontological* understanding of *historicality*."[7] For Heidegger, regular "world" history presupposes a prior relation rooted in the historical nature of Dasein's existence: "Historicality, as a determinate character, is prior to what is called "history" (world-historical historizing). "Historicality" stands for the state of Being that is constitutive for Dasein's 'historizing' as such; only on the basis of such 'historizing' is anything like world-history possible or can anything belong historically to world-history."[8]

This historicality of Dasein is differentiated from that of mere objects belonging to the world, which are "world-historical," by means of a structure of what we above called "temporal difference." The objects of everyday history are considered by Heidegger to be "secondarily historical," whereas Dasein is "primarily historical."[9] The distinction between primary and secondary historicality expresses the relation between the rapidly shifting system of historically determined human meanings, on the one hand, and on the other hand the sense-giving structures of the world that determine what we do and how we live while themselves continuing to change but at a comparatively *glacial pace*. According to Heidegger, ordinary "factual" conceptions of history have reversed this priority, regarding the historicality of objects as primary and attempting to understand Dasein's historicality secondarily on the basis of this objectivity. Historicity is exhibited by restoring the primary historicality of Dasein while continuing to respect the irreducible temporal difference between lived time and secondary "world-historical" time.

It is no accident that this difference between temporalities, if we notice it at all, tends to become evident when familiar spatiotemporal objects in our lives suddenly shift – to describe it in Heideggerian terms – from being ready-to hand to revealing aspects that appear to us as merely present-at-hand. *Suddenly* I notice the wear-and-tear on the armchair I sit in every day, and remember the time when it was new. But it did not *age with me* – I did not encounter its aging with every sitting, and it did not seem – as might, e.g., my own body – to be getting a little older each day. It is only suddenly, *now*, that it strikes me as having aged. Its historical change *crept up on me*, so to speak, so slowly that I did not (could not) notice it in the intervening instances of use. Because of the position of the inquirer *within* history, the character of historicity remains hidden from ordinary objective analysis.

Heidegger suggests that this is at least partially responsible for the conceptual difficulties of an account of historical knowledge. Any analysis of history from the objective perspective of the scientist will ultimately fail because the objects the scientist would treat are already themselves historical and thus cannot tell us anything about the underlying conditions of historicity.

> Even if the problem of history is treated in accordance with a theory of science, not only aiming at the 'epistemological' clarification of the historiological way of grasping things (Simmel) or at the logic with which the concepts of historiologial presentation are formed (Rickert), but doing so with an orientation towards 'the side of the object,' then, as long as the question is formulated this way, history becomes in principle accessible only as the *Object* of a science. Thus the basic phenomenon of history, which is prior to any possible thematizing by historiology and underlies it, has been irretrievably put aside.[10]

The basic phenomenon of history must be prior to all particular historical objects because historicality, as an "essential constitutive state" of historical subjects, ultimately concerns historical ontological conditions *not* only for the objects of the world but also, and more primarily, for Dasein. The positivist, in conceiving history as an object for scientific analysis akin to any other, ignores the fact that history is a phenomenon that occurs for me not primarily as an object in the world but as an actively temporalizing subject engaged in basic relations of equipmental use, relations whose immediate possibilities are structured by the broader horizon of historical objects present at hand. We must recognize *both* the independent historicity of the object – the armchair's aging "when I wasn't looking" – *and* the fact that it is nonetheless an historical artifact only in relation *to me*: "What is primarily historical is Dasein. That which is secondarily historical, however, is what we encounter within-the-world – not only equipment ready-to-hand, in the widest sense, but also the environing nature as 'the *very soil* of history'"[11]. It is no accident that Heidegger refers here to the "soil of history" [*geschichtlicher Boden*]. Moving away from Heidegger for a moment, we can easily recognize that geology, viewed as a field of scientific inquiry in the everyday sense, takes as its object a set of natural spatiotemporal structures in which *nothing* is completely fixed. Even the soil that is most compacted, even that which is "set in stone" will not, from the strictest physico-chemical standpoint, last forever. Even the oldest of geological formations are changing from the standpoint of the "*long durée.*" Indeed, the study of geology has been of great value to branches of human knowledge far removed from its own arena of inquiry precisely because of its ability to function as a *measure of change and of time* from the standpoint not of days or years but of millennia or eons. Importantly, it is only capable of measuring these broad changes through evidence presented in the changes to *itself*: The sedimentary layers of rock *represent* geological change by themselves manifesting it. They serve as a yardstick of the passing of time only because they are *also themselves affected by* it, albeit at a scale very different from the temporal experience of individual human beings. If the geological were not itself capable of historical change it could not serve as a record of history, but compared to the more "primordial" temporality of Dasein, "nothing present-at-hand 'in-time,' whether passing away or still coming along, could ever – by its ontological essence – be temporal in such a way."[12]

The geological tropes are illustrative of this temporal difference precisely because they are an immediately recognizable but at the same time *extreme* case. As beings of the modern scientific world, we recognize that the aging of the rockface is *in principle* not different from the aging of my easychair. But the *sublimity* of the rate of change, as we might put it, in the geological, merely present-at-hand case makes it all the more striking in relation to our own historical being as equipmentally involved subjects in the world. For the geological manifests its wear and tear only on the scale of eons, whereas the change in the condition of my armchair is noticeable in the space of just a few seasons of use.

Stated schematically, then, geological tropes point to a temporal difference between two levels or systems of historical entities. On one level we have our immediate and meaningful experience as historical subjects. At the second level, we have those *relatively* constant and *relatively determinant* persistences of the world-historical on the basis of which the continuity of meaningful conscious experience depends, even as this objective historicality is ultimately derived from our own. This temporal difference is from a phenomenological standpoint the very structure of historicity. But this structure is also never completely closed off or determined: it holds open a place for the characteristic contingency of lived experience in the face of historical determination.

III. Sedimentation in Husserl and Merleau-Ponty: Historicity as Determined and Spontaneous

In addition to the formal structure defined by temporal difference, geological tropes also help to further specify the role of the contingent in the historicity of experience: for the historical is always manifested through a particular content that is never completely determined by the historical formations from which it arose. In Husserl's *Crisis*, this interplay of historical determination and experiential contingency arises in descriptions of the relative constancy that pervades the lifeworld despite its constant alteration: "the world of life... is, to be sure, related to subjectivity throughout the constant alteration of its relative aspects. But however it changes and however it may be corrected, it holds to its essentially lawful set of types, to which all life, and thus all science, of which it is the "ground," remain bound."[13] Historicity is for Husserl, as for the early Heidegger, the structure of temporal difference through which we understand the *constant alteration* of the relation between the lifeworld and subjectivity. Despite the constant flux of experience, the historical phenomena of the lifeworld nonetheless hold to an essential – for Husserl this means ultimately transcendental – lawfulness. But this "a priori of history" is only visible to us because of the historical *sedimentation* of layers of meaning built up according to it. Again, then, as for Heidegger, history can be understood only as a phenomenon *for us, as subjectivities,* and in this sense history is "from the start nothing other than the vital movement of the coexistence and the interweaving of original formations and sedimentations of meaning" according to a structurally determinant formal law.[14]

But, as Husserl acknowledges in one of the *Beilagen* to the main texts of *The Crisis,* this seems to suggest a sort of paradox:

> Here a peculiar question arises. When we methodically and systematically bring to recognition the a priori of history, is this itself a facticity of history? Does it not then presuppose the a priori of history? The a priori is related to the being of mankind and the surrounding world that is valid for it in experience, thinking, and acting. But the a priori is something

ideal and general, which on the one hand refers to men themselves as objects and on the
other hand is a *structure within men*, in us who form it.[15]

If meaning only exists within our subjective and intersubjective lifeworld,
which is itself a result of the conceptual possibilities established by the sedimentation of meaning structures acquired throughout history, the determining
structures *for* this lifeworld could never themselves have distinguishable dis-
crete meanings. Indeed, Husserl generally refers to this all-important, underlying a priori lawfulness in very broad and nonspecific terms, as a "general
ground" or "immense structural a priori" or something "ideal and general." In
a sense, its structuring role relegates it to the status of *mere posit*. Like Heidegger's "historicality, as a logical structure underlying both history and the
lifeworld, the a priori of history is prior to both, and thus, it would seem, prior
even to any categories needed to further define it.

The account of "Galileo's mathematization of nature" in the first part of *The
Crisis* is an illustration of this conception of historicity. Despite the fact that
we each perceive the world somewhat differently, and have different "ontic
validities," we nonetheless tacitly agree about some qualities of the world we
share. The subject of this agreement is in a given "thematic" reflection usually
a specific element of cultural formation or of our now habitually scientific
lifeworld, but in each case the regularity depends upon more basic universally
accepted structures ascribed to the pre-scientifically self-given and "obvious"
characteristics of the world of experience.[16] Husserl's principal point is not so
much that the "original geometer" is capable of discovering such self-evident
structures, but that geometry itself can only be understood insofar as it is *built
upon* them. As he puts it, "The whole of the cultural present, understood as a
totality, 'implies' the whole of the cultural past in an *undetermined but structurally determined* generality."[17]

What does it mean for the generality of our present – as a totality – to imply
our past – again, as a totality – in a way that is at once undetermined but *structurally* determined? Is this not an obvious contradiction, another version of the
paradox of the a priori of history noted above? For Husserl the paradox is only
apparent, and arises from a failure to distinguish between the dual temptations
of historical relativism and historical determinism. The relation of our cultural
present to our cultural past is undetermined, insofar as we can never establish
perfect one-to-one correlations or exact causal links between past events and
present ones. This is a phenomenon very familiar to the historian: to say that

the Great War was "caused" by the assassination of Franz Ferdinand is not to say that this was its sole and exclusive cause. Indeed, many historians would claim that it is impossible, *even in principle*, to map out completely the complex interplay of causes that led to such an event, and perhaps, by extension, to any event. To think that such a perfect mapping of causes to effects is possible is to succumb to a version of historical determinism, since it implies that the present is *nothing more than* the totality of properly understood past causes. Husserl's claim that the cultural present stands in a relation of *undetermined* generality to the cultural past instead admits the contingency of history and of happenings; the fact that historicity as a lived phenomenon does not consist of a series of one-to-one causes and effects but is structured not only by past horizons (retentions) but also by future possibilities (protentions).

At the same time, Husserl claims, the cultural present *in its totality* is related to the cultural past *in its totality* in a *structurally determined* way. Despite the indeterminacy of individual relations between past objectivities and present subjective experience, there is still a *general* dependency: in a *very general sense*, it is correct to say that my cultural present is *structurally* dependent upon my cultural past. Meaningful experience does not exist in a vacuum, and does not amount to an historical relativism of "one damn thing after another" only to be made sense of by means of the generalizations of an external observer. As Heidegger showed, the temporal difference between the primary historicality of subjects and the secondary historicality of objects holds open a horizonal structure of anticipation for the subject, who experiences history from *within* history. Husserl emphasizes that this structure in each case depends upon the actual events of the past despite the specific relations within the structure never being completely predetermined, or even similarly determined for different individual subjectivities. The relation between the cultural present and the cultural past is thus *formally fixed* because of sedimentation, which manifests the structural determinacy of the historical, but never completely determined in its content: in the case of any specific subject's tracing back of evidences, an undetermined element – the specific material that fulfills the structurally determined meaning intention in a given case – is always something there to be discovered.

It may seem strange to refer to a "content" or *material* here, since we are not dealing directly with fixed meanings or objects but with elements in an experiential *relational structure*. But Husserl recognizes that this structure must – in a *logical* sense – have material as well as formal components, and it is precisely this insight that distinguishes these accounts of history from speculative accounts described above. Since our phenomenological investigations always begin from the now-moment, there is not – even in principle – any final God's eye view from which historical events could be exhaustively explained in terms of an unfolding of fully determinant ideal laws. The understanding of historicity in its constantly changing manifestations in lived experience is thus a central and defining element of the broader project of phenomenology as an ongoing methodological movement or "infinite task." For Husserl, transcendental logic is never fixed, and we cannot rest content with a once-and-for-all deduction of the categories of meaning because this contradicts the evidence of lived experience.

To the suspicious critic, such formally defined but materially open space in the structure of history will look like a loophole in the theory; an unjustified posit that "lets in" an outside element or an undesirable "opening" in what is expected to be a closed logical system. But such suspicion arises from an expectation that the relation between that which is historically determined and that which does the determining must be fixed in all respects, either as decided through a process of external scientific observation or as intuited from within as a momentary glimpse of the whole.

Husserl's phenomenological investigation of history recognizes not only specific experienced historical facts but also the structural, "formal" regularities of the experiencing itself, the characteristic historicity that governs the sedimentation of meaning in time. This recognition of the complex interplay of the formal and the material manifests phenomenology's radical break with the way history and epistemology were previously understood: as Husserl writes, "the ruling dogma of the separation in principle between epistemological elucidation and historical, even humanistic-psychological explanation, between epistemological and genetic origin, is fundamentally mistaken..."[18] In *The Crisis,* historicity thus plays a central role in the phenomenological analysis of constitutions, "the tracing of the historical meaning-structures given in the present, or their self-evidences, along the documented chain of historical back-references into *the hidden dimension of the primal self-evidences which underlie them.*"[19] History consists of *sedimentations* on the basis of self-evidences, but these sedimentations can be examined *both* in terms of their specific content *and* in their structural and formal generality, but in a way that never ignores the manifest openness of lived experiencing.

Husserl's analysis thus shows that the gap between historical facticity as fixed object of study and historicity as formal condition of subjective being-in-the-world is filled out by contingent logically material *variables*, just as, in geology, less "durable" elements such as water and air are gradually compressed out, evaporated, or otherwise expelled in a *variety of processes* as the underlying geological layers become more compacted, resulting in an ever-more-hardened and more-durable – though never eternally fixed – layer of the natural historical record. This variety of processes is always partially but never entirely determined by the geological elements that both affect and are affected by it, just as there is never an exact and perfect founding of one level of the geo-historical record upon the other: the geological functions as historical record not only by means of a regular pattern of sedimentation according to the fixed logic of gravity but also through eruptions, through erosions, and even through tectonic shifts. The relationship between the levels of the geological record is thus structurally necessary but not fixed in its content or manner of appearing.

Thus, as Merleau-Ponty notes in his taking up of Husserl's seminal historical concept in *The Phenomenology of Perception*,

> this word 'sedimentation' must not trick us: this contracted knowledge is not an inert mass at the foundation of our consciousness... My acquired thoughts are not an absolute acquisition; they feed off my present thought at each moment... The acquired, then, is only truly acquired if it is taken up in a new movement of thought, and a thought is only situated if it itself assumes its situation. The essence of consciousness is to provide itself with one or many worlds, to make its own thoughts exist *in front of* itself like things, and sketching out these landscapes and abandoning them indivisibly demonstrates its vitality. The structure 'world,' with its double movement of sedimentation and spontaneity, is at the center of consciousness...[20]

Sedimentation as an historical phenomenon is not primarily an object but a vital activity, one which always involves *two* movements: that of settling into passivity and that of "spontaneity." Sedimentation is thus *never complete determination*: "Were it possible to unfold at each moment all of the presuppositions in what I call my 'reason' or my 'ideas,' then I would always be discovering experiences that have not been made explicit; weighty contributions of the past and of the present and an entire 'sedimented history' that does not merely concern the genesis of my thought, but that determines its *sense*."[21] The result of such a conception of history would be a *one-dimensional* sedimentary structure, in which the formal laws of the "a priori of history" were the sole and exclusive defining feature of historicity. This would be complete historical determinism.

At the same time, Merleau-Ponty emphasizes, the constant flux of the playing out of history seen in total abstraction from its sedimented meanings would amount to mere raw action; to the positivist's claim that time simply passes bringing with it an unordered confusion of "one damn thing after another." Thus despite – and indeed *because of* – the founding of history in the structure of temporal difference, historical knowledge presupposes a certain deference to determining sedimentary structures even as it demands the experiential spontaneity of the subject:

> [H]ere again, we must recognize a sort of sedimentation of our life: when an attitude toward the world has been confirmed often enough, it becomes privileged for us. If freedom does not tolerate being confronted by any motive, then my habitual being in the world is equally fragile at each moment... The rationalist alternative—either the free act is possible or not, either the event originates in me or is imposed from outside—does not fit with our relations with the world and with our past. Our freedom does not destroy our situation, but gears into it: so long as we are alive, our situation is open, which implies both that it calls forth privileged modes of resolution and that it, by itself, lacks the power to procure any of them.[22]

The trope of sedimentation illustrates the phenomenological insight that freedom and its containment are always codependent parts in the structure of historicity: experience as an historical structure for individual and collective subjectivities manifests both predetermination and spontaneity. It is the need for such spontaneity, for a *contingency in the system,* that a phenomenological account of history (as opposed to a deterministic conception) recognizes. It takes it as a given that our experience often has the character of *thrownness* or subjection to the unexpected. And yet, unlike the positivist's conception of history as a series of otherwise random facts made sense of from the outside, phenomenology recognizes that our accounts of history are always structured by the internal logic of own historicity. The word "sedimentation" is thus not a vague, catch-all metaphor covering up a lack of descriptive exactness, but a description offered in fidelity to the lived reality of the things themselves.

IV. Conclusion: Phenomenology's "Grounding" of History in the Movement of Historicity

In our brief treatment of phenomenology's use of the geological trope, we have seen the same basic conception of historicity expressed in Heidegger's explication of the structure of temporal difference in terms of the "soil of history," and in Husserl's and Merleau-Ponty's reflections on "sedimentation" as the structure of the past's "undetermined but structurally determined generality."[23] We have argued that these geological tropes point to a middle path in the philosophy of history, one that avoids both positivist conceptions of history and the speculative historical determinism they arose in reaction to, but does so by orienting its account to the internal movement of temporality instead of an external and immutable ground.

This internal movement of temporality occurs in a context of temporal difference, but one in which, as Heidegger shows, the lived temporality of the subject is always primordial against the background of the secondary historicity of objects and facts. This temporal difference resists a complete determinism about history, leaving itself partially open to the spontaneous character of lived human experience while remaining grounded by the hardened sedimentation of past events. Considered reflectively, history is thus a structure of constraint, since it has always-already limited what counts as meaningful and valuable in what we say and do, but this constraining role is never complete: As Merleau-Ponty insists, our spontaneity "gears into" our determined situation. It is the *inherent inconstancy of the geological* as much as its durability and duration that is definitive of its use in phenomenological accounts of history. It is only because of the internal temporality of geological processes – the fact that the long-lasting determining structures themselves erode, compact, shift and sediment – that allows them to function as a measure of the much more rapid change of other elements of our lived environment. The geological, despite its glacial pace of change, represents an ultimately shifting "bedrock."

These two opposed and complementary aspects of the geological trope suggest a characterization of history that is not metaphysically grounded in something external, objective, and timeless. Phenomenology's "grounding" of historical knowledge is thus ultimately "Copernican" in the Kantian sense: while it acknowledges the (relative) fixity and historical facticity of objects and events, it argues for the dependence of this historicity on the more primordial historicity of the experiencing subject. But since this very primordial historicity is understood in terms of the ongoing task of investigating the changing structures of lived experiencing, and not in terms of categories determinable once-and-for-all, this is no simple stable ground, but a movement, an infinite task whose center of gravity is not any object "out there," but the lived temporality of human historical experience: the always-eventful sedimentation of the soil of history.

Notes

1. The historical overview offered here is indebted to that of W. H. Walsh, *Philosophy of History: An Introduction* (New York: Harper Torchbooks, 1960), pp. 42ff.
2. Cf. David Carr, *Time, Narrative, and History* (Bloomington, IN: Indiana University Press, 1986), p.1.
3. I take this description to also apply, for example, to the work of Foucault, with his accounts of the "shifting sands" and "fault lines" of historical epistemes in *The Order of Things*, and even to the later Wittgenstein's description of the "riverbed of thoughts" in the manuscripts collected in *On Certainty*. Although not phenomenologists per se, it is no accident that both authors bear important and complicated relationships to the phenomenological tradition. I explore their uses of the geological trope alongside more extended discussions of Heidegger, Husserl, and Merleau-Ponty in a longer paper on this topic currently in preparation.
4. Cf. Søren Gosvig Olesen, *Transcendental History*, trans. David Possen (New York: Palgrave Macmillan, 2013), p. 108.
5. As Carr has put this goal in his recent and largely phenomenological work on history, "descriptively we must strike a balance between two extremes: over-stressing our inherence in the present by treating it as an isolating *from* past and future, and over-stressing our openness to past and future by treating it as a supra-temporal perspective" (*Time, Narrative, and History*, p. 42).
6. A conception investigated at great length, though in a manner different from that presented here and not directly concerned with questions of history, in Lee Braver, *Groundless Grounds: A Study of Wittgenstein and Heidegger* (Cambridge, MA: MIT Press, 2012).
7. Martin Heidegger. *Being and Time*, trans. John Macquarrie and Edward Robinson (San Francisco: Harper and Row, 1962), p. 427, italics in original.
8. Ibid, p. 41.
9. Ibid, p. 433.
10. Ibid, p. 427, italics in original.
11. BT 433, my emphasis.
12. Ibid, p. 433.
13. Edmund Husserl, *The Crisis of European Sciences and Transcendental Phenomenology*, trans. and ed. David Carr (Evanston, IL: Northwestern University Press, 1970), p. 173.
14. Ibid, p. 371, my emphasis.
15. Ibid, p. 349, my emphasis.
16. Ibid, pp. 23–24.
17. Ibid, p. 371, my emphasis.
18. Ibid, p. 370.
19. Ibid, p. 373.
20. Maurice Merleau-Ponty, *Phenomenology of Perception*, trans. Donald A. Landes (New York: Routledge, 2012), pp.131–132.
21. Ibid, p. 416.
22. Ibid, pp. 466–467.
23. Ibid, p. 371.

„ICH HABE KÖNIGSBERG BRENNEN SEHEN"

Überlegungen zur Responsivität geschichtlicher Erfahrung und den Erfahrungscharakter der Responsivität

Thomas Schwarz Wentzer

Inwiefern ist ‚Geschichte' ein Phänomen? In welchem Sinne ist Geschichte als Phänomen gegeben, d.h. erfahrbar und erlebbar? Wie gibt sich und gibt es Geschichte?

Die folgenden Überlegungen versuchen, das Phänomen Geschichte als *geschichtliche Erfahrung* zu beschreiben. Ich möchte also fragen, was es heißt, geschichtliche Erfahrung zu machen, d.h. geschichtliche Erfahrung zu teilen, zu erleiden und zu deuten. Ich gehe davon aus, daß Menschen geschichtliche Wesen sind, insofern das, was Menschen heute oder morgen erfahren, bestimmt ist durch die Art und Weise, wie sie oder bestimmte andere Menschen (ihrer Familie, Generation, sozialen Gruppe, Kultur, Religionsgemeinschaft, Sprache, Nation, Hautfarbe etc.) lebten und gelebt haben. Alles, was Menschen erleben, findet unter bestimmten historischen Bedingungen statt, die zu einer bestimmten Zeit an einem bestimmten Ort gelten. Neue Erfahrungen mögen den Horizont erweitern oder bisherige Traditionen sprengen. Doch sie sind neu bloß vor dem Hintergrund einer bereits zugänglichen Sicht der Dinge, die Deutungsangebote liefert. Erfahrungen machen heißt demnach, nie bei Null anzufangen. Die These – Menschen sind geschichtliche Wesen – meint also zunächst trivialerweise, daß es keine menschliche Lebensform gibt, die nicht irgendwie im weitesten Sinne kulturell geprägt ist. So verstanden beschreibt 'Geschichtlichkeit' ein gleichsam anonymes, historisch flexibles Apriori, das relativ zu bestimmten Variablen wie Religion, Geschlecht, Sprache oder soziale Herkunft das komplexe Hintergrundgefüge individueller wie kollektiver Existenz ausmacht. Wie Husserl einmal salopp formuliert: „Jedes Volk und Völkchen hat seine Welt [...] und danach [...] ,sein' Apriori."[1]

Wenn Geschichte selbst aber als Phänomen gegeben sein soll, so muß diese geschichtliche Bedingtheit selbst erfahrbar sein. Eben dies ist die leitende Hypothese der folgenden Überlegungen. Ich gehe also davon aus, daß sich Geschichtlichkeit erfahren läßt, daß es mithin Erfahrungen gibt, in denen wir uns als geschichtlich erfahren, und die deshalb geschichtliche Erfahrungen genannt werden dürfen. Geschichtlichkeit bezeichnet folglich nicht nur das Sediment einer durch Sozialisation und Überlieferung vermittelten sozio-kulturellen Kompetenz, das als die vielbeschriebene 'zweite Natur' des Menschen beschrieben werden kann. Geschichtlichkeit meint darüber hinaus die Fähigkeit, sich selbst geschichtlich zu erfahren. Diesem emphatischeren, stärkeren Begriff von geschichtlicher Erfahrung nach sind Menschen geschichtliche Wesen, weil sie ihre geschichtliche Existenz als solche erfahren, weil sie also eine Erfahrung mit ihrer Geschichte machen und diese ihre Geschichte als solche ausdrücklich wird. Eben dies meint geschichtliche Erfahrung. Und in eben dieser Perspektive kann man von der Gegebenheit des Phänomens ‚Geschichte' sprechen. – Was das heißen kann, sollen die folgenden Überlegungen, die ihren Ausgangspunkt in einer autobiographischen Fallstudie nehmen, beispielhaft anzeigen.

Ich bewege mich mit diesem Anliegen im Niemandsland zwischen einer Theorie der Geschichte von Droysen bis Koselleck, einer Philosophie der Geschichte von Hegel bis zu Benjamin, einer Phänomenologie des Historischen von Husserl und Heidegger bis zu Gadamer, einer Poetik oder Narratologie des Historischen von Schapp und Ricoeur bis zu David Carr.[2] In dieses theoretische Feld möchte ich den Begriff der *Responsivität* einbringen, wie er insbesondere von Bernhard Waldenfels entwickelt wurde,[3] auf dem Gebiet des Historischen und der geschichtlichen Erfahrung jedoch noch keine Anwendung fand. Weil das Anliegen dieses Beitrags eher darin besteht, dem Phänomen Geschichte nachzudenken, als bestimmte Theorien über Geschichte und Geschichtlichkeit zu referieren, werde ich mich den genannten und anderen Repräsentanten eher sporadisch, und nicht exegetisch widmen. Es geht mir schlicht darum, meine eigene geschichtliche Erfahrung zu artikulieren und philosophisch zu verstehen.

Die folgenden Überlegungen gliedern sich in fünf Abschnitte:
1) Hegel und die Erfahrung
2) Flucht aus Ostpreussen
3) Geschichtliche Erfahrung als Erfahrung diachroner Distribution
4) Substitution und Responsivität geschichtlicher Erfahrung
5) Epilog

Hegel und die Erfahrung

In der Einleitung zu Hegels *Enzyklopädie der philosophischen Wissenschaften* von 1830 finden wir folgende berühmte Formulierung:

„Das Prinzip der Erfahrung enthält die unendlich wichtige Bestimmung, daß für das Annehmen und Fürwahrhalten eines Inhalts der Mensch selbst *dabei sein* müsse, bestimmter, daß er solchen Inhalt mit der *Gewißheit seiner selbst* in Einigkeit und vereinigt finde. Er muß selbst dabei sein, sei es nur mit seinen äußerlichen Sinnen, oder aber mit seinem tiefern Geiste, seinem wesentlichen Selbstbewußtsein." [4]

Das *Dabeisein* unterscheidet also Hegel zufolge die Erfahrung von anderen kognitiven Aneignungsprozessen. Für das Prinzip der Erfahrung gilt eben dies, daß man sie selbst macht. Dieses Dabeisein darf nicht, wie Hegel präzisiert, als gleichsam unbeteiligtes Zuschauen mißverstanden werden. Dabeisein bedeutet, den Erfahrungsgehalt selbst als gehaltvoll zu erkennen und anzueignen. Was ich aufgrund von Erfahrung weiß oder kann, habe ich mir angeeignet, so daß ich mir auch über den Ursprung meines Wissens oder Könnens bewußt bin, nämlich aus meiner eigenen Erfahrung. Wie Hegel richtig sieht und als ‚Gewißheit seiner selbst' ausdrückt, ist Erfahrung eine *reflexive Leistung*; Erfahrung ist immer die Einheit der Erfahrung von etwas und der Erfahrung seiner selbst. Ich erfahre mich also als ein Wesen, das Erfahrung macht; und in diesem Satz beschreibt das Verbum nicht das Entgegennehmen einer Kenntnis oder Information, sondern eine Vollzugs- oder Erlebnisqualität.

Wie steht es nun mit geschichtlichen Erfahrungen? In einem trivialen Sinne sind alle unsere Erfahrungen historisch, insofern sie in der Zeit und unter bestimmten historischen Bedingungen stattfinden. Geschichtlich in eigentlichem Sinne sind sie aber dann, wenn sie nicht nur unter solchen Bedingungen stattfinden, sondern diese selbst zu Erfahrung bringen und ausdrücken. Eine geschichtliche Erfahrung besteht diesem Gedanken nach darin, sich selbst als geschichtliches Wesen zu erfahren. Wenn wir der Hegelschen Bestimmung noch einmal folgen wollen, so bedeutet dies, daß wir selbst dabei sind, wenn wir historische Bedingungen als unsere eigenen annehmen und fürwahrhalten. Wir erfahren dann Geschichte, indem wir *uns* als geschichtlich erfahren. Wir erfahren nichts über Geschichte, sondern wir erfahren Geschichte, und wir erfahren uns als die-Geschichte-Erfahrenden. Wir lauschen nicht fremden Erzählungen in ästhetisch objektivierender, unbeteiligter Distanz, sondern sind dabei, mittendrin, in unserer Geschichte. Es mag deshalb für deutsche Ohren angemessener scheinen, von *geschichtlicher* Erfahrung anstatt von *historischer* Erfahrung zu sprechen. Denn *historia* meint zunächst die Kunde, die *fama*, die Erzählung, die zuweilen aus zweiter Hand erzählt, wohingegen ‚Geschichte' etymologisch auf das Geschehen selbst verweist, das die *historia* nur bekundet.

Allerdings ist dieser feine Unterschied eher von vorläufiger Gültigkeit. Wie im Folgenden deutlich werden wird, besteht die geschichtliche Erfahrung gerade in der Aufhebung oder Dekonstruktion des Unterschieds von *res gestae* und *historia rerum gestarum,* von Geschichte und Historie.

Flucht aus Ostpreußen

Meine Überlegungen zum Phänomen der Geschichte, die sich um geschichtliche Erfahrung bemühen, nehmen ihren Ausgangspunkt in einer Art Fallstudie, einer autobiographischen Erzählung. Die Familie meines Vaters stammt aus dem früheren Ostpreußen, einer Region, die von Anbeginn der Gründung eines deutschen Nationalstaates unter Bismarck 1871 zum Reichsgebiet zählte. Nach dem Ersten Weltkrieg eine Exklave, wurde Ostpreußen in den Potsdamer Verträgen 1945 zwischen der Sowjetunion und Polen aufgeteilt; freilich verblieb es gemäß dem Völkerrecht deutsches Staatsgebiet bis zur deutschen Wiedervereinigung 1990 und dem sogenannten Zwei-plus-Vier Vertrag. Der nördliche Teil Ostpreußens unter dem Namen ‚Oblast‘ gehört heute zu Russland und ist eine Enklave auf dem Gebiet der EU, gelegen zwischen Litauen und Polen. Seine Hauptstadt heißt Kaliningrad, das frühere Königsberg.

Die Familie also stammt aus einer Ortschaft in der Nähe von Tilsit, heute Sovetsk, in Sichtweite der Memel, dem Grenzfluss zu Litauen, ein Fluß, der vor dem Zweiten Weltkrieg die äußerste nordöstliche Grenze des Deutschen Reiches ausmachte. Die Eltern betrieben einen kleineren Bauernhof, gerade groß genug, um die große Familie ernähren zu können. Mein Vater, geboren 1938, war das zwölfte von insgesamt dreizehn Kindern. Er hätte, so erzählte er, wohl ein Schmied (oder Automechaniker) werden sollen, wäre nicht der Krieg und die Flucht dazwischen gekommen. Hitler begann den Krieg gegen Polen 1939 und überfiel die Sowjetunion im Juni 1941. Die Grenzzone Ostpreußens wurde Frontgebiet, zunächst als Aufmarschzone, dann als eine der am heftigsten umkämpften Regionen des deutschen Kernlandes, die Hitler immer wieder als ‚Festung‘ deklarierte, die sich niemals ergeben und bis zuletzt verteidigt würde. Trotz des Zusammenbruchs der deutschen Ostfront nach der Schlacht bei Stalingrad und des Vormarsches der Roten Armee war es Zivilisten untersagt, zu fliehen; denn man kämpfte ja an der Heimatfront, und auch hier war es bei Strafe untersagt, zu desertieren.

Im Dezember 1944, mitten im bitterkalten Winter, machte die Familie sich endlich auf zur Flucht, kurz bevor die Rote Armee im Januar 1945 die Memel überschritt. Die Familie – das waren zu diesem Zeitpunkt die Mutter mit ihren vier kleinsten Kindern, hierunter mein Vater—floh gen Westen; die Mutter hoffte irgendwie, auf eines der zivilen Flüchtlingsschiffe zu gelangen, die aus Pillau und aus Danzig Flüchtlinge evakuierten, übrigens auch nach Schweden und Dänemark.

Mein Vater war zum Zeitpunkt dieser Flucht gerade sechs Jahre alt. Er hat mir oft von den Ereignissen der Flucht erzählt, von der Flucht über das gefrorene Haff, den abgefrorenen Zehen, den Tieffliegerangriffen auf die Flüchtlingstrecks, den Pferdekadavern am Rande, den Kindergräbern aus Steinen auf festgefrorener Erde, den schneeweißen Nächten und den russischen Soldaten, den Suppen aus Kartoffelschalen. Er hat all dies immer aus der Perspektive des Kindes erzählt, sehr lebendig, übrigens nie aus Ressentiment oder Bitterkeit, weder gegenüber dem Regime der Nazis und ihrer Kriegswut noch den russischen Verteidigern, die zu brutalen Eroberern geworden waren. Er sprach nie wie jemand, dessen Welt in den Feuern des Krieges untergegangen war. In all diesen Erzählungen kam irgendwann der Satz vor ‚Ich habe Königsberg brennen sehen.‘ Ich weiß nicht, wann ich diesen Satz zum ersten Mal gehört habe. Ich weiß aber noch, daß mein Vater diesen Satz immer mit besonderem Nachdruck formulierte, als Fazit gleichsam, und zugleich mit der Autorität des Augenzeugens, der ein historisches Ereignis mit eigenen Augen gesehen hat. ‚Ich habe Königsberg brennen sehen‘.

Was für ein Satz. Was bedeutet dieser Satz? So oft mein Vater diesen Satz formulierte, so oft stellten sich bei mir innere Bilder ein. Als ob ich selbst eine brennende Stadt sehen würde, im sicheren Abstand gewissermaßen, als vorbeiziehender Reisender. Bilder von Rauchsäulen am Horizont, Feuergeläut von den Glocken der zerstörten Gotteshäuser, vor sich hin schwelende Ruinen von ehemaligen Häusern einer Stadt, die einmal die blühende Hauptstadt Ostpreußens war. Ein Junge, der seine Mutter fragt: „Mama, was ist das?" – „Da, mein Junge, brennt Königsberg."

Was weiß ich, was wußte mein Vater denn eigentlich von Königsberg? Was sah er, als er Königsberg brennen sah? Auf welches Ereignis bezieht sich der Satz ‚Ich habe Königsberg brennen sehen‘? Was ist der Erfahrungsgehalt, den dieser Satz ausdrückt? Für meinen sechsjährigen Vater, der Königsberg vor seiner Zerstörung nie kennengelernt hatte, war Königsberg wahrscheinlich der Inbegriff einer großen Stadt, der Stadt, die bereits eine Reise weit weg war, die Stadt, in der die ältere Schwester wohnte, die ihm vielleicht mal Süßigkeiten oder eine Postkarte mitgebracht hatte. Für ihn war diese Stadt wahrscheinlich eine Kinderprojektion, eine Stadt mit Schloß und Kirchtürmen, Brücken und Flüssen, Autos und Straßenbahn. All das brannte. Für mich bedeutete dieser Satz immer etwas anderes und immer mehr, je älter ich wurde. War es zunächst nur eine Stadt in der Heimat meines Vaters, so wurde es im Laufe meines Studiums die Stadt E.T.A. Hoffmanns und Käthe Kollwitz', aber vor allem die Stadt Immanuel Kants. Des Mannes, dessen Ethik den Gipfel der Philosophie der Aufklärung darstellt, die die Würde des Menschen in seiner Autonomie begreift, in der Fähigkeit also, über alle kontingenten Verhältnissen hinweg die Autorität praktischer Vernunft zu behaupten, und in dieser moralischen Behauptung unbedingt gut, d.h. frei zu sein. Kant behauptete die unverletzbare moralische Würde jedes einzelnen Menschen qua Mensch innerhalb der deutschen Philosophie. Wenn ich den Satz meines Vaters jetzt höre – ‚Ich habe Königsberg brennen sehen' – so beschreibt er das Fanal des Untergangs der europäischen Aufklärung, der Vernichtung der Menschenwürde, der Zerstörung des Guten, nicht zuletzt der moralischen Integrität alles dessen, was in irgendeiner Weise mit der deutschen Kultur zusammenhängt. Es brennt dann nicht nur Königsberg. Es brennt eine Welt. Es brennt das Projekt der europäischen Aufklärung und das Versprechen der Moderne, ausgedrückt vielleicht am eindrücklichsten in der Formulierung Hegels, demzufolge Geschichte der Fortschritt im Bewußtsein der Freiheit sei.[5]

Das Bild des brennenden Königsbergs, der Satz meines Vaters, ist für mich eine persönliche Erinnerung an ein grausames Jahrhundert, seine Weltkriege, die weitestgehende Vernichtung der europäischen jüdischen Kultur und die Ermordung ihrer Menschen, an die Entfesselung der Atombombe und die Erfindung der Vernichtung des Bruttosozialproduktes durch Wettrüsten. Es ist ein Symbol für die Zerstörungswut und die Grausamkeit menschlicher Zivilisation. So genommen verdichtet sich in diesem Satz wie in einem Prisma die Geschichte der Aufklärung und ihres Fortschrittsversprechens ebenso wie die Geschichte ihres Untergangs durch Selbstzerstörung. Dieser Satz erzählt die Geschichte des Untergangs der Geschichte. Er ist para-geschichtlich, kommentiert sich selbst, indem er das Ereignis der Verunmöglichung von Geschichte in der Form geschichtlicher Erfahrung formuliert. In den Flammen von Königsberg geht sie, Geschichte, in Rauch auf. Was bleibt, sind ihre Ruinen, die Erinnerung an vergangene Städte und ihre Versprechen; eine ‚Schädelstätte' (gemäß dem Zyniker im Geiste Hegel)[6] und ‚zum Himmel wachsende Trümmerhaufen'[7] (gemäß dem Benjaminschen Engel der Geschichte).

Geschichtliche Erfahrung als Erfahrung diachroner Distribution

Doch ist obige Reflexion gerechtfertigt? Ich habe, das gebe ich gerne zu, in gewisser Weise übertrieben; ich wollte mit Absicht einen Sinn provozieren, der den ursprünglichen Erlebnisgehalt übersteigt. Ich habe eine Aussage, die ursprünglich auf ein Wahrnehmungserlebnis bezogen war, mit einem Gehalt gefüllt, der sie von der ursprünglichen Wahrnehmung und ihrer Erinnerung ablöst, so daß die Aussage gar nicht mehr jenes Wahrnehmungserlebnis oder seine Erinnerung ausdrückt, sondern meine Deutung. Ich behaupte trotzdem, daß meine Interpretation den eigentlichen Gehalt jener Aussage widergibt. Die Aussage meines Vaters, eine minimale Geschichte im Sinne von Wilhelm Schapp, wurde also von mir aufgegriffen und ausgedeutet, mancher wird meinen, defätistisch aufgebläht oder apokalyptisch verfremdet. Darf man das? Mein Vater war ein Kind; er hat nicht den Verlust des Projekts der Moderne betrachtet. Auch seine Mutter, meine Großmutter, die nur vier Jahre in die Schule ging, hat keineswegs die europäische Aufklärung und ihr durch Kant verbrieftes Menschenbild brennen sehen. Zumindest war sie sich dessen nicht bewußt. Mutter und Kind haben jene historische Identifikation, die das erlebte Ereignis als Zeichen eines größeren, umfassenderen Zusammenhangs deutet, nicht vollzogen. Ist meine Deutung deshalb ‚falsch'? Wohl kaum. Ist sie ‚richtig'? Wer weiß, wahrscheinlich sind ‚richtig' und ‚falsch' unzureichende Kategorien. Es findet eine Umbesetzung des Erfahrungsgehaltes statt, die – folgt man Ricoeur, Blumenberg und anderen – das Herz der *Metapher* und damit des sprachlichen Verstehens ausmacht. Ich will diese Spur der Metaphorologie oder der Allegorese, im allgemeineren Sinne, der Symboltheorie hier nicht weiter verfolgen. Mir geht es um die diachrone Dissoziation von Aussage und Erfahrungsgehalt, die sich einstellt, wenn ich mir den Satz meines Vaters vergegenwärtige. Ich, der ich zuhöre, erfahre mich dabei nicht bloß als passiver Zuhörer, der eine Information einfach nur zur Kenntnis nimmt. Meinem Vater lauschend, erfahre ich seine, erfahre ich meine Geschichte. Ich habe teil an einem Erfahrungsgehalt, der längst nicht mehr nur meinem Vater gehört, sondern an dem auch ich teilhabe, und an dem ich erfahrend mitwirke, indem ich ihn verstehe. Vielleicht ist dieser distributive Aspekt der gemeinsamen Teilhabe an der geschichtlichen Erfahrung meines Vaters der eigentliche, geheime Grund für das Pathos seiner Erzählung. Das Pathos formuliert einen Appell, einen Anspruch, den ich beantworte, indem ich die Erfahrung imaginativ teile. Ich verstehe, daß es eben auch *meine* Geschichte ist, die mein Vater stellvertretend für mich erlebt hat. Noch bevor ich geboren wurde, hat mein Vater für mich Königsberg brennen sehen.

Aber: *wer* ist denn dann eigentlich *bei was* ‚dabei‘? Worin besteht eigentlich der Erfahrungsgehalt, den der Satz ‚Ich habe Königsberg brennen sehen?‘ ausdrückt? Ist dieser Satz eine Aussage, die einen propositionalen Gehalt wiedergibt? Ist dieser propositionale Gehalt identisch mit dem Erfahrungsgehalt? Wohl kaum. Vielleicht muß man doch wie bereits oben die Terminologie der *Logischen Untersuchungen* Husserls bemühen: Handelt es sich um ein Wahrnehmungserlebnis, das dieser Satz ausdrückt? Kommt das in diesem Satz Gemeinte zu originärer Gegebenheit in der Wahrnehmung meines Vaters? In diesem Falle wäre mein Vater Inhaber der Deutungskompetenz des Erfahrungsgehaltes, und wenn ich oder jemand anders die Erzählung meines Vaters widergibt, wäre dieser Gehalt nur symbolisch gegeben, in signitiver, nicht originärer Anschauung. Der Satz meines Vaters wäre ein ‚Anzeichen‘, dessen Funktion die Vergegenwärtigung eines Wahrnehmungsgehaltes darstellt, das gegenwärtig gegeben war eben im Akt des ursprünglichen Wahrnehmungserlebnisses. Derridas Lektüre dieser Zusammenhänge in *La voix et le phénomène* hat die paradoxe Grundlage dieser Theorie aufgezeigt. Mich interessiert nicht so sehr die Dekonstruktion der Husserlschen Sprachtheorie als solche, sondern der Hinweis auf die Vorurteile der Metaphysik der Präsenz, die auch in einer allzu naiven Vorstellung von geschichtlicher Erfahrung liegen mögen.

Die Erfahrung, um die es mir geht, entzieht sich dem Schema von Proposition und propositionalem Gehalt, von *idea* und *impression* im Sinne Humes oder dem von Bedeutungsintention und Erfüllungsintention im Sinne Husserls, dem Dreischritt Diltheys von Erlebnis-Ausdruck-Verstehen. Geschichtliche Erfahrung erfüllt sich nicht im Wahrnehmungserlebnis oder einer Urevidenz. Mein Verstehen ist nicht die inverse Operation zum Erleben meines Vaters. Am Beispiel meines Vaters formuliert: Die geschichtliche Erfahrung besteht nicht darin, die Wahrnehmung einer brennenden Stadt zu artikulieren oder sich in diese einzufühlen. Der Satz ist keine Aussage, die einen eindeutigen Sachverhalt oder propositionalen Gehalt wiedergibt. Die in ihm geschilderte Erfahrung beschränkt sich nicht auf ein singuläres lokalisierbares Ereignis, sondern auf den Zusammenbruch einer Welt; und das Subjekt dieses Satzes, jenes ‚ich‘ meines Vaters, weist eine analoge Offenheit auf, die trotz der expliziten Autorschaft jener Erfahrung gerade nicht als Exklusivität verstanden werden darf, die die beschriebene Erfahrung privatisierte. Jener Satz schöpft die Erfahrung nicht aus. Es scheint mir, als ob mein Vater genau dies erzählen wollte, wenn er seinen Satz formulierte. Als ob es eine Erfahrung gab, deren diffuser Reichtum die Vorstellungskraft sowohl des erlebenden Sechsjährigen wie die des sie nacherzählenden Vierzig- oder Fünfzigjährigen als auch die des zuhörenden Zwanzigjährigen übersteigt. Die sich in jenem Satz artikulierende Erfahrung besteht gerade in dem doppelten Appell an meinen Vater, ihrem Erzähler, und an mich, seinem Zuhörer. Sie besteht darin, das Ereignis des brennenden Königsbergs als Ereignis einer kollektiven Erfahrung zu artikulieren, die mein Vater sozusagen stellvertretend, nicht zuletzt für mich, gemacht hat. Es ist eine Erfahrung, die durch meinen Vater zu Worte kommt, zu der er sich responsiv verhält, indem er jenen Satz äußert, und an der ich teilhabe, wenn ich sie deute und so erfahre. In dieser Beschreibung wird der Satz meines Vaters zu einer gemeinsamen Erfahrung. Das brennende Königsberg ist dann auch meine Erfahrung. Auch ich bin dabei, teilnehmend, zuhörend, eingenommen von einer Erfahrung, deren Bedeutung das Erleben übersteigt.

Dieser Gedanke läßt sich noch etwas weiter verfolgen. Das Dabeisein, von dem Hegel sprach, begründet Autorschaft und Autorität. Keine Erfahrung ohne die Autorität des Dabeiseins, ohne die Augenzeugenschaft, ohne das Ausgesetztsein in die Unbilden eigenen Erlebens. Hierauf gründet sich der subjektive Wahrheitsanspruch, das Recht, den Erfahrungsgehalt sich selbst zuzuschreiben und entsprechend zu artikulieren. Erfahrung verleiht Kompetenz. Im Beispiel meines Vaters ist aber der Erfahrungsgehalt überdeterminiert.[8] Das, was da brennt, läßt sich gar nicht eingrenzen; und ebenso gibt das Pathos des Erzählens zu verstehen, daß mein Vater selbst gar nicht genau weiß, was das, was er gesehen hat, eigentlich bedeutet. Nur, *daß* es etwas bedeutet, und zwar so, daß es von geschichtlicher Bedeutung ist, also auch mich betrifft, das ist meinem Vater klar, und eben diese Überdeterminiertheit wird in seiner Erzählung zum Ausdruck gebracht. Mit anderen Worte, der Satz ,*Ich habe Königsberg brennen sehen*' ist elliptisch, denn er läßt offen, was genau der Gehalt der Erfahrung ist, die er artikuliert. Er unterstreicht den Ereignischarakter jener Erfahrung und überläßt es mir, der ich zuhöre, den genauen Erfahrungsgehalt zu erfassen. ,*Ich habe Königsberg brennen sehen*' meint dann, ,*Ich habe Königsberg brennen sehen, und es brannte nicht nur Königsberg, und es war nicht nur ich, der dies sah, als er all das sah und nicht sah*'. Wenn ich meinen Vater erzählen lasse und den Satz ,*Ich habe Königsberg brennen sehen*' höre, empfange ich also keineswegs eine Information über einen Sachverhalt. Vielmehr werde ich zum Teilnehmer jener ursprünglichen Erfahrung. Ich bin selbst dabei. Es ist dann keineswegs so, daß nur mein Vater geschichtliche Erfahrung

macht oder erleidet, die ich dann emphatisch nacherlebe oder kognitiv verar-
beite. Ich werde selbst zum Subjekt der Erfahrung, insofern die Überbestimmt-
heit des Satzes und das Pathos seiner Erfahrungsqualität mich zum Dabeisein
auffordern. Ich kann nicht anders, als Dabeisein zu müssen, als selbst zu erfahren – wenn schon nicht „mit [meinen, TSW] äußerlichen Sinnen" so doch mit
meinem „tiefern Geiste, [meinem, TSW] wesentlichen Selbstbewußtsein".

Geschichtliche Erfahrung ist, so meine These, diachron distributiv. D.h. daß
zu ihrer Qualität als Erfahrung gehört, geteilt zu werden, nie nur privat, sondern notwendig kollektiv zu sein. Die Distribution geschichtlicher Erfahrung
geschieht diachron, also über die Zeit. Mein Vater und ich teilen so gesehen
eine Erfahrung, und in jeder Vergegenwärtigung jenes Satzes anerkenne ich
meine Teilnahme an der geschilderten Erfahrung. Es ist meine Geschichte, die
da brannte, als mein Vater Königsberg brennen sah.

Substitution und Responsivität geschichtlicher Erfahrung

Das Dabeisein, das Hegel als das Charakteristikum der Erfahrung ausmachte,
ist in meiner Deutung geschichtlicher Erfahrung also durch seinen Stellvertre-
tercharakter gekennzeichnet. Es ist substitutiv. Jemand macht Erfahrungen für
jemand Anderes. Die Erfahrung wäre keine geschichtliche Erfahrung, wenn sie
privat bleiben würde. Das Erzählen alleine ist dabei nicht hinreichend, individuelle Erfahrungen zu kollektiven und historisch bedeutsamen Erfahrungen zu
machen. Narrativität gründet nicht geschichtliche Erfahrung. Denn wir erzählen von vielen Dingen, die wir im Laufe unseres Lebens erfahren haben und die
biographisch von entscheidender Bedeutung sein mögen – die Geschichte meines ersten Autounfalls und meiner Verletzungen, meiner ersten Liebe und meines gebrochenen Herzens, meines zweiten Hamsters und seines plötzlichen
Ablebens etc. – ohne, daß wir sie als geschichtliche Erfahrungen begreifen
würden. Der Satz meines Vaters jedoch, ‚Ich habe Königsberg brennen sehen‘,
betont gerade durch die Hervorhebung des Ichs, wie wichtig es war, daß diese
Erfahrung für uns, für mich, gemacht wurde. Ich kann mich in ihr wiedererken-
nen und selbst dabei sein, insofern ich mich als Adressat eines in diesem Satz
mit ausgesagtem Appell erkenne. Das Familienband von Vater und Sohn unterstreicht so gesehen bloß die diachrone Kollektivität geschichtlicher Erfahrung.
Ich begreife mich als geschichtliches Wesen, eben weil ich vergangene Erfahrungen als zu mir gehörige Erfahrungen, als Erfahrungen meiner Geschichte,
begreife. Ich verhalte mich also responsiv, indem ich auf eben diesen Appell

antworte, so ich die Geschichte meines Vaters als meine Geschichte begreife. Substitution und Responsivität sind in dieser Deutung also die beiden Charakteristika geschichtlicher Erfahrung.

Ich sehe in dieser Struktur übrigens den Kern christologischen Denkens. Denn die Passionsgeschichte Jesu ist in ihrem Kern eine Geschichte der Stellvertretung. Der Gekreuzigte stirbt den Tod am Kreuze stellvertretend und im Voraus für alle Gläubigen. Je nach Konfession ist Christus als das Lamm Gottes sowohl Opfer wie Erlöser, der stellvertretend für uns Leiden und Sünden dieser Welt auf sich nimmt und uns abnimmt. Erlösung heißt, von Sünde und Leid befreit zu sein. An dieser Tat hat je nach Konfession Anteil, wer getauft ist oder, wie bei Luther, glaubt. Sowohl Taufe wie der Glaube allein sind aber dann Rezeptionshandlungen, die auf das Substitutionsereignis der Heilstat Jesu *antworten*. Der Substitutionsgedanke setzt also den Responsivitätsgedanken voraus, denn der Gläubige muß den Tod Jesu als ein Ereignis deuten, das *für ihn*, den Gläubigen, eintraf. Christlicher Glaube in diesem Sinne ist responsiv, insofern der Gläubige durch den Gottestod angesprochen wird oder sich angesprochen fühlt, sich als Angesprochener erkennt und entsprechend, lutherisch religiös gesprochen: glaubend, antwortet.

Ich sehe im Tod Christi daher das Urphänomen geschichtlicher Erfahrung. Die Heilsbotschaft des Evangeliums baut geradezu auf die Logik geschichtlicher Erfahrung, die obigen Überlegungen zufolge darin besteht, daß ein Mensch sich aus einer Erfahrung versteht, die er nicht selbst ursprünglich initiierte, und die er aber doch als seine eigene weiß, als etwas, was für ihn erfahren wurde, woran er folglich selbst teilhat. Geschichte ist also nicht etwas, was Menschen machen, sondern etwas, was Menschen als für sie gemacht erfahren oder erfahren müssen. Es ist übrigens kein Zufall, daß Hegel und Schleiermacher, die unabhängig voneinander den Begriff ‚Geschichtlichkeit' etwa zeitgleich erfunden haben, diesen Begriff an der Menschwerdung Gottes in der Person Jesus Christus erläutern.[9]

Das Verhältnis von Substitution und Responsivität liegt also dort zugrunde, wo die Spätgeborenen sich als von der Vergangenheit Angesprochene erkennen und sich entsprechend dieser Erkenntnis verhalten. Wir sind geschichtliche Wesen, insofern wir auf entsprechende Einladungen, Anforderungen oder Ansprüche antworten, die uns wie Botschaften aus der Vergangenheit erreichen. Vergangene Ereignisse werden in geschichtlicher Perspektive zu Erfahrungsangeboten, zu Anforderungen oder Ansprüchen, also zu etwas, zu dem wir uns immer schon verhalten und auf das wir angemessene Antworten finden müssen, sobald wir einen solchen Anspruch als solchen vernehmen.

Mit den Begriffen Substitution und Responsivität lege ich mir jedenfalls meine eigenen Erfahrungen zurecht, wenn ich als Deutscher etwa über die Stolpersteine im Kopfsteinpflaster stolpere, die in vielen deutschen Städten an die vertriebenen und ermordeten Juden erinnern. Ich werde hier angesprochen, und zwar so, daß ich nicht nur gleichsam beiläufig wie bei der Lektüre einer veralteten Todesanzeige von der Ermordung anderer Menschen erfahre. Sondern so, daß ich jenen Stolperstein als Teil meiner Geschichte erfahre, als etwas, was sich an mich richtet, weil jemand anders an meiner statt erfahren mußte, was es heißt, verfolgt und rechtlos in einem Unrechtsstaat zu sein. Ich kann gar nicht anders, als zu antworten, d.h. Verantwortung zu übernehmen, mich ansprechen und angehen zu lassen, und so wiederum mich für Erfahrung zu öffnen.

Die eigentümliche Nachträglichkeit geschichtlicher Erfahrung und die These ihrer Responsivität kennt noch eine Steigerung. Eine Passage aus Benjamins zweiter sogenannter These Über die Geschichte liest sich wie folgt:

„Die Vergangenheit führt einen heimlichen Index mit, durch den sie auf die Erlösung verwiesen wird. Streift denn nicht uns selber ein Hauch der Luft, die um die Früheren gewesen ist? Ist nicht in Stimmen, denen wir unser Ohr schenken, ein Echo von nun verstummten? Haben die Frauen, die wir umwerben, nicht Schwestern, die sie nicht mehr gekannt haben? Ist dem so, dann besteht eine geheime Verabredung mit den gewesenen Geschlechtern und unserem. Dann sind wir auf der Erde erwartet worden. Dann ist uns wie jedem Geschlecht, das vor uns war, eine *schwache* messianische Kraft mitgegeben, an welche die Vergangenheit Anspruch hat. Billig ist dieser Anspruch nicht abzufertigen. Der historische Materialist weiß darum." (Benjamin, GS I.2., 693 f.)

Auch Benjamin zufolge läßt sich eine Art Band zwischen vergangenen Ereignissen und der Gegenwart ausmachen, die als Verpflichtung oder als Anspruch der Vergangenheit erfahren werden kann. Anders als im christlichen Erlösungsverständnis und seinem immer bereits gegebenem Heilsversprechen ist Benjamins Messianismus jedoch selbst responsiv. Nicht *wir* sind die Profiteure am Erlösungsversprechen; vielmehr erfahren wir uns selbst als Agenten oder Akteure im Erlösungsgeschehen, das sich an gewesenen Geschlechtern abspielt. Dabei ist klar, daß diese Reflexion Benjamins eine säkulare, historische Reflexion ist, keine religiöse. Der historische Materialist weiß um die Legitimität jener Ansprüche, die vergangene Geschlechter an uns stellen mögen. Die schwache messianische Kraft, von der Benjamin spricht, ist eine Kraft des historischen Bewußtseins, das sich über die Zeiten hinweg mit vergangenen Geschlechtern verbunden weiß, als gäbe es eine Verabredung. Im Benjaminschen Modell antwortet jede Gegenwart auf die Ansprüche der Vergangenheit, indem sie sich nicht nur als Angeredete erkennt, sondern Verantwortung für die Vergangenheit übernimmt. Nicht um des eigenen Seelenheils oder Glückes wegen, sondern weil sie sich immer schon als geschichtlich in die Verantwortung genommen erfährt. Folgen wir Benjamin, so hat mein Vater nicht nur für mich an meiner Statt Königsberg brennen sehen. Er hat einen Anspruch darauf, daß ich Verantwortung für diese Erfahrung übernehme und sie ihm abnehme.

Die Erlösungstat besteht danach in der Weitergabe des Erfahrungsgehaltes an die jeweils kommenden Generationen, besser gesagt, in der ausdrücklichen Übernahme des Erfahrungsgehaltes durch die jeweils aktuelle Generation. Folgen wir Benjamin, so besteht geschichtliche Erfahrung nicht nur in der diakronen Distribution geschichtlicher Erfahrung, die sich in der Logik von Substitution und Responsivität vollzieht. Sondern in einer Art Kompetenzübertragung, insofern ich mich von nun an als verantwortliches Subjekt jener Erfahrung begreife, die sich zunächst in meinem Vater, und ab jetzt in mir, Geltung verschafft. Insofern gibt es keine Gnade der späten Geburt, die mich von der Bürde der Vergangenheit entbindet, sondern Verantwortung als das Resultat ihrer responsiven Aneignung.

Man mag Zweifel haben, ob man Benjamins Vorschlag bis zum Ende gehen will, ob das responsive Verhalten der Gegenwart tatsächlich als messianische Kraft verstanden werden muß, und insbesondere, welche ethischen Implikationen dieser Vorschlag enthalten mag. Allerdings hilft mir Benjamins Beschreibung, mein eigenes Gefühl zu deuten, nämlich das Gefühl der Verantwortung vor der Vergangenheit; geschichtliche Erfahrung besteht dann gerade darin, sich von vergangenen Erfahrungen in die Pflicht genommen zu fühlen, auch und gerade dann, wenn man noch nicht weiß, welche konkreten Verpflichtungen oder ethischen Maximen sich daraus entnehmen lassen.

Obige Überlegungen lassen sich wie folgt zusammenfassen:

1) Es gibt so etwas wie geschichtliche Erfahrung, d.h. Erfahrungen der eigenen Geschichtlichkeit

2) Diese Erfahrungen sind qua Erfahrungen gekennzeichnet durch ihren Vollzug, d.h. durch das, was Hegel das ‚Dabeisein‘ nannte.

3) Dieses Dabeisein ist aber nicht individuell oder privat beschränkt, sondern

diachron distribuiert, d.h. auf mehrere Subjekte (evt. kollektive Identitäten wie Familien, Gruppen, soziale Verbände, Generationen etc.) über die Zeit verteilt.

4) Die Logik dieser Distribution läßt sich durch die Begriffe der Substitution und der Responsivität kennzeichnen. Das geschichtliche Subjekt ist danach einer Erfahrung ausgesetzt, die jemand anders an seiner Statt für es gemacht oder erlebt hat. Es erfährt sich als angesprochen und antwortet auf diesen Anspruch durch die Übernahme einer Verantwortung für den erfahrenen Gehalt.

5) Zwei Anmerkungen:

a. Was ich als Familiengeschichte und noch dazu als eine Art Leidensgeschichte erfahren habe, ist weder auf Familie noch auf Leid beschränkt. So habe ich in der Schule meiner Töchter vom Mauerfall und dem Revolutionsjahr 1989 erzählt und versuche, selbst den dänischen Kindern diese Geschichte als Teil *ihrer eigenen* jüngeren europäischen Geschichte zu erzählen.

b. Und noch eine wichtige Anmerkung: Die Logik von Substitution und Responsivität führt nicht in die Heldenverehrung oder die Hagiographie von Märtyrern. Sie beschreibt zunächst bloß die Möglichkeit, sich selbst aus der Erfahrung Anderer zu verstehen, indem diese Erfahrung zur eigenen wird, trotz des Zeitenabstands, der zwischen einer ursprünglichen substitutiven und einer nachträglichen responsiven Erfahrung liegen mag.

Epilog

Mein Vater starb vor drei Jahren. Ich habe erst nach seinem Tod begonnen, mich eingehender mit seiner Geschichte zu beschäftigen und ein wenig zu recherchieren. Ich habe die zwei noch lebenden älteren Schwestern meines Vaters interviewt. Dabei stellte ich folgendes fest:

Königsberg wurde bereits im August 1944 von englischen Geschwadern bombardiert und durch Phosphor-, also Brandbomben weitestgehend zerstört. Etwa 200.000 der 320.000 Einwohner wurden obdachlos. Die Stadt wurde im April 1945 von russischen Verbänden nach heftigen Kämpfen erobert.

Die Familie meines Vaters flüchtete aber im Dezember, vier Monate nach den Luftangriffen der Briten im August, und vier Monate vor der Eroberung der Roten Armee. Die britische Zerstörung kann mein Vater also gar nicht gesehen haben, denn da war die Familie noch am heimatlichen Bauernhof. Bei dem Beschuß durch die russische Artillerie war die Familie bereits in Danzig. Außerdem ergab die Rekonstruktion der Fluchtroute, daß die Familie etwa 30 Kilometer südlich an Königsberg vorbeizog. Mein Vater hat Königsberg also nie gesehen, weder vor den Bombardements, noch hinterher, und schon gar nicht brennend. Woher aber kam der Eindruck?

Wie ich aus meinen Interviews erfuhr, war die ältere Schwester seit Oktober 1943 Krankenschwesterschülerin in Königsberg. Sie erlebte die Bombardements; sie mußte unzählige Brandopfer versorgen. Sie erzählte mir von den Feuerorkanen, die durch die Stadt fegten, von einem Königsberg also, das tatsächlich über mehrere Tage brannte. Diese Schwester war damals 16 Jahre alt und floh Ende August traumatisiert aus dem Königsberger Krankenhaus. Sie konnte ihren Dienst einfach nicht mehr ausführen. Anstatt nun selbst direkt gen Westen zu fliehen, kehrte sie zurück zum heimatlichen Hof. Sie muß von ihren Erlebnissen erzählt haben, so eindringlich, daß mein Vater glaubte, er selbst habe Königsberg brennen sehen. Meine Geschichte beginnt also mit einer Substitution. Bereits mein Vater war im eigentlichen Sinne kein Augenzeuge, aber eben doch dabei.

Notes

1 E. Husserl, *Die Krisis der europäischen Wissenschaften und die transzendentale Phänomenologie,* Vol. 6, Den Haag: Nijhoff, 1954, S. 382.

2 Vgl. Droysen, J. G., *Historik: Vorlesungen über Enzyklopädie und Methodologie der Geschichte* (R. Hübner Ed. 4., unveränd. Aufl. ed.). München: Oldenbourg, 1960, R. Koselleck, *Vergangene Zukunft: zur Semantik geschichtlicher Zeiten* (1. Aufl. ed.), Frankfurt am Main: Suhrkamp, 1979, G. W. F. Hegel, *Vorlesungen über die Philosophie der Geschichte*, Stuttgart: Reclam, 1989, W. Benjamin, *Gesammelte Schriften* (R. Tiedemann & H. Schweppenhäuser Eds. [Werkausgabe] ed. Vol. Bd. 1), Frankfurt am Main: Suhrkamp, 1991, E. Husserl, *Die Krisis der europäischen Wissenschaften*, M. Heidegger, *Sein und Zeit* (17. Aufl., unveränd. Nachdr. der 15., an Hand der Gesamtausg. durchges. Aufl. mit den Randbemerkungen aus dem Handex. des Autors im Anh. ed.), Tübingen: Niemeyer, 1993, H.-G. Gadamer, *Wahrheit und Methode: Grundzüge einer philosophischen Hermeneutik*. Tübingen: Mohr, 1960, W. Schapp, *In Geschichten verstrickt: zum Sein von Mensch und Ding* (4. Aufl. ed.), Frankfurt am Main: Klostermann, 2004, P. Ricoeur, Temps et récit, Paris: Edition du Seuil, 1985, D. Carr, *Time, narrative, and history*, Bloomington u.a.: Indiana University Press, 1986.

3 Insbesondere in B. Waldenfels, *Antwortregister*, Frankfurt am Main: Suhrkamp, 1994.

4 G. W. F. Hegel, *Die Wissenschaft der Logik: mit den mündlichen Zusätzen Werke* (E. Moldenhauer & K. M. Michel Eds. Werke ed. Vol. 8), Frankfurt am Main: Suhrkamp, 1981, Werke 8, 49 f.

5 Vgl. Hegel, *Die Wissenschaft der Logik*, Werke 12, 77.

6 Vgl. Hegel, *Die Wissenschaft der Logik*, Werke 3, 591.
7 Vgl. *Gesammelte Schriften*, GS 1.2., 698.
8 Man könnte hier im Sinne Waldenfels' von einer hyperbolischen Erfahrung und der Geschichte folglich als einem Hyperphänomen sprechen, vgl. B. Waldenfels, *Hyperphänomene. Modi hyperbolischer Erfahrung*, Frankfurt am Main: Suhrka, 2012.
9 Hierzu vgl. L. v. Renthe-Fink Renthe-Fink, *Geschichtlichkeit. Ihr terminologischer und begrifflicher Ursprung bei Hegel, Haym, Dilthey und Yorck*, Göttingen: Vandenhoek und Ruprecht, 1964, Noch einmal: Zur Herkunft des Wortes ,Geschichtlichkeit', *Archiv für Begriffsgeschichte*, 15, 1974, 306–312.

Danish Yearbook of Philosophy, Vol. 48–49 (2013–2014), 169–184

ZWISCHEN DEN DISKURSEN ODER INMITTEN DER ERFAHRUNG, WIE UND WO ENTSTEHT GESCHICHTE?

MAREN WEHRLE

Geschichtswissenschaft zwischen Diskurs und Erfahrung

Spätestens seit den 1980er Jahren lässt sich eine Umkehrung in der Geschichtswissenschaft erkennen. Geschichte gilt nun immer weniger als Ausdruck einer großen einheitlichen Erzählung, die an wenigen Daten und Personen orientiert ist.[1] Statt sich an politischen Akteuren zu orientieren, die die Geschichte mit ihren Entscheidungen sozusagen „von oben" initiieren, versucht man nun die einzelnen Geschichten „von unten" zu erzählen und die Erfahrungen der Beteiligten in den Mittelpunkt zu rücken. Solche alltäglichen Erfahrungen und Ereignisse drücken sich nicht in expliziten Reden oder Handlungen aus, sondern implizit in Diskursen und Praktiken. Erfahrungen und Ereignisse formieren und stabilisieren sich in den wiederholenden Diskursen und Praktiken und bestimmen damit den Lauf der Geschichte in *impliziter* aber nichtsdestotrotz machtvoller Weise.

Diese, wie ich sie nennen möchte, *implizite Geschichte*, geht dabei auf das Konzept einer *Genealogie* zurück, dass Foucault im Anschluss an Nietzsche entwirft.[2] Die Genealogie als Ereignisgeschichte betont im Gegensatz zu hermeneutischen Positionen die Einmaligkeit, Unerwartbarkeit und fehlende Finalität von Ereignissen. Statt den verborgenen Sinn und die Kontinuität hinter den historischen Quellen zu suchen, soll nun gerade die *Zufälligkeit* von Ereignissen zum Ausgangspunkt werden. Geschichte als Genealogie beschäftigt sich mit den positiven und zufälligen Fakten und Ereignissen einer Zeit und muss zurückfragen nach deren *Ermöglichungsbedingungen*. Genealogie ist in diesem Sinne eine positive Wissenschaft, d.h. sie untersucht die ermöglichende Funktion von Diskurs und Ordnung. Sie fragt danach, welche Diskursordnung gerade diese Aussagen, Erfahrungsformen und Subjekte möglich macht. Ergänzt werden soll dies laut Foucault von einer Kritik, die die negative, d.h. einschränkende und ausschließende Funktion derselben Ordnung untersucht. Also welche Aussagen, Erfahrungen, Subjektkonstitutionen von derselben Ordnung ausgeschlossen oder gar unmöglich gemacht werden.

Geschichtswissenschaft verstanden als Genealogie muss den Ereignissen also gerade dort auflauern, „wo man sie am wenigstens erwartet und wo sie keine Geschichte zu haben scheinen – in den Gefühlen, der Liebe, dem Gewissen, den Instinkten". Dagegen richtet die traditionelle Geschichtsschreibung ihren Blick „gern in die Fernen und in die Höhen: auf die vornehmsten Epochen, auf die höchsten Formen, auf die allgemeinsten Ideen, auf die reinsten Individuen" [3]. Die wirkliche Historie zeigt sich dagegen nur im Blick auf „das Nächste": „den Leib, das Nervensystem, die Ernährung und Verdauung" [4]. Scheinbare biologische oder naturhafte Tatsachen wie der *Körper* weisen insofern eine Genealogie auf.

Zeitgenössische historische Disziplinen wie die Körper- und Patientengeschichte versuchen sich nun nach obigem Vorbild mit den „niederen Bereichen des Alltags" zu beschäftigen. In ihrer praktischen Arbeit sind sie dabei auf *Erfahrungsberichte* von Subjekten als deren „Quellen" angewiesen. [5] Der Begriff der *Erfahrung* hat in der Genealogie jedoch einen *ambivalenten Charakter*, einerseits muss sie als *Ausgangspunkt der geschichtlichen Betrachtung* fungieren und andererseits ist sie (nur) Ausdruck von geschichtlichen Diskursen, Normen und Konventionen.

Innerhalb der von Foucault inspirierten Ansätze – also Geschichte „von unten" zu untersuchen – gibt es insofern eine noch immer während Debatte darüber, welche Rolle man der Erfahrung innerhalb der geschichtlichen Untersuchung zugestehen soll. Diskursanalytische Ansätze nach dem *linguistic turn* wenden sich gegen einen Begriff von Geschichte, der sich auf objektivierbare Fakten und rekonstruierbare Tatsachen stützt. Zugleich zeichnen sich diese Ansätze durch eine anti-hermeneutische und anti-phänomenologische Haltung aus, die nicht in die „Fallen einer Subjektphilosophie, der Bewusstseinszentriertheit und des Intentionalismus" [6] tappen möchte. Viele diskursorientierte Geschichtswissenschaftler beschäftigen sich daher nur mit sprachlichen ‚Tatsachen' und lehnen jede Thematisierung von außer- oder nicht sprachlichen Dimensionen als Konstruktion eines Essentialismus entschieden ab. Trotzdem nimmt die Erfahrung einzelner Subjekte in einer *Genealogie* bzw. Geschichtsschreibung „von unten" eine wichtige Rolle ein, auf die in der Körper- und Geschlechtergeschichte, sowie der Patienten- und Medizingeschichte nicht verzichtet werden kann.

Der Streit um Diskurs vs. Erfahrung zeigt sich dabei besonders in der feministischen Geschichtswissenschaft. Hier wird seit den 1980er Jahren Kritik am Essentialismus einer „angeblich biologisch präfigurierten Geschlechtsidentität" [7] geübt. Auf der anderen Seite stehen GeschichtswissenschaftlerInnen, die den Körper (der Frau) als letzte Referenz und Grundlage von Erfahrung und *Agency* außerhalb des omnipräsenten Spiels der Diskurse ansehen (möchten).[8] Eine solche *radikale Gegenüberstellung* der kritischen Diskurswissenschaft gegenüber einer essentialistischen Erfahrungswissenschaft scheint nun aber weder genealogisch noch kritisch im Sinne Foucaults zu sein.[9]

Wie kann man also Erfahrung einen Stellenwert für die Bildung von impliziter Geschichte einräumen, ohne auf einen eindeutigen Ursprung oder objektive, biologische und zugleich wahre Natur rekurrieren zu müssen? Und wie lassen sich die Einflüsse der Diskurse nicht nur aufeinander und innersprachlich, sondern auch auf die Erfahrung, Wahrnehmung und den Körper selbst, besser beschreiben? Die (genetische) Phänomenologie Husserls und die Leibphänomenologie von Merleau-Ponty bieten hier ein differenziertes Konzept von Erfahrung und Subjektivität. Hier lassen sich einige Anknüpfungspunkte für eine „implizite Geschichtskonzeption", einer „Geschichte von unten" finden.

In einer solchen phänomenologischen Form der Genealogie, die ihren Ausgang in der sensuellen und leiblichen Erfahrung des Subjekts nimmt, wird deutlich, dass Geschichte bereits inmitten der Erfahrung entsteht. Zusätzlich zur *individuellen Erfahrungsgeschichte* zeigt sich hier eine *überindividuelle Geschichte von Normen, Diskursen und Ordnungen*, die die leibliche Erfahrung von Beginn an mitbestimmt. Diskursanalytische Ansätze können hier hilfreich sein, um zu beschreiben, wie Diskurse sich in die Erfahrung einschreiben. Eine *phänomenologische Genealogie* muss in diesem Sinne durch eine *genealogische Phänomenologie* ergänzt werden.

Phänomenologische Genealogie: Geschichte inmitten der Erfahrung

Nachdem Husserl sich zunächst um die Aufklärung von höherstufigen, d.h. aktiven intentionalen Leistungen bemüht hatte, interessiert ihn in späteren Texten mehr und mehr die passive Seite der Erfahrung. Hier betont er, dass jede Aktivität der Vernunft „notwendig als unterste Stufe [...] eine vorgebende Passivität"[10] voraussetzt. Dass das Subjekt unmittelbar ein einheitliches Objekt erfahren kann, verdankt es einer „wesensmäßigen Genesis" von passiven Synthesen, durch die das Subjekt auf eine Vorgegebenheit von Erfahrungsgegenständen zurückgreifen kann.

Die formale Struktur des Zeitbewusstseins als *Urimpression*, *Retention* und *Protention* ermöglicht dabei eine *zeitliche Synthese* der Sinnesdaten. Der Quellpunkt, mit dem die jeweilige Wahrnehmung oder Konstitution eines dauernden Gegenstandes beginnt, ist dabei die (Ur)*Impression*. Nimmt man Husserls Beispiel des Hörens einer Melodie, wäre dies das Ton-Jetzt. Da sich das Bewusstsein aber in stetiger Veränderung befindet, wandelt sich das Ton-Jetzt sogleich in einen soeben-gewesenen Ton, in eine *Retention* des nun vergangenen Ton-Jetzt. Durch die Retention werden die auftretenden Daten auch nach ihrer tatsächlichen Empfindung in modifizierter Form im Bewusstsein behalten. Das aktuelle impressionale Bewusstsein geht so „ständig fließend über in immer neues retentionales Bewusstsein"[11]. In dem von Husserl beschriebenen Kontinuum von Retentionen steht dabei jede Retention in modifizierender Verbindung zu allen vorangegangenen Retentionen. Jede Retention muss also wiederum selbst eine „kontinuierliche Modifikation" sein, die „in Form einer Abschattungsreihe das Erbe der Vergangenheit in sich trägt"[12]. Auf der Basis von vergangenen Impressionen und Retentionen baut sich die Funktion der *Protention* auf, die beim Hören einer Melodie automatisch den nächsten Ton antizipiert. Jede Impression ist demnach nicht nur in einen retentionalen, sondern auch in einen protentionalen Horizont eingebettet. Solange ein Ton oder eine Melodie erklingt, gehört zum zeitkonstituierenden Prozess daher notwendig eine „vorgerichtete Intentionalität". Im Ablauf einer Zeitwahrnehmung stellt sich damit „immerfort ‚Erwartung'"[13] ein, wenn diese auch nicht als explizite Erwartung missverstanden werden darf. Trotzdem lässt sich diese automatische Gerichtetheit und ‚Erwartung' auf den nächsten Ton nicht so einfach mit formalen Kriterien beschreiben, sondern muss ebenfalls inhaltlich bestimmt sein. Wie und ob sich ein leibliches Subjekt implizit auf zukünftige Sinnesempfindungen richten kann, hängt von den Inhalten seiner früheren Erfahrungen ab.

   Zugleich mit den formalen Synthesen müssen also auch inhaltliche Spuren im Bewusstsein verbleiben, um *assoziative Synthesen* des Gegebenen nach Ähnlichkeit und Kontrast motivieren zu können. Das solchermaßen für sich Abgehobene entwickelt dann eine affektive Kraft, die die Aufmerksamkeit des Subjektes wecken kann. Auf der untersten Stufe der Passivität ist die zustande kommende Affektion für Husserl einerseits durch die relative Größe des Kontrasts bestimmt und andererseits von „bevorzugenden sinnlichen Gefühlen" und „instinktive[n], triebmäßige[n] Bevorzugungen"[14].

   Diese grundlegenden passiven Synthesen bieten die Grundlage dafür, dass jede Erfahrung bleibende Spuren hinterlässt. Dies tut sie in Form von erworbenem Gegenstandssinn und *Sedimentierungen*[15] sowie habitualisierten Erfahrungsverläufen und Bewegungsmustern. Jede Erfahrung des Subjekts hinterlässt so auf der *noematischen Seite* einen zeitlichen und inhaltlichen Horizont, der jede weitere Wahrnehmung mitbestimmt. Auf der *noetischen Seite* erhält das Subjekt aus früheren Konstitutionen bleibende passive Erwerbe, Verhaltensmuster und *Habitualitäten*.

Gehören Sedimentierungen und Erwerbe zu den rein passiven Niederschlägen der Erfahrung, thematisiert Husserl mit dem Konzept der Habitualität den personalen Charakter des Subjekts. Eine Habitualität wird bei Husserl zunächst aktiv erworben und wirkt hernach passiv auf den weiteren Gang der Erfahrung. Personale Akte der Stellungnahme oder Wertung werden so zu bleibenden Überzeugungen des Subjekts, wie etwa die Entscheidung für eine bestimmte Politik oder Lebensweise, die zukünftig die gesamte Erfahrung auch in passiver, d.h. impliziter, Weise prägt. Die Wirkung von personalen Habitualitäten kann dabei im Gegensatz zu den rein passiven Erwerben vom Subjekt – zumindest teilweise – kontrolliert werden: So kann eine Gesinnung oder Lebensweise bewusst aufgegeben werden und in der Folge verändern sich auch die damit verbundenen Habitualitäten. Anders verhält es sich dagegen mit passiven Sinnstiftungen: Ist der Sinn und Zweck eines Gegenstandes, z.B. als Schere, einmal gestiftet, werden Gegenstände solcher Art immer unmittelbar in diesem Sinne (als Schere) aufgefasst.

Ähnlich fundamental wirken auch die leiblichen Habitualitäten, also Bewegungsmuster und Fähigkeiten (sogenannte *skills*). Merleau-Ponty spricht in diesem Zusammenhang auch von *Gewöhnungen*. Sein Begriff des *Körperschemas*[16] umfasst dabei nicht nur die Bewegungspotentialitäten, sondern auch ein operatives Wissen, um unsere Position, Lage und Statur. Darüber hinaus kann man von einem leiblichen und sensuellen Gedächtnis sprechen, in dass sich nicht nur Fähigkeiten und Bewegungsmuster, sondern auch angenehme und schmerzhafte Erlebnisse einschreiben, die bei ähnlichen Umständen automatisch aktualisiert werden. Dieser *habituelle Leib*[17], wie Merleau-Ponty es nennt, macht es dem *aktuell agierenden Leib* erst möglich sich in der Welt zu orientieren und sorgt für eine Kontinuität der Erfahrung. Obwohl der Leib damit als Voraussetzung für Wahrnehmung überhaupt gilt und jede konkrete Wahrnehmung begleitet, bleibt er selbst jedoch zumeist in seinem Fungieren unthematisch sowie teilweise unsichtbar. Gleiches gilt auch für seine Habitualitäten – Reaktionsweisen, Bewegungsabläufe, Wegesysteme – sowie seine biologischen Grundlagen und Prozesse. Der habituelle Leib trägt unsere gesamte passive Erfahrungsgeschichte in und mit sich, auch diejenige, zu der wir selbst nie bewusst Zugang hatten, wie etwa unsere eigene Geburt.

Diese Erfahrungsgeschichte generiert nun den individuellen und selektiven Wahrnehmungsstil des Subjekts: Die Selektivität der Wahrnehmung zeigt sich dabei nicht nur im Bereich der expliziten Aufmerksamkeit, sondern bereits im Bereich der Affektivität. Die Erfahrungsgeschichte bestimmt dabei nicht nur *wie* wir etwas wahrnehmen und erfahren, sondern auch, *was* wir zu einem gegebenen Zeitpunkt überhaupt bemerken und erfahren können. Die bleibenden Spuren der Erfahrung bilden damit wiederum den Maßstab für die Selektionskriterien der weiteren Erfahrung. Welche Reize uns affizieren oder, in Husserls Worten, „wecken" können, hängt insofern von den jeweiligen leiblichen oder personalen Interessen ab.

Ein solchermaßen ausgebildeter Erfahrungsstil ist aber nicht nur individuell, sondern Teil einer Tradition, das Subjekt ist ein „Kind seiner Zeit" und „Erbe" einer Kultur.[18] Das Interessenprofil ist insofern nicht nur einzelsubjektiv bestimmt, sondern beinhaltet auch überpersonale Faktoren, wie etwa *intersubjektive Normalitätsmuster*. Ob uns beispielsweise eine Gestalt als Puppe oder Mensch erscheint – um ein bekanntes Beispiel Husserls herauszugreifen – hängt nicht nur von den jeweiligen Wahrnehmungsumständen ab, sondern wird ebenfalls von kulturellen Normen beeinflusst, die definieren, was innerhalb einer Kultur- und Lebenswelt als typisch menschlich oder eben als typisch mechanisch gilt. Die (implizite) ‚Bewertung' des Gegebenen als ‚Mensch' oder ‚Puppe' wird dabei nicht nachträglich ausgesprochen, sondern lenkt bereits implizit unseren Blick: Sie bestimmt das, was uns jeweils auffällt oder das, was von uns regelrecht übersehen wird. Intersubjektive Normen drücken sich insofern auf der Ebene der subjektiv-leiblichen Wahrnehmung als eine Art *sensuelle Normativität* aus, z.B. in Form einer Typik des Aufmerksamkeitsverhaltens. Auf der einen Seite handelt es sich dabei um habituell wirkende ‚Scheuklappen', auf der anderen Seite ermöglicht die Prägung durch intersubjektive und normative Maßstäbe in der Praxis eine unmittelbare Verständigung von Subjekten, die eine ähnliche Lebenswelt teilen.

Sedimentierung und Habitualität können insofern als passive Voraussetzungen für das Haben einer Geschichte angesehen werden: Sie ermöglichen bleibende Sinnbestände und Erfahrungsstile im Subjekt, die aufgrund ihrer intersubjektiven Bedeutung, eine Ebene der gemeinsamen Aufmerksamkeit und Verständigung von Individuen eröffnet. Durch die habituell und kulturell geprägte Verhaltenstypik wird darüber hinaus Orientierung in der Welt und eine Antizipation des Verhaltens von anderen Subjekten ermöglicht. Man könnte also argumentieren, dass hier inmitten der Erfahrung so etwas wie eine individuelle und intersubjektive Geschichte entsteht.

Zugleich schreibt sich aber auch eine *überindividuelle Ebene von Geschichte*, in Form von Kultur und Normen in die individuelle Erfahrung mit ein. Dieser Einfluss von überindividuellen Normen lässt sich mit Merleau-Ponty durch unsere leibliche Situierung in der Welt begründen. Diese führt einerseits zu einer positiven Verankerung in der Welt, andererseits ist damit eine gewisse Determination und die Unmöglichkeit einer absoluten Freiheit verbunden: Das leiblich situierte Subjekt wird in eine intersubjektive und geschichtliche Welt hinein geboren. Diese ist als Vorgeschichte Teil des habituellen Leibes. Aber auch der aktuelle Leib als „Gegenwartsfeld" ist nicht nur eine Gegenwart bei sich selbst, sondern vor allem bei der Welt und den Anderen. Die leibliche Gegenwart vollbringt somit die „Vermittlung des Seins-für-sich und des Seins-für-Andere, von Individualität und Generalität"[19]. Zugleich kann der *aktuelle, spontane Leib*, die gegebenen Strukturen übersteigen, um daraus andere zu schaffen. Dies ist möglich, da die Welt zwar bereits immer konstituiert ist, aber eben niemals vollständig konstituiert ist.[20]

Genealogische Phänomenologie: Die Diskursivierung der Erfahrung

Der oben erwähnte Einfluss von überindividuellen Faktoren und Strukturen auf die Erfahrung und insbesondere den Leib oder Körper möchte ich als *Diskursivierung der Erfahrung* bezeichnen. Der Leib fungiert hierbei als ‚Brücke' zwischen phänomenologischen und diskursorientierten bzw. genealogischen Ansätzen. Für beide Richtungen stellt er den Ort da, wo Geschichte ihren konkreten Ausdruck findet, sich zeigt. Nietzsche betont etwa, dass sich erst am Leib die wirkliche Genealogie ablesen lässt[21], und Foucault fügt ergänzend hinzu, dass die Genealogie als Analyse der Herkunft dort steht, „wo sich Leib und Geschichte verschränken". Die Genealogie muss zeigen können, „wie der Leib von der Geschichte durchdrungen ist und wie die Geschichte am Leib nagt".[22]

Aus genealogischer Perspektive ist mit Geschichte aber nicht die individuelle Erfahrungsgeschichte gemeint, die sich in der Interaktion mit der Welt und anderen Subjekten bildet, sondern vielmehr überindividuelle Diskurse, Ordnungen und Strukturen, die sich mit Gewalt und vermittels Praktiken in den Leib einschreiben. Leibliche Erfahrung wird damit zu einer determinierten und determinierenden Kraft aus der Begierden, Konflikte und Irrtümer erwachsen:

Ereignisse schreiben sich nach Foucault regelrecht „in das Nervensystem, in das Temperament, in den Verdauungsapparat"[23] ein, „am Leib findet man das Stigma der vergangenen Ereignisse"[24].

Beispiele für solche gewaltsamen Einwirkungen der Geschichte bzw. einer *Diskursivierung der Erfahrung* finden wir insbesondere dort, wo Machtdispositive sich den Körper nutzbar machen: Mit Praktiken und Techniken wird hier eine Unterwerfung oder gar allererst eine Konstitution des Subjektes vollzogen. Im 18. Jahrhundert geschieht dies nach Foucault etwa durch die räumliche, zeitliche und funktionale Individualisierung und effektive Organisation von Körpern. In der Konstruktion von sogenannten „Tableaus" findet in Spitälern, Schulen oder beim Militär eine räumliche und qualitative Anordnung der Körper statt, die dem Motto folgt: „Jedem Individuum seinen Platz und auf jeden Platz ein Individuum"[25].

Dies wird weiterhin flankiert von einer zeitlichen Kontrolle der Körper und der Zergliederung ihrer Tätigkeiten, wie sich anhand von militärischen Manövern oder sportlichen Übungen zeigen lässt. Beim „Manöver" wird etwa durch wiederholte Einübung eine strikte Korrelation zwischen dem Subjekt und dem benutzten Objekt (dem Gewehr) hergestellt: Körper und Objekt werden „fest aneinander gebunden" und bilden hernach einen einzigen Komplex aus Körper und Maschine.[26] Das Objekt schreibt sich insofern regelrecht in den Körper ein bzw. wird – mit Merleau-Ponty gesprochen – Teil des Körperschemas. Die Tätigkeiten des Körpers werden dabei im Rahmen einer Übung in einzelne Elemente zerlegt, deren Reihenfolge und zeitliche Dauer genau festgelegt ist. Am Ende einer solchen Übung steht eine Prüfung, die festhält, ob die jeweiligen Teilziele innerhalb der vorgegebenen Zeit erreicht wurden. Ähnliche Strukturen findet man im Schulunterricht oder anderen Formen des Lernens, die dem Prinzip der *analogen Wiederholung* folgen. Hier vollzieht sich sowohl eine Vereinheitlichung und Beherrschung der Zeit als auch des Körpers. Die Kontrolle der Verteilung, der Tätigkeiten und des Zusammenspiels von Körpern gewährleistet den Gehorsam der Individuen, eine bessere Ökonomie von Zeit und Energie, sowie eine Organisation, die „aus den unübersichtlichen, unnützen und gefährlichen Mengen geordnete Vielheiten" macht.[27]

Im Falle des Sexualitätsdispositivs, das Foucault in *Sexualität und Wahrheit* beschreibt, wird der Körper zusätzlich problematisiert und mit Hilfe von Institutionen wie der Familie oder der professionalisierten Medizin klassifiziert und reguliert. Es erfolgt daher nicht nur eine Disziplinierung einzelner Körper(-gruppen) durch „Dressur, Intensivierung und Verteilung der Kräfte"[28], sondern darüber hinaus eine überindividuelle Regulierung der Bevölkerung: „Die Mechanismen der Macht zielen auf den Körper, auf das Leben und seine Expansion, auf die Erhaltung, Ertüchtigung, Ermächtigung oder Nutzbarmachung der ganzen Art ab."[29] Hier wird besonders deutlich, wie individuelle und überindividuelle Faktoren, genetische und genealogische Aspekte im Körper bzw. Leib verschränkt sind und ihn gerade deshalb zum Angriffspunkt der Macht werden lassen.

Die vergangenen Ereignisse und übergreifenden Normen und Machtdispositive, die hier inkorporiert werden, entziehen sich gerade einer expliziten subjektiven Erfahrung und Thematisierung. Die Geschichte des Körpers ist insofern durch seine Anonymität und Determiniertheit gekennzeichnet, wie auch Judith Butler betont: „Ein Körper zu sein, heißt in gewissem Sinne, eine vollständige Erinnerung des eigenen Lebens zu entbehren. Mein Körper hat also eine Geschichte, an die ich keine Erinnerung haben kann"[30]. Die Geschichte in Form von Diskursen, die sich an ihm niederschlagen, bilden somit zwar Möglichkeitsbedingung für spezifische Formen der Erfahrung und des Subjektseins, können aber nicht reflexiv von eben diesem Subjekt selbst eingeholt werden, da Sie eine andere Zeitlichkeit besitzen: „Die Normen […] sind nicht wirklich meine. Sie kommen nicht mit mir in die Welt; die Zeitlichkeit ihres Erscheinens deckt sich nicht mit der Zeitlichkeit meines eigenen Lebens."[31]

Eine ähnliche Ansicht vertritt auch Merleau-Ponty, der hier als Vermittler zwischen der subjektzentrierten Position Husserls und den diskursorientierten Ansätzen fungieren kann. Für ihn hat die Leiblichkeit ebenfalls eine Ambivalenz und Anonymität, in dem der aktuell engagierte Leib immer mit dem habituellen Leib verschränkt ist. Der habituelle Leib hat hier eine „Vorgeschichte", die auch nicht-individuelle Momente, wie biologische Dispositionen, die eigene Geburt und den kulturellen und historischen Horizont umfasst. Aufgrund der Situierung des Leibes in der Welt beeinflusst die überindividuelle Geschichte als seine Vorgeschichte implizit jede Erfahrung des Subjekt, kann jedoch nie explizit erfahren oder erinnert werden: Sie ist eine Vergangenheit, „die niemals Gegenwart war"[32].

Geschichte und Philosophie zwischen Erfahrung und Diskurs

Die grundsätzliche Aufgabe der Philosophie als „Aufklärung" besteht nach Foucault in Genealogie und Kritik. Und damit dem Versuch anders wahrzunehmen, anders zu denken, als man – innerhalb der épisteme oder des herrschen-

den Machtdispositives – wahrnimmt und denkt. Es handelt sich um die Erkenntnis, dass alle Wahrheiten und Ordnungen, die für uns selbstverständlich
und somit in „Fleisch und Blut" übergegangen sind, auch ganz anders hätten
sein können. Diese Einsicht kann nach Foucault nur im Umweg über die Geschichte erlangt werden. Die Zeugnisse von früheren Erfahrungen, Handlungen und Ereignissen zeigen, dass das, was für uns heute selbstverständlich ist,
früher anders war. Geschichte als Genealogie liefert damit Beweise für die
Relativität und zeitliche Begrenztheit von jeweils gültigen Ordnungen, indem
sie auf ihre (zufällige) Entstehung zurückweist.

In diesem aufklärerischen Duktus und dem methodischen Versuch einer
„Ausschaltung" von bestehendem Wissen und Vorurteilen gleichen sich
Foucault und Husserl auf eigenartige Weise, auch wenn die Art der Durchfüh-
rung und die daraus gezogenen Folgerungen ganz andere sind. Versucht
Foucault und die an ihm orientierte Geschichtswissenschaft gegebene Ordnungen anders zu sehen, möchte Husserl hingegen die zugrundeliegenden Strukturen der Erfahrung und des Bewusstseins aufdecken. Sucht der eine die Zufälligkeit und die Brüche von Erfahrungsordnungen sichtbar zu machen, strebt
der andere danach, die zugrundeliegende Kontinuität, Universalität und Teleo-
logie derselben aufzuzeigen. Für beide Richtungen, Phänomenologie wie Genealogie oder Diskurswissenschaft, spielt dabei das Konzept der Konstitution
eine zentrale Rolle. Auch wenn Konstitution jeweils ganz anders definiert
wird, ist beiden die Einsicht gemein, dass konkrete Subjekte, die Welt und die
Gesellschaft für uns nicht einfach ‚da' sind, sondern vielmehr Produkte eines
wie auch immer gearteten Prozesses der Sinnbildung, Konstitution oder gar
Konstruktion.

Während in der Phänomenologie das (transzendentale oder leibliche) Subjekt oder die Gemeinschaft von Subjekten (Intersubjektivität) diese *Konstitution* „leistet", erfolgt sie in den diskursanalytischen Ansätzen durch Machtkonstellationen und Diskurse. Hier ist das Subjekt nicht der Akteur, sondern
vielmehr das Produkt der Konstitution. Dies wird dabei durchaus ontologisch
verstanden: Für Butler gibt es beispielsweise kein Subjekt außerhalb oder vor
einer diskursiven Konstitution, sondern unser Subjektsein materialisiert sich
erst in einer solchen, wie z.B. in der binären Konstitution des Geschlechts. Die
phänomenologische Konstitution hat hingegen eher epistemologische Bedeutung, sie konstituiert den Sinn, nicht jedoch die Existenz der Welt, der Anderen
und des Subjektes selbst. Die Konstitutionsleistungen des Subjekts hinterlas-

sen dennoch bleibende, und das heißt auch, ontologische oder materiale, Spuren wie dies oben dargestellt wurde.

Konstitution ist phänomenologisch gesehen also ein positiver und notwendiger Vorgang, eine „Leistung"[33] des Subjekts oder der Subjekte. In den passiven Schichten der Erfahrung vollzieht sich diese Sinnbildung jedoch automatisch bzw. operativ: sich wiederholende Vorgänge und Tätigkeiten führen zu Kontinuität und bleibenden personalen Fähigkeiten und Eigenschaften. Getragen wird diese Kontinuität formal durch die Struktur des Zeitbewusstseins und inhaltlich durch die passive Synthesis der Assoziation, die Gegebenes nach Kontrast und Ähnlichkeit selektiert und integriert. Merleau-Ponty knüpft hier an, verschiebt aber die Bedeutung der Konstitution, weg von einer transzendentalen Leistung hin zu einer Sinnbildung, die sich zwischen dem leiblichen Subjekt und seiner Interaktion mit der Welt vollzieht. Konstitution im phänomenologischen Sinne ist demnach die Bedingung für einheitliche (d.h. temporal und inhaltlich strukturierte) Wahrnehmung und einen gelungenen Weltbezug. Sie bildet damit zugleich die Voraussetzung für die Ausbildung und Stabilisierung eines personalen Ichs.[34]

Die Konstitution wird dabei nicht vom Subjekt allein geleistet, sondern ist von Beginn an eine intersubjektive Sinnbildung. Einheitlichkeit und Objektivität kann insbesondere auf der Ebene kultureller Güter und Normen nur durch die ständige Abstimmung und Verifizierung durch Mitsubjekte erreicht werden. Husserl spricht in diesem Sinne auch von einer *Gemeinschaftshabitualität*[35] sowie *Gemeinschaftsleistungen*[36]. Gerade ersteres kann jedoch nicht nur auf explizite gemeinsame Tätigkeiten wie etwa Handlungen oder Kommunikation zurückgeführt werden, sondern muss bereits vor jeglicher expliziter Aktivität einzelner oder mehrere Subjekte in impliziter Weise vorhanden sein. Die Kultur, Geschichte oder das jeweilige soziale Milieu, in das ein konkretes Subjekt hineingeboren wird, prägt in diesem Sinne seine spezifischen Traditionen, Gewohnheiten, Umgangsformen, Normen und Werte. Dies geschieht von Geburt an in der Interaktion mit den Eltern, dem näheren Umfeld und dem Einfluss eines umfassenderen Weltbildes, das über Medien vermittelt wird. Durch wiederholende Einübung werden so die bestehenden Normen vom heranwachsenden Subjekt inkorporiert, erlernt, passiv übernommen und später auch aktiv bestätigt oder abgelehnt.[37]

In den meisten diskursorientierten Ansätzen werden nun hauptsächlich die negativen, d. h. einschränkenden Aspekte, der Konstitution betont. Hier produziert, wie bei Butler, die geltende Werte- und Normenmatrix, was ein Subjekt sein darf und in welcher Weise es konstituiert wird. Zugleich schreiben sich die Diskurse und damit die herrschenden Machtkonstellationen gewaltsam in die Körper ein. Beide Formen der Konstitution funktionieren jedoch nach demselben Prinzip: der performativen Wiederholung. Im Falle der Subjektkonstitution bei Butler, aber auch bei Foucault, muss das Subjekt in seiner Geschlechtsidentität stets aufs neue benannt werden und diese Anrufung selbst wiederholen. In *Sexualität und Wahrheit* bildet sich das Subjekt durch den wiederholten Zwang, über sich selbst die Wahrheit zu sprechen. Besonders wichtig bzw. radikal ist das Prinzip der Wiederholung jedoch im Falle der körperlichen Disziplinierung. Kann in der diskursiven Konstitution noch ein subversives Element festgemacht werden, da sich in den Wiederholungen der jeweilige Sinn beständig verschiebt, ist dies bei der körperlichen Einschreibung von Diskursen schon schwieriger. Eine Veränderung von körperlichen Verhaltensweisen und Gewohnheiten, etwa die Art, wie wir gelernt haben zu sitzen oder zu gehen, kann nur schwer wieder rückgängig gemacht werden. Dies gelingt nur in einer expliziten ‚Gegenkonditionierung‘, in der andere Bewegungsmuster mühsam eingeübt werden, wie dies etwa bei der Rehabilitation der Fall ist. Konstitution aus Sicht der diskursorientierten Ansätze steht demnach für Gewalt, Macht, Normierung und Exklusion von Minderheiten. Ihre Gefahr besteht darin, dass Sie ihre Existenz verleugnet und die Produkte einer geschichtlichen, d.h. zeitlich relativen, Konstitution als objektiv, universal gültig und natürlich ausgibt.

Um diesen Umstand zu erklären, könnten die Beschreibungen und Einsichten von diskursorientierten Ansätzen wie die von Foucault und Butler helfen. Sie zeigen, wie allgemeine Normen- und Machtsysteme zum Teil unseres Subjektseins selbst gemacht werden bzw. immer schon sind. Diese überindividuellen Wertesysteme beeinflussen insofern alle Bereiche der Erfahrung von Beginn an: Sie bestimmen dasjenige, was wir bemerken und wahrnehmen, fühlen, wollen und denken. Die leitende Frage dieser Ansätze besteht also mit den Worten Foucaults darin, ob es (überhaupt) möglich ist, anders wahrzunehmen, als wir wahrnehmen, und anders zu denken, als wir (innerhalb unserer Normenmatrix) denken. Wie die Phänomenologie verstehen sie sich damit als Erkenntniskritik und Aufklärung, gehen darin aber noch einen Schritt weiter und weisen die Phänomenologie auf ihren blinden Fleck hin. Dieser besteht darin, dass Phänomenologie methodisch aus epistemischer Redlichkeit von der eigenen Erfahrung ihren Ausgang nehmen muss, diese aber bereits kontaminiert ist von impliziten Nomen- und Diskurssystemen, die ihrer eigenen skeptischen Methode entgehen.[38]

Erfahrung dagegen als Gegenpol zum Diskurs zu begreifen, setzt nur eine binäre Denkweise fort, die ja gerade kritisiert werden soll. Diskurse sind nur deshalb so mächtig, wirksam, langlebig und verbergen nur deshalb ihre geschichtliche Relativität und Entstehung so effektiv, weil sie Teil unserer Erfahrung sind: Nicht nur in der Weise, wie wir uns selbst und andere *als Körper wahrnehmen*, sondern sie sind auch Teil unseres *operativen Leibseins*, wie wir uns bewegen, was uns auffällt, was wir wollen und fühlen. *Diskurse* sind in dieser Hinsicht zwar meist *nicht explizit* greifbar oder *erfahrbar*, aber dafür immer schon *Teil unserer Erfahrung* und machen deren impliziten geschichtlichen Charakter aus. Diese implizite Basis teilen wir mit den Menschen, die ähnliche Erfahrungen gemacht haben (dasselbe reale oder virtuelle Umfeld haben). Aus diesem Grund sind uns ähnliche Dinge wichtig oder unwichtig, können wir uns verstehen und übereinkommen oder gemeinsam handeln. Hierdurch begreifen wir auch erst gewisse Ereignisse und Entwicklungen als unsere gemeinsame explizite Geschichte. Mit dieser expliziten Geschichte können wir uns nun verbunden fühlen, uns an ihr abarbeiten, uns gegen sie abgrenzen: In diesem Verhalten zur Geschichte vollzieht sich eine gewisse überpersönliche Identität, z.B. einer Generation.

Dieselben Prozesse und Mechanismen, die so zu Kontinuität, Sozialität und Identität einer Kultur gehören, führen nun zugleich zu Normierung und Ausschließung. Die *Diskursivierung der Erfahrung* als implizite Geschichte bestimmt demzufolge, welche Personen, Ereignisse, Subjekte und Körper für uns in einer gewissen Zeit „von Gewicht"[39] sind und welche nicht. Gewisse, nicht in diese Raster fallenden, Erfahrungen und Subjekte werden nicht gesehen und gehört oder gar gewaltsam ausgeschlossen. Die implizite Geschichte oder die *Diskursivierung der Erfahrung* aktualisiert und stabilisiert so beständig gewisse Normensysteme, ohne dass uns diese Vorgänge transparent werden.

Geschichte lässt sich in diesem Sinne in ähnlicher Weise charakterisieren, wie Foucault einst die Funktion des Diskurses beschrieben hat: Einerseits hat sie eine ermöglichende (in Form von Sozialität und Kultur), andererseits eine beschränkende Funktion. Philosophie als Arbeit des Denkens an sich selbst ist wiederum nur über den Umweg über die eigene Geschichte möglich: In der Hoffnung, dass die „Arbeit, seine eigene Geschichte zu denken, das Denken von dem lösen kann, was es im Stillen denkt, und inwieweit sie es ihm ermöglichen kann, anders zu denken."[40]

Notes

1   Vgl. P. Sarasin: *Geschichtswissenschaft und Diskursanalyse*. Frankfurt a. Main 2003, 13–14.

2   Vgl. M. Foucault: *Nietzsche, die Genealogie, die Historie*. In: Michel Foucault. Von der Subversion des Wissens. Hrsg. und übers. von W. Seitter. Frankfurt a. Main 2000, 69–91.

3   M. Foucault: *Nietzsche, die Genealogie, die Historie*, 81.

4   Ebd.

5   Diese Beschreibungen der eigenen Erfahrung und des Körperempfindens sind für die betreffenden Personen jedoch meist keine ganz willkürlichen Ereignisse: Sie sind ein integrativer Teil innerhalb der impliziten Erfahrungsgeschichte der Person. Wenn die Person diese Erfahrungen in Worte fassen will, kommt zusätzlich eine narrative Leistung hinzu. Das Subjekt benutzt bestimmte kulturell konnotierte Metaphern und Ausdrücke und liefert Gründe für sein Befinden oder seine Handlungen. Um aus diesen Beschreibungen von individuellen Erfahrungen also die geforderten zufälligen Ereignisse mit Verzicht auf jegliche Finalität zu machen, müssen diese erst mühsam dekonstruiert und von ihrer inhärenten Struktur und Kontinuität befreit werden. Um nicht in die Falle vorgegebener kultureller Denk- und Ordnungsmuster zu tappen, wird versucht, das gesammelte Material gleich archäologischen Funden innerhalb einer neuen, zufälligen Anordnung zu betrachten. Vgl. B. Duden: *Geschichte unter der Haut: ein Eisenacher Arzt und seine Patientinnen um 1730*. Stuttgart 1987.

6   ` P. Sarasin: *Geschichtswissenschaft und Diskursanalyse*, 28.

7   Ebd., 24.

8   Vgl. B. Duden: *Die Frau ohne Unterleib: Zu Judith Butlers Entkörperung. Ein Zeitdokument*. In: Feministische Studien 2, 1993, 24–33; J. Scott: *The evidence of experience*. In: Critical Inquiry 3, 1991, 773–797; L. Roper: *Jenseits des linguistic turn*. In: Historische Anthropologie 7, 1999, 452–466; P. Sarasin: *Mapping the body: Körpergeschicht zwischen Konstruktivismus, Politik und ‚Erfahrung‘*. In: Historische Anthropologie 7, 1999, 437–451.

9   Die diskurswissenschaftlichen Ansätze betonen dabei zu Recht, dass es keine diskursfreie bzw. Ordnungs- oder Normfreie Wirklichkeit gibt. Dies ist aber nicht gleichbedeutend mit der Annahme, dass keine sprachfreie oder vorsprachliche Dimension von Wirklichkeit existiert. Vielmehr können sich geltende Normen gerade in diese vorsprachliche Erfahrungsebene, den Körper, einschreiben. Darüber hinaus könnte man von einer *impliziten Normativität* der Erfahrung selbst sprechen, die sich in wiederholten Interaktionen mit der Umwelt, Wahrnehmungen und Bewegungsabläufen (Praktiken) generiert. Erfahrung in diesem Sinne ist zwar nicht sprachlich, aber dennoch normativ. Zugleich spielt sich Erfahrung und Körperlichkeit nicht außerhalb des Spiels der Diskurse ab, sondern vielmehr mittendrin bzw. die Diskurse werden zum Teil der Erfahrung selbst. Diskurse, Ordnungen oder Macht müssen in irgendeiner Form *Teil des Subjektseins* werden, um *überhaupt wirksam sein* zu können – und das nicht nur auf sprachlicher, sondern eben auch auf körperlicher Ebene.

10   Husserl, E.: *Cartesianische Meditationen und Pariser Vorträge*. In: Husserliana Bd. I. Hg. von S. Strasser. Den Haag 1950, 112.

11   E. Husserl: *Zur Phänomenologie des inneren Zeitbewusstseins (1893-1917)*. In: Husserliana Bd. X. Hg. von R. Boehm. Den Haag 1966, 29.

12   E. Husserl: *Zur Phänomenologie des inneren Zeitbewusstseins (1893-1917)*. In: Husserliana Bd. X. Hg. von R. Boehm. Den Haag 1966, 29f.

13   E. Husserl: *Die Bernauer Manuskripte über das Zeitbewusstsein (1917/18)*. In: Husserliana Bd. XXXIII. Hg. von R. Bernet u. D. Lohmar. Dordrecht 2001, 7.

14   E. Husserl: *Analysen zur passiven Synthesis. Aus Vorlesungs- und Forschungsmanuskripten 1918–1926*. In: Husserliana Bd. XI. Hg. von M. Fleischer. Den Haag 1966, 150.

15 Die gegenständlichen *Erwerbe/Sedimente*, die den inhaltlichen Kern dieses Horizontes bilden, sind dabei nicht auf das Einzelbewusstsein beschränkt, sondern beziehen sich auf Vorgänge und Resultate gemeinsamer Sinnkonstitutionen (z.B. Kulturgebilden). Sedimentierungen weisen nach Husserl also auf eine aktive (Ur)Stiftung zurück, in dem der Sinn eines Gegenstandes allererst aufgefasst wird. Ist dieser Zweck eines Gegenstandes, z.B. als Schere, aber einmal *gestiftet*, werden solche Gegenstände immer unmittelbar als Schere aufgefasst. Der einmal gestiftete Sinn kann in der Folge auf ähnliche Dinge passiv-assoziativ übertragen werden Vgl. E. Husserl: *Cartesianische Meditationen*, 141. Insbesondere bei kulturellen Erwerben, ist die „ursprünglich leistende Sinngebung" jedoch meist „vergessen" und fungiert lediglich als passiver Horizont der Erfahrung der Einzelsubjekte. Vgl. E. Husserl: *Die Krisis der europäischen Wissenschaften und die transzendentale Phänomenologie*. In: Husserliana XXIX. Hg. von R.N. Smid. Dordrecht 1993, 345. In beiden Fällen handelt es sich um einen Sinn, ob aktiv erworben oder operativ wirksam, auf den man immer wieder als Einzelsubjekt oder als Gemeinschaft zurückkommen kann und der so eine ‚bekannte' Welt und intersubjektive Verständigung ermöglicht.

16 Für Merleau Ponty bezeichnet der Terminus ‚Körperschema' mehr als die bloße Summe der Informationen der verschiedenen Körperfunktionen. Er zielt vielmehr auf die ganzheitliche Organisation des Leibes hin, der immer schon auf eine Welt gerichtet ist. Die einzelnen Glieder des Leibes sind dabei nicht lose miteinander verknüpft, sondern man hat seinen Leib „in einem unmittelbaren Besitz" und weiß um die Lage seiner Glieder unmittelbar „durch ein allumfassendes Körperschema". M. Merleau-Ponty: *Die Phänomenologie der Wahrnehmung*. Übers. von R. Boehm. Berlin 1966, 123.

17 Vgl. M. Merleau-Ponty: *Die Phänomenologie der Wahrnehmung*, 12, 107f., 109, 253, 280.

18 E. Husserl: *Zur Phänomenologie der Intersubjektivität. Texte aus dem Nachlass. Zweiter Teil*: 1921–1928. Hrsg. von I. Kern. Dordrecht 1973, 223.

19 M. Merleau-Ponty: *Die Phänomenologie der Wahrnehmung*, 513.

20 Vgl. Ebd., 514.

21 Vgl. Nietzsche: *Zur Genealogie der Moral*. In: Sämtliche Werke. Kritische Studienausgabe. Band 5. München 1980, 392.

22 M. Foucault: *Nietzsche, die Genealogie, die Historie*, 75.

23 Ebd., 74.

24 Ebd., 75.

25 M. Foucault: *Überwachen und Strafen. Die Geburt des Gefängnisses*. Übers. von W. Seitter. Frankfurt a. Main 1994, 83, vgl. 89.

26 Ebd., 197.

27 Ebd., 190.

28 M. Foucault: *Der Wille zum Wissen. Sexualität und Wahrheit I*. Übers. von W. Seitter. Frankfurt a. Main 1983, 140.

29 Ebd., 142

30 J. Butler: *Kritik der ethischen Gewalt*. Übers. von R. Ansén u. M. Adrian. Frankfurt a. Main 2007, 55.

31 Ebd., 50.

32 M. Merlau-Ponty: *Die Phänomenologie der Wahrnehmung*, 283.

33 Gerade die Sinnbildung in intellektuellen Akten wird gern als aktive Leistung bezeichnet, obwohl diese wiederum in passiven Vorgängen fundiert sind. Vgl. M. Wehrle: 'Konstitution des Sozialen oder soziale Konstitution'. In: *Phänomenologische Forschungen 2013*, 301–319. Dieser Absatz ist hier in ähnlichem Wortlaut bereits publiziert, siehe 314.

34 Das wiederholte leibliche und geistige Tätigkeiten bleibende materiale Spuren hinterlassen,

sieht sich in der aktuellen Neurowissenschaft unter dem Stichwort „neuronale Plastizität" bestätigt. Nach dem Verlust körperlicher und geistiger Fähigkeiten durch Unfall oder Krankheit, ermöglicht eine solche Plastizität eine fast vollständige Rehabilitation der Fähigkeiten, durch eine langwierige Bewegungstherapie, in der die entsprechenden Fähigkeiten wieder und wieder wiederholt werden. Dasselbe Prinzip der wiederholten Interaktion, die zu bleibenden (neuronalen) Strukturen und damit Handlungsmustern führt, kann sich auch negativ auswirken, in Form von Sucht und Abhängigkeit. Vgl. D.V. Buonomano, M.M. Merzenich: *Cortical plasticity: from synapses to maps.* Annual Review of Neuroscience 21 (1998), 149-186; B. Draganski, C. Graser, G. Kempermann, H.G. Kuhn, J. Winkler, C. Büchler, A. May: *Temporal and spatial dynamics of brain structure changes during extensive learning.* Journal of Neuroscience 27 (2006), 6314–6317.

35 E. Husserl: *Zur Phänomenologie der Intersubjektivität. Texte aus dem Nachlass. Zweiter Teil,* 230.

36 Ebd., 207, 198, 221.

37 Husserl selbst thematisiert die passive Genesis/Dimension dieser Gemeinschaftsintentionalität nicht, für ihn steht die explizite Übereinkunft und Kommunikation der Subjekte im Vordergrund. In seinen Vorlesungen zur Intersubjektivität betont er mehrfach, dass man Ansichten und Normen anderer nicht einfach passiv übernehmen darf, sondern sich diese explizit zu eigen zu machen muss, um diese zu eigenen Normen zu machen. Trotzdem erscheint eine solche gemeinsame Intentionalität und Habitualität die Voraussetzung von Kommunikation und Übereinkunft jeglicher Art zu sein, auch wenn es sich nur um eine geteilte Sprache handelt.

38 Phänomenologie muss zunächst vom eigenen Bewusstseinsleben ausgehen: Nur in diesem sind uns Dinge, andere Subjekte und die Welt gegeben. Es bietet insofern den evidenten epistemischen Ausgangspunkt, von dem man später durch eidetische Variation zu den allgemeinen Strukturen des Bewusstseins gelangen kann. Zu dem Bewusstsein von anderen Subjekten habe ich dagegen keinen unmittelbaren Zugang, genauso wenig wie zu einer ‚objektiven' Welt, die sich uns immer nur perspektivisch zeigt und nur in dieser Korrelation mit einem wahrnehmenden Bewusstsein verständlich wird. So wichtig diese Erkenntniskritik ist, entsteht hier doch ein blinder Fleck: Das Bewusstsein, dem die Welt jeweils gegeben ist, ist ein konkretes Subjekt, mit einer bestimmten Erfahrungsgeschichte, die nicht nur die individuellen Erfahrungen umgreift, sondern zugleich ein System überindividueller Normen repräsentiert. Der unbeteiligte Beobachter und die Einklammerung aller Vorurteile bleiben demnach eine Utopie. Seit der (Post)Moderne kommt man nicht umhin, mit dem Zweifel zu leben, dass die Erkenntnis sog. allgemeiner Strukturen, in ihrer Tragweite oder ihrem Inhalt abhängig ist, von dem jeweiligen Normensystem und den daraus resultierenden Interessen, welche das Denken des philosophierenden Egos mitbestimmen.

39 Vgl. J. Butler: *Körper von Gewicht. Die diskursiven Grenzen des Geschlechts.* Übers. von K. Wördemann. Frankfurt a. Main 1997. Vgl. M. Wehrle: 'Konstution des Sozialen oder soziale Konstitution', 316. In diesem Artikel wird mit Bezug auf Butler dieselbe Schlussfolgerung für den Bereich der Sozialität gezogen. Die folgenden acht Zeilen haben dementsprechend einen ähnlichen Wortlaut.

40 M. Foucault: *Der Gebrauch der Lüste. Sexualität und Wahrheit 2.* Frankfurt a. Main 1989, 16.

Notes for Contributors

Danish Yearbook of Philosophy publishes contributions in English, German and French. The journal mainly publishes articles relating to Danish philosophy, or by authors with ties to Danish philosophy. Articles for consideration and all editorial communications should be sent to *Danish Yearbook of Philosophy*, University of Copenhagen, Department of Media, Cognition and Communication, Karen Blixens Vej 4, DK–2300 Copenhagen S, Denmark. The journal will only consider manuscripts accompanied by the auther's certification that, while under consideration with this journal, they will not be submitted elsewhere.

Articles should normally not exceed 20 pages of 2700 characters. Articles which are considerably longer than 20 pages may be accepted, if it is considered that their length is appropriate to their topic and that they are of suffiently high quality throughout. Articles must bear the title of the contribution, name(s) of the author(s) and the address where the work was carried out. Sections should be numbered by Roman numerals. The full postal address of the author who will check proofs and receive correspondence and offprints should also be included. All pages should be numbered. Footnotes to the text should be kept to a minimum.

Table and figures. Tables and figures must be separate from and not included as part of the text. The approximate position of tables and figures should be indicated in the manuscript.

References should be indicated in the text by giving the author's name, with the year of publication in parentheses. If several papers by the same author and from the same year are cited, a,b,c, etc. should be put after the year of publication. The reference should be listed in full at the end of the paper in the following standard form:

For books:	Parfit, Derek (1984). *Reasons and Persons* (Oxford: Oxford University Press).
For articles:	Mackie, P. (1987). "Essence, Origin and Bare Identity". *Mind*, 96, pp. 173– 201.
For chapters within books	Pastin, M. (1978). "Modest Foundationalism and Self-warrant". In: G. Pappas & M. Swain (eds.), Essays on Knowledge and Justification (Ithaca/ London, Cornell University Press).

Journal titles should *not* be abbreviated.

Proofs will be sent to authors. They should be corrected and returned to the editorial secretary within one week. Major alterations to the text cannot be accepted.